The Challenge of C
Physical Educa

Dear David,

Thank you for your contribution, support and encouragement during the preparation of this book.

Your generous comments were much appreciated.

All good wishes for the future.

Ida.

The Challenge of Change in Physical Education:

Chelsea College of Physical Education – Chelsea School, University of Brighton 1898–1998

Ida M. Webb

Ida M. Webb
28th May, 1999

UK   Falmer Press, 1 Gunpowder Square, London, EC4A 3DE
USA   Falmer Press, Taylor & Francis Inc., 325 Chestnut Street, 8th Floor,
        Philadelphia, PA 19106

First published in 1999

A catalogue record for this book is available from the British Library

ISBN 0 7507 0976 6

**Library of Congress Cataloging-in-Publication Data are available on
request**

Jacket design by Caroline Archer

Typeset in 10/12pt Times by
Graphicraft Ltd., Hong Kong

*Printed in Great Britain by Biddles Ltd., Guildford and King's Lynn on
paper which has a specified pH value on final paper manufacture of not
less than 7.5 and is therefore 'acid free'.*

Contents

Contents

List of Figures

Acknowledgments

First, I must express my sincere appreciation to the infinite number of Chelsea Old Students and members of staff, for many posthumously, who regularly contributed to the Chelsea Old Students' magazines and newsletters, and to those who completed questionnaires. Their articles, achievements, reminiscences, news, views and reports have provided a very rich source of original material, which has been drawn on liberally, in the preparation of this book.

Secondly, I am grateful to the following heads of the College, the School or the parent institution: Audrey Bambra (Chelsea College of Physical Education), Gillian Burke (Chelsea School of Human Movement), Patricia Kingston (Chelsea School of Human Movement), Elizabeth Murdoch (Chelsea School of Physical Education, Sports Science, Dance and Leisure), Geoffrey Tyler (East Sussex College of Higher Education), Geoffrey Hall (Brighton Polytechnic) and David Watson (University of Brighton) for their written submissions and comments on the first draft.

Thirdly, I would like to thank the current members of the academic and administrative staff of the Chelsea School: Ann Cole, Barry Copley, Jonathan Doust, Jerry Fairclough, Ann-Marie Latham, Udo Merkel, Paul McNaught-Davis, Fiona Smith, Alan Tomlinson, Edward Twaddell, Joan Williams, Dawn Carey, Eve Moore, Linda Turner and Karen Wise, for providing information on request and for unfailingly answering innumerable questions.

Fourthly, I wish to recognize the cooperation of former members of staff: Biddy Burgum, Wendy Burrows, Hilary Corlett, George Deacon, Clive Griggs, Diane Tatlock, Varina Verdin, Sheila and Trevor Wood, which has been invaluable in innumerable ways.

Fifthly, I identify the service I have received from the following members of staff of the University of Brighton: Michael Bandle, John Kitcher, Diane Lace, Linda Miles, Maureen Taylor and Marion Trew, which enabled me to complete this study.

Sixthly, I am indebted to the following individuals who are external to the institution: John Alderson, David Bayman, Frances Anne Cocker, Bill Dorkings, Beryl Furlong, Olivia Harding, Paula Harding, Peter Harrison, Victoria Holtby, Ingrid Lackajis, Gillian Murton, Catriona Parratt, Valerie Preston-Dunlop, Gordon Rideout, Marcus Robinson, Eric Saunders, D Sparkes, Patricia Shenton, Kelvin Street, Michael Thomas, Peter Wickens and Peter Williams for their communications.

Seventhly, I wish to pay tribute to Judy Herbert, who designed the Chelsea centenary logo, which has been used in creating the artwork for the cover.

Eighthly, I must praise the stamina, skill and expertise of Lisa Carroll in deciphering my longhand copy and as the long-suffering typist of the first and redrafted manuscript.

Ninthly, I record the generosity of the University of Brighton for access to the Chelsea archives and for permission to reproduce material, photographs and logos.

And, finally, I acknowledge the role Malcolm Clarkson has played through stimulating discussion and resolution of difficult issues, editorial guidance, constructive advice and encouragement to complete the task.

The author and publisher are grateful to the Royal Borough of Kensington and Chelsea (Chelsea Library) for permission to use the map of Chelsea 1901.

Preface

The following narrative describing the history and development of Chelsea College of Physical Education, now the Chelsea School, University of Brighton, during its first 100 years is, of necessity, a selective and in no way exhaustive personal interpretation of factually based information extracted from primary and secondary sources. Nevins (1962) in *The Gateway to History* wrote, 'Most historical work, though by no means all of it, is important by virtue of its ideas; that is, its interpretations'. As far as humanly possible, an objective and critical stance has been taken, but with any living institution different interpretations of the same event are inevitably coloured by personal expectations, experience and perceptions.

No one book, and certainly not one examining a century of continuous development, can be a definitive work. There are, for example, unused student records that provide original material for a more sociological based study, or course documents, particularly from 1976, for a more detailed analysis of the curriculum and review of programmes of study currently available at the Chelsea School or material identifying the role and contribution of the Chelsea School within Brighton Polytechnic and the University of Brighton.

This Chelsea case study has been set within the wider context of the specialist women's physical education colleges. In *Women First The Female Tradition in English Physical Education 1880–1980*, Sheila Fletcher (1984) opened a new perspective when she examined the work and achievements of the women pioneers, with close reference to the history of Bedford College of Physical Education. She set her work in the wider context of educational history. Colin Crunden (1974) in *A History of Anstey College of Physical Education 1897–1972* brought to life the ever changing character of the College. He related its history to wider perspectives of social and professional change which took place in the late nineteenth and twentieth centuries. Albert Pomfret (1985) in *Dartford College 1885–1985* recorded the history of the first college specializing in the training of women teachers of physical education. I C Maclean (1976) in *The History of Dunfermline College of Physical Education* conveyed the unique association of the College with Andrew Carnegie and the developing scene which influenced its progress.

I have attempted to interpret Chelsea's history through the professional lives of its eight women heads. This biographical approach has been used to reveal and, in some ways, recreate, as vividly as possible, the different personalities and traits of the leaders of the College and the School. It has also been used as a method by which their contributions to the development of Chelsea and its main foci, whether the latter be in physical training, physical education, movement studies, dance, sports science, leisure, recreation, health, teacher training, related vocations, scholarship or research, could be identified and located. Each incumbent can be viewed as a *force*; a force that inspired *change* appropriate to the stage of development of the institution and the subject of physical education in keeping with the educational, political and social climates and parameters of the day.

The institution is, however, more than the role and contributions of its heads, perhaps the whole is even greater than the sum of the parts. While it has not been possible to identify and include the specific impact of each member of staff and each student, nevertheless by reference to the work, achievements, aspirations and views of as many as possible, their influence on the corporate outcome has been included in the four main chapters (2–5).

The *Foundation* of the College, to provide opportunities for women to train as teachers of gymnastics and games, with access to a relatively new profession in the Victorian era, required vision, faith, focus and strength on the part of its Head Mistress with generous support and understanding from staff, students and the parent polytechnic institution.

Its *Transition*, especially during the turbulent, uncertain times of evacuation in the Second World War, both externally at national level and internally within the parent institution, demanded dedication, foresight, courage and persistence to cope with enforced changes and to resolve what must, at times, have seemed to all concerned with the College, insolvable problems.

With *Expansion* came innumerable openings and possibilities for innovation that required drive, perception, conviction and insistence for more ambitious, identified goals to be achieved. This 'purple patch' heralded the beginning of further fundamental differences in institutional allegiance and what might have been viewed by some as the demise of the Chelsea College of Physical Education.

During *Incorporation*, at first, a sense of loss of identity was experienced by staff and students in what were perceived as complex organizations of multistructures and unnecessary bureaucratic procedures. As Gillian Burke wrote, 'Occasionally, gradual evolution and steady progress give way to a major step forward and a radical reorganization'. Adaptability, ruthlessness, patience and appreciation were all required; first, to grasp and secondly, to take advantage of and profit from, the opportunities that appeared, initially on the horizon and later, within realistic reach of the Chelsea School.

So what does the *future* hold for the Chelsea School? There will be a place for teaching, for learning, for scholarship and for research. Boldness, resourcefulness, enterprise and, above all, flexibility will be required so that advantage can be taken of changed and changing circumstances. Standards, quality assurance and accountability will have to be met. Perhaps there will be a greater contribution towards a unified physical education profession, whilst not losing sight of basic vocational requirements and allied interests.

It has been a privilege to be entrusted with the preparation of this text. At times, however, it has been difficult to be totally impartial, having been an integral part of the physical education profession since 1947. Any factual errors, or any differences of view from those of the contributors or the readers' perceived perspectives are, therefore, my personal responsibility.

Nevins (1962) indicated that a factually accurate text should reflect 'consideration to the living and truth to the dead'. I hope this book has respected those two briefs in indicating Chelsea's rightful place in higher education and recording its contribution to physical education and allied professions. I also hope that it has helped, in a small way, to celebrate 100 years of achievements and, at the same time, looked forward to the future of the Chelsea School with justified optimism.

Ida M Webb
September 1998

1   Introduction

South Western Polytechnic, Chelsea   Location, 1898

'. . . creating new opportunities for women'.

Chelsea College of Physical Education was founded by Fräulein Dorette Wilke in 1898 at the South Western Polytechnic, Manresa Road, Chelsea, London, as a Department for the training of gymnastic and games teachers to hold posts in girls' schools, in connection with the Polytechnic's Day College for Women.

Chelsea was the third college of its kind to be founded towards the end of the nineteenth century. Collectively, these colleges and the subsequent foundations, up to a maximum of nine by 1953, were first known as the 'specialist' women's physical training colleges and later, 1958, as the 'specialist' women's colleges of physical education. No one date can be ascribed to the use, or change of usage, of 'training' and 'education' either in the names of the colleges or in the theory and practice of their primary focus. At times the two words have been interchanged and at other times a clear distinction has been attributed to their meaning.

The original six colleges were founded between 1885 and 1905 and the last three between 1938 and 1953. The first college, initially named the Hampstead Gymnasium, was founded by Martina Bergman, a graduate from the Royal Central Gymnastic Institute, Stockholm in 1881. Miss Bergman based the training of her students on Ling's Swedish gymnastics. Against financial advice, she purchased 1 Reremonde, Broadhurst Gardens, Hampstead in 1885. In her own words,

> . . . to train a teacher who will give her whole time and interest to a school, a leader in the games field as in the gymnasium, one who will guard the children's development, prevent deformities and keep an eye on the whole hygiene of the school.

1

In 1886, she married Dr Edvin Per Wilhem Österberg and, from that time, she was known as Madame Bergman Österberg. Conditions at Hampstead soon became restricted and restrictive. She moved the, by then, renamed Hampstead Physical Training College to Kingsfield, Dartford in 1895 and called it the Bergman Österberg Physical Training College. It was not until 1939 when the College was evacuated to Newquay, Cornwall, that it was called Dartford College of Physical Education.

The second college was founded by Rhoda Anstey, who had been trained by Madam Bergman Österberg at Hampstead from 1893 to 1895, at The Leasowes, Halesowen in 1897. Here, although the College stood in 16 acres of grounds, opportunities for teaching practice were limited in and around Halesowen. In 1907, she moved her college to Yew Tree House, Chester Road, Erdington with easy access to a greater number of schools in Birmingham, but with limited grounds for the development of facilities at later stages of the College's history. Anstey Physical Training College was renamed Anstey College of Physical Education in 1947, coinciding with the Golden Jubilee celebrations.

The fourth, Liverpool Gymnasium Training College, was privately founded by Irene Mabel Marsh in 1900. She had attended the Southport Physical Training College and Gymnasium, 1893 to 1895, run jointly by Mr and Mrs Alec Alexander, who were eminent members of the National Physical Recreation Society. In 1895, Miss Marsh qualified as a teacher and after a few years she became the Director of Women's Classes at the Liverpool YMCA Gymnasium; a post she retained until her death in 1938. With the sum of £100 as her capital, she rented 110 Bedford Street, Liverpool and trained one of her sisters, Salome, together with Pearl Taverner and Muriel Pert. Although she had purchased additional houses by 1919, student numbers had so increased that a new building with grounds for further expansion was essential. Therefore, in 1920, she moved the Liverpool Physical Training College to Barkhill House, Liverpool. In 1939, when it was run by Trustees, it was retitled the I M Marsh College of Physical Education by the new Principal, Miss Marie Crabbe, to honour the founder.

The fifth was founded by Margaret Stansfeld who had attended classes in London, held by Martina Bergman, in 1881. Between 1885 and 1888 she was an instructor at the Hampstead College and also continued her gymnastics teaching at several of the Girls' Public Day School Company Schools, including the High School for Girls, Bedford. In 1903 she bought a house, The Wylams, 37 Lansdowne Road, Bedford, and started Bedford Physical Training College. It became Bedford College of Physical Education in 1952, when the Bedfordshire Education Authority took it over.

The sixth college, the Carnegie Dunfermline Trust College of Hygiene, was inaugurated in 1905 at Dunfermline and was known as the Dunfermline College of Hygiene and Physical Training, with Flora Ogston (Chelsea, 1901–1903) as its first Principal. It was retitled Dunfermline College of Hygiene and Physical Education in 1946 and Dunfermline College of Physical Education, Aberdeen in 1951. Aberdeen was dropped from the title when the College moved to purpose built accommodation at Cramond, Edinburgh in 1966.

In the early days, with the foundation of 'rival' colleges, the need was felt by old students of the Bergman Österberg Physical Training College for a national association for teachers trained in the Swedish gymnastic system. On 9 January 1899, Mary Hankinson, trained at the Bergman Österberg Physical Training College from 1896 to 1898, met together with 30 of Madame Bergman Österberg's old students at the Hampstead Gymnasium and formed 'The Association of Swedish Physical Educationists'. Madame Bergman Österberg was invited to be the President, an honour she declined because of 'the ridiculous title' chosen for the Association. Even after the name was changed to the Ling Association in April 1899, she again refused the honour. Initially, the Association admitted all women who held a certificate from Madame Bergman Österberg or anyone trained at the Royal Central Gymnastic Institute, Stockholm.

The objects of the Association were to:

(a) band together teachers of Swedish Gymnastics in the British Isles;
(b) ultimately obtain a registered list of those duly qualified to teach Swedish Gymnastics and give Massage scientifically;
(c) arrange meetings and holiday courses at different times; and
(d) publish a list of vacant posts.

Chelsea College was inspected by the Ling Association on 27 November 1912 and the following resolution was passed at the Fourteenth Annual General Meeting of the Association in January 1913.

That CPTC be recognised by the Ling Association, and all future graduates be eligible for membership.

Although three of the first colleges were privately founded and funded, the position of women principals of women's colleges had been strengthened in 1908, when,

An important step has been taken by the Board of Education in relation to the Headship of Women's Colleges. They are convinced that a large number of questions that have to be determined by the principal of such institutions are such as are best treated by a woman; and experience has clearly shown that there is no lack of capable women who can most effectively undertake the responsibilities of the Headship of a Residential College, both on its administrative and its instructional sides. The Board will accordingly require that, as vacancies occur, they will be filled by the appointment of women.

The main elements of Chelsea's history have been identified in this '*Introduction*' and these will be developed in the main text.

The foundation stone of the South Western Polytechnic was laid by HRH the Prince of Wales on Thursday 23 July 1891 and the Polytechnic opened, without ceremony, in 1895. From its inception the Polytechnic had programmed gymnastic classes for women in keeping with object 5 of the institution 'to provide instruction and practice in gymnastics, drill, swimming and other bodily exercises'. These took place on two evenings per week, originally taken by Miss Stuart Snell of Queen Alexandra's Gymnasium.

Fulfilment of object 5 was also achieved through the provision of gymnastic classes for boys and men.

The College was established 'to give a sound education in Physical Training' for it was Dorette Wilke's belief that '. . . to educate the mind without educating the body could only end in failure, for what was knowledge at the mercy of a weak, undisciplined body?'. The first course was broadly based with a sound theoretical foundation complemented by educational visits and external lectures to support the core of practical studies. Students were to understand scientific and physiological principles which underpinned the systems of gymnastics in vogue in different main-land European countries at the end of the nineteenth century. Dorette Wilke also believed that the scientific approach was essential '. . . for all whose task in after life will be to teach others and to design and to adapt exercises and games for children and adults under different conditions of physique and environment'. It was significant that, from the inception of the first course, the knowledge acquired during study was always meant to be adapted and used according to prevailing conditions.

In the early days, the College was very aware of the 'poor' physique of many pupils, particularly those in city elementary schools, whose boys and girls were lucky if they had one hour of physical exercise or drill each week, often taken by untrained teachers. The College was also aware of the general lack of facilities for physical training. As one Old Student commented, 'A happy, healthy physical development of children was our aim, with relaxed and correct deportment and a watchful eye for those who needed special physical correction'. Dorette Wilke believed, '. . . prevention was better than cure' and advocated dancing, games and gymnastics for every pupil every week with, if possible, 'good educational gym-nastics' daily.

The work of both the early pioneer physical educationists and their successors was assisted through the permissive legislation or statutory obligations approved by the government of the day. The 1870 Education Act had laid the groundwork for the establishment of a national system of elementary education in England and new opportunities had been created for physical education. For girls, separate second-ary education was available only to a minority of fee paying pupils at endowed grammar and independent schools for girls. The number of professions open to women at the end of the nineteenth century was limited, but, with the opening of Chelsea, professional opportunities for trained women physical educationists had been increased. It is of interest to note that the average starting salary for trained teachers was £100 per annum. The Gymnastic Teachers' Course had to be self-financing from tuition fees, which led to a paucity of specialist facilities, although Chelsea was fortunate to have access to the facilities of other departments in the Polytechnic, which were in receipt of generous equipment grants from the London County Council.

The 1918 Education Act enabled local authorities to provide school and holiday camps, centres and equipment for physical training, playing fields, swimming baths and other facilities for social and physical training in the day or evening.

Although no formal educational qualifications were demanded of the first entrants, prospective students, nevertheless, had to satisfy the Head Mistress that they were capable of completing the course and suitable for training as prospective teachers. Emphasis was placed on qualities such as 'suitable', 'personality', 'calibre of the individual', 'professional integrity', 'total commitment to teaching' and 'dedication'. Those who were 'not gifted for the profession', 'unsuitable for the profession', 'not strong enough for the work' or just 'not accepted' often left at the end of the first term, the 'trial' term. This decision was reached after the Head Mistress had decided the advisability of the students continuing their course. If progress or conduct was not satisfactory, students were asked and required, at any time, to withdraw.

By 1902–03 entrants to the College were expected to hold matriculation of the London University, the Oxford or Cambridge Senior or Higher Local Examination or the Oxford and Cambridge Joint Board. Later, in 1913, Matriculation Examination of any University in the United Kingdom, or an examination accepted by such a university in lieu of matriculation, became the entry qualification.

Subsequently, as changes were made in school examinations, the requirement became first, a School Certificate Examination of a recognized examining body, secondly, by 1951, the General Certificate of Education and, thirdly, by 1988, the General Certificate of Secondary Education. Specific levels also changed from first, a pass in five subjects to, secondly, a minimum of five 'O' level passes provided that there was evidence that other courses had been studied beyond the age of 16 and, thirdly, to two 'A' level grades, normally at least a B and a C. By the 1990s, 'A' level grades were scored and a minimum of 18 points was the required entrance qualification. All candidates for the teacher training courses were interviewed by the Head of the College (later the School) and were required to demonstrate physical aptitude for the course, except during the Second World War if they were interviewed in London.

By 1930, the College was in the process of moving from principally internal to both internal and external validation, although some examinations of external bodies had always been taken. For example, students at the turn of the nineteenth century sat examinations set by the St John's Ambulance Association in First Aid to the Injured and in Home Nursing and the Board of Education South Kensington Examinations in Physiology, Hygiene and Elementary Science of Common Life. This practice continued throughout the 100 years, with changes in awards appropriate to professional demands, and the development of umpiring, coaching and officiating awards in games and sports from the national governing bodies of sport.

Between 1929 and 1958, there were major changes in the structure of courses at Chelsea, with a corresponding development of subject content. Students, whilst being trained to teach, were also given an '. . . opportunity for research work . . .', together with experience in, and appraisal of, new methods in physical education. These processes continued, indeed at times they were accelerated, particularly with programmes for diversified courses, throughout the remainder of the century.

As the physical training profession expanded and the subject developed, the heads of five of the six women's physical training colleges felt the need to meet regularly, to share views, ideas and concerns and to examine policies. On Thursday 21 November 1935, the Association of Principals of Physical Training Colleges was formed when,

> A meeting of Principals of Physical Training Colleges, whose Diplomas are recognised for membership of the Ling Association of Teachers of Swedish Gymnastics was convened by Miss May Fountain (Chelsea) at the Cowdray Club at 3.00 pm by invitation of Miss Margaret Stansfeld (Bedford). Miss R Hope Greenall (Bergman Österberg) and Miss Marion Squire (Anstey) also attended. Apologies were received from Miss Helen Drummond (Dunfermline).
>
> The business of the meeting was to discuss the formation of an Association of Principals of Physical Training Colleges. Its objects:
> 1 To further the common aims and requirements of the Physical Training Colleges.
> 2 To establish a representative body to whom reference can be made on all matters concerning the training of students.

Miss Greenall had trained from 1909 to 1911 at the Bergman Österberg Physical Training College, Miss Squire at Bedford Physical Training College from 1913 to 1915 and Miss Drummond at the Bergman Österberg Physical Training College from 1913 to 1915; she had also gained an MA (Cantab). Miss Marsh was not invited to the meeting; the Diploma of her College had not been recognized as qualifying her students for membership of the Ling Association.

An exclusive, but authoritative, Association had been established. It was consulted and its collective opinions were respected on numerous occasions by many recognized national and international bodies such as: the Chartered Society of Massage and Medical Gymnastics (later the Chartered Society of Physiotherapy); the Society of Medical Officers of Health (School Health Group); the Ling Physical Education Association (later the Physical Education Association of Great Britain and Northern Ireland); the Association of Teachers of Colleges and Departments of Education; the Association of Head Mistresses of Recognised Independent Schools and the International Association of Physical Education and Sport for Girls and Women.

Nonington College of Physical Education, the seventh 'specialist' college to be founded, had been opened officially by the Archbishop of Canterbury, at St Albans Court, Nonington on 23 July 1938. Its founder and first Principal was Miss Gladys Wright who had trained at the Silkeborg Physical Training College, Denmark and the Royal Central Gymnastic Institute, Stockholm, Sweden.

The Principal of Liverpool, Miss Marie Crabbe, who had trained at the Bergman Österberg Physical Training College from 1922 to 1925 and Miss Wright, were invited to become members of the Association of Principals of Physical Training Colleges in 1942.

The eighth college to be founded was the Lady Mabel College of Physical Education, named after Lady Mabel Smith, County Councillor, daughter of Viscount

Milton, eldest son of the sixth Earl Fitzwilliam. It was the first college of physical education to be opened by a local education authority, the West Riding of Yorkshire. The College started in October 1949 in a hotel in Harrogate, and moved to its permanent site in the magnificent mansion of the Fitzwilliam family at Wentworth Woodhouse in January 1950. Miss Nancy Moller, MA, was appointed Principal and attended her first meeting as a member of the Association of Principals of Physical Training Colleges on 4 November 1949.

The ninth college, the Ulster College of Physical Education, was established by the Northern Ireland Ministry of Education in Dalriada House, Belfast, whose purchase had been negotiated by the Belfast Corporation, in September 1953. Miss Oonah Pim, who had trained at the Bergman Österberg Physical Training College from 1931 to 1934, had been appointed Principal in the spring of 1953. She was invited to join the Association of Principals of Physical Training Colleges on 16 November 1953 and attended her first meeting on 29 December 1953.

The Association changed its name to the Association of Principals of Women's Colleges of Physical Education on 11 October 1958. It formally ceased on 29 April 1976. By this time, seven of the women's colleges of physical education had either been incorporated into larger institutions or discussions about proposed mergers were at an advanced stage. Anstey was incorporated into Birmingham Polytechnic (1975); Bedford into Bedford College of Higher Education (1976); Chelsea into East Sussex College of Higher Education (1976); Dartford into Thames Polytechnic (1978); I M Marsh into Liverpool Polytechnic (1981); Lady Mabel into Sheffield Polytechnic (1977) and Ulster into Ulster Polytechnic (1972). Dunfermline and Nonington remained as free-standing institutions at this stage.

During the 1930s, the promotion of social and physical welfare were matters of national concern. They were partially addressed by the government through the Physical Training and Recreation Act 1937, which was welcomed by the physical education profession as it marked a milestone in the national development of recreation in meeting the physical needs of post-school youth. Under the Education Act 1944, it became the duty of every local education authority to provide adequate facilities for recreation, social and physical training for primary, secondary and further education.

An increase in the number of teachers and leaders qualified in physical training, education and recreation had been signalled. Initially, a formal teacher training in physical education was open only to those students whose parents could afford to pay the fees of the newly-established institutions, including Chelsea. With financial support from grants made by various trusts to individuals in 1913 and the introduction of County Scholarships in 1920, the opportunity to train became available to an increased number of girls. It was not until the 1940s, with the recognition of colleges by the Ministry of Education, under the Further Education and Training Scheme, that students were eligible to receive free tuition and maintenance grants based on assessment of parental income. Students in receipt of this grant were, however, required to teach in state schools on completion of their initial course of training. 'The Ministry of Labour and National Service require a declaration that you intend to teach at the end of your training; I should be glad to have this and your National Registration Identity Number'. This requirement was later withdrawn. In the meantime, however, the Ministry of Education, '. . . will follow with great interest the careers of men and women who have held awards under the above scheme and, for the purpose of the record, you will be asked in about three years' time if you will be good enough to give some particulars of your career subsequent to the expiry of your award under the Scheme'. The *Declaration* that students signed read,

> I . . . hereby declare that I intend to complete the course of training for which I have been admitted to the . . . College and, thereafter, to adopt and follow the profession of teacher in a grant aided school or other institution approved for the purpose by the Minister and I acknowledge that, in entering on this course, I take advantage of the public funds by which it is aided, in order to qualify myself for the said profession and for no other purpose.

Such a student was referred to as a 'recognized' student, as compared with the 'private' student who paid full fees for tuition and residence and did not sign, on entry, a 'Declaration of Intention to Teach'.

Chelsea was recognized on 1 April 1945, when it was administered by the London County Council; it was the first of the Specialist Women's Colleges of Physical Education to attain this status. Anstey was grant-aided in 1955 when the Staffordshire Education Authority took responsibility for the administration of the College, Bedford in 1952 under the Bedfordshire Education Authority, Dartford was recognized for grant aid as a Voluntary College in 1951 and it came under the Inner London Education Authority in 1961, I M Marsh in 1947 under Lancashire Education Authority and Nonington in 1951 under the Kent Education Authority.

Between 1958 and 1976 the Chelsea curriculum had two complementary aims: first, a liberal education to enable the student to realize her full potential as an individual and as an educator and, secondly, a professional preparation based on an understanding of the educational needs of children, together with an appreciation of the vital part which movement plays in their growth and development.

The 'new' emphasis on 'movement' had been inspired by the perceptions of Rudolf Laban who 'created a new myth of movement for our century'. Movement was accepted as 'an aspect of man's individuality' and the study of human movement was aimed beyond 'the development of the individual's potential for movement towards his deeper understanding of himself and others'. From 1942, Lisa Ullmann and Rudolf Laban worked together in Manchester where, in 1946, Lisa Ullmann founded the Art of Movement Studio. She had been a pupil of Laban in Berlin and said that under his guidance,

> I learned how to use my body in turning, jumping and leaping, how bendings and stretches created beautiful lines and patterns in space, and how strong, gentle, sudden, slow, large or small movements can produce the most exciting rhythms in the flow of movement.

The Laban Art of Movement Guild was formed in 1946 to safeguard the teaching qualifications of those taking modern educational dance in the Manchester schools. By September 1948, the first one-year course for women teachers who had received a two-year or emergency training was approved by the Ministry of Education. Subsequently, as the number and range of courses expanded, the Studio, as the Laban Art of Movement Centre, moved to Addlestone, Surrey, in 1953 and as the Laban Centre to Goldsmith's College, New Cross, London, in 1974.

At the beginning of the twentieth century the elementary school physical education curriculum could best be described as drill and physical exercises. With the training of women as specialist teachers of games and gymnastics the gradual introduction of a more comprehensive programme of physical training took place in the girls' high and public schools.

By the middle of the twentieth century physical education, including dancing, games, gymnastics, athletics and swimming, was an integral part of the school curriculum for primary and secondary pupils. Whilst allocation on the timetable varied between schools, the majority of pupils received at least three hours per week with many receiving more than five hours a week.

At the end of the twentieth century the National Curriculum, controlled by the School Curriculum and Assessment Authority, was in place and, contrary to the recommendations of the Physical Education Working Group under the chairmanship of Ian Beer, pupils at Key Stage I (5–7 years) received 36 hours per year, Key Stage II (7–11 years) received 45 hours per year, Key Stage III (11–14 years) received 45 hours per year and at Key Stage IV (14–16 years) only 5 per cent of the timetable was allocated for physical education activities. The original recommendations had been: Key Stages I–III five of the six areas of activity selected from athletics, dance, games, gymnastics, outdoor and adventurous activities and swimming and, at Key Stage IV, for those not taking physical education as a General Certificate of Secondary Education subject, at least two activities per week.

The Education Reform Act 1988 provided for the establishment of a National Curriculum of core subjects (English, mathematics, science) and foundation subjects (art, geography, history, music, physical education, technology, modern foreign language) for pupils of compulsory school age in England and Wales. Welsh was designated a core subject in Wales and religious education throughout the school and sex education at Key Stages III and IV were statutory requirements.

In 1997 the English Sports Council published *England, The Sporting Nation: A Strategy*, in which one of its targets was, 'to increase curriculum time for Physical Education' to at least two hours per week for all pupils.

From September 1998 the government proposes to relax the National Curriculum Physical Education Order for Key Stages I and II. In the future, schools will be asked to give '. . . due regard to physical education'.

By the end of the century, the Chelsea School aimed to create a good learning and working environment for students pursuing courses with vocational relevance in either education, sport, recreation or leisure.

Importance has often been placed on institutional and course titles and the meaning(s) they convey. During the first 100 years, the College has been known as the Gymnastic Teachers' Training Department (1898–1902), the Gymnastic Teachers' Training College for Women (1902–1908), Chelsea Physical Training College

(1908–1920), Chelsea College of Physical Education (1920–1976), Chelsea School of Human Movement (1976–1990) within East Sussex College of Higher Education (1976–1979) and Brighton Polytechnic (1979–1990) and Chelsea School of Physical Education, Sports Science, Dance and Leisure (1990–1998) within Brighton Polytechnic (1990–1992) and the University of Brighton (1992–1998).

The other colleges who had changes in their titles were, for example: Anstey became a Department of Physical Education in 1975; Bedford became the School of Human Movement Studies in 1976, the Department of Physical Education, Sport and Leisure in 1990, the Department of Physical Education, Sport and Leisure in the School of Humanities, Sport and Education within De Montfort University, Bedford, in 1994 and, finally, the School of Physical Education, Sport and Leisure, De Montfort University, Bedford in 1996.

With regard to Dunfermline on 17 July 1986, the Secretary of State for Scotland, Malcolm Rifkind, announced to Parliament that,

> ...the training of physical education teachers, both men and women, will be centralised on the site of the present Dunfermline College of Physical Education and, accordingly, the training of men PE teachers at Jordanhill College of Education will cease. Dunfermline College will, itself, be merged with Moray House College of Education under a single governing body.

The enlarged Moray House College of Education was formally instituted on 1 April 1987 and incorporated the Scottish Centre for Physical Education, Movement and Leisure Studies at Cramond. Moray House became the Institute of Education of Heriot–Watt University in 1991.

The Ulster Polytechnic was incorporated with the University of Ulster in 1984 when the former School of Physical Education and Recreation was known first, as the School of Specialist Studies, secondly, in 1986 as the Department of Pre-Service Education and, finally, in 1994, as the School of Leisure and Tourism.

Dartford became Dartford College of Education in 1968 to reflect more accurately its work in training primary and middle school teachers, as well as secondary teachers of physical education and another subject. In 1978, it became the Dartford Faculty of Education and Movement Studies of Thames Polytechnic and, together with Nonington, it closed when the fourth year students graduated in 1986.

I M Marsh was known as the Department of Physical and Outdoor Education, whilst in Liverpool Polytechnic and retitled the Centre for Physical Education, Sport and Dance when the Polytechnic became Liverpool John Moores University in 1992.

Lady Mabel was incorporated into the Faculty of Environment, Sheffield Polytechnic as the Department of Leisure and Environmental Studies in conjunction with the Faculty of Education in 1977. In 1992, the Polytechnic was renamed Sheffield Hallam University and the Department became the School of Leisure and Food Management in conjunction with the School of Education.

The development, both expansion and contraction, of Chelsea has been influenced by its physical environment, its management and its curriculum. The College/School has had three geographical locations: London 1898 to 1939, Borth

1939 to 1948 and Eastbourne from 1948, and four governing authorities: South Western, later Chelsea Polytechnic, London County Council (1898 to 1947), Eastbourne Education Authority (1947 to 1974), East Sussex Education Authority (1974 to 1989) and Brighton Polytechnic, later University of Brighton (1989 to 1998).

Changes in structure, content and direction of courses were clearly reflected in titles of awards from the Diploma of the College; through the London Diploma in the Theory and Practice of Physical Education; Teachers' Certificate, University of London; Certificate in Education, University of Sussex; to Bachelor Degrees of the University of Sussex, the Council for National Academic Awards and the University of Brighton and higher degrees of the latter two institutions.

The curriculum has had four distinct phases, moving from subject-centred to child-centred through society-based to experience-based courses. However, practical experience has always been central to the development of a thorough professional training, complemented by theoretical studies and combined with a sound personal education. This policy has been followed, irrespective of whether the outcome was viewed as physical culture, physical training, physical education, movement education or, more recently, physical education, sport, dance, leisure or recreation.

Learning may have been product and/or process oriented, but independence in terms of the individual's development of thought, self-discipline, professional attitude and responsibility, which may be termed the 'hidden curriculum', has always been encouraged.

Throughout Chelsea's history the overriding impression that has led to its success has stemmed from the leadership, strength, influence, outstanding ability and dominance of its charismatic personalities, particularly its Women Heads. These leaders have been very ably supported by the staff and students, both women and men, who have contributed specifically to the work of the College and, more generally, to physical education, health, sport, dance, leisure and recreation.

The four historical eras, 1898 to 1929, 1929 to 1958, 1958 to 1976 and 1976 to 1998, into which Chelsea's history can be divided, coincide with changes in leadership and/or institutional allegiance, and have been encapsulated in the four words: 'Foundation', headed by Dorette Wilke, 'Transition', mainly guided by May Fountain with Gwyneth Cater and Annie Rogers in charge for shorter periods of time, 'Expansion', steered by Audrey Bambra, and 'Incorporation' under the leadership of Patricia Kingston, followed by Gillian Burke and Elizabeth Murdoch.

If the length of service of the individual Heads of the nine specialist women's colleges of physical education is taken as the criterion for division into eras, each will be different. All the colleges have, however, been affected in their development by, for example: the Education Acts of 1870, 1918, 1944 and 1988; official reports, such as McNair (1944), Robbins (1963) and Dearing (1997); validation processes of examining bodies, such as the Board of Education, the Ling Association, universities and the Council for National Academic Awards; political policies of the government of the day and by social reforms.

There are many factors that influence secondary school pupils when they decide to continue their education beyond the statutory school leaving age and apply for a place in a higher education institution. Students' choice of Chelsea College/School has, more often than not, been influenced by personal contact and recommendation, 'My PE staff was Chelsea trained', and 'Students at the College persuaded me to join them!'. Other factors have included 'I was able to live at home' or 'with friends' or 'relatives', or 'I was attracted by the opportunity to live in London' or 'by the sea', or 'I had an opportunity to take a degree course', or the College was 'recognized'.

The preceding brief factual statements open doors to a fascinating journey and living story of the ongoing development in physical education, dance, sport, recreation and leisure in England. The journey spans a period of time that stretches from the end of the Victorian era, a time when so many differences were polarized, to the present day, the dawn of the third millennium, at one nationally and internationally recognized institution.

In the *Conclusions*, the 'essence' of Chelsea has been identified, and the various themes and threads that characterize its history and development, have been brought together. It is, therefore, possible to view this history as one example of a case study and '**. . . to use it as a template**'.

2   Foundation: 1898–1929

Dorette Wilke
Head Mistress

'To know her was a liberal education.'

Dorette Wilke was born, a subject of the German Empire, on 14 June 1867, at Stendal, Magdeburg, Bezirk, Prussia, of Prussian parents Friedrich and Dorothea Wilke. In spite of many enquiries, little is known of her early life or how she came to England. We do know, however, that she arrived in England in 1885 a penniless, delicate, sensitive, but receptive, teenager, suffering from lateral curvature of the spine. Acting on a doctor's advice, she took up gymnastics to effect a cure; her professional career had been determined. Enthusiasm for gymnastics led her to enrol at the fashionable Training School of Adolf A Stempel's Gymnasium, Albany Street, Regent's Park, London. Here she received two years free training in the theory and practice of all published systems of physical education, together with lessons in fencing under French masters and sixteenth century fencing under Captain Alfred Hutton, complemented by private tuition in anatomy and physiology. Her teaching practice was very varied, from infants' classes to classes for elderly ladies. After gaining a First Class Diploma at the end of the course and by way of repayment, she taught unsalaried for a year at Stempel's and its connected schools. 'I am so grateful, you see, for what gymnastics have done for me, that I want to make them a means of doing good to as many people as possible'.

On leaving Stempel's Gymnasium in 1888, Dorette Wilke went first as an Assistant to the Misses Evelyn and Beatrice Bear at Queen Alexandra's Gymnasium, which was located in the basement of Queen Alexandra House, opposite the Albert Hall, Kensington. These two remarkable Australian sisters were famous for their skill with the foil. They became well known members of the British College of Physical Education, following its foundation in 1898. Initially, priority was given to British gymnastics in the students' course; later, Swedish gymnastics became the main focus. Dancing, games and swimming, supported by theoretical subjects and teaching practice, completed their curriculum. Secondly, in 1891, when frustrated at being called away from her classes to treat individuals, often important personages, Lady So and So, Dorette Wilke was appointed to the staff of Battersea Polytechnic. Finally, in 1896, following the resignation of Miss Stuart Snell to get married at the end of 1895, she joined the staff of the South Western Polytechnic. This last appointment was at a much lower salary, but with the active support of the Principal, Herbert Tomlinson, and the governors, Dorette Wilke had an opportunity to establish a training department and so to achieve her dream, her ambition, her 'raison d'être'.

> Surely it was my fate to come to Chelsea? I had been at Battersea some four or five years, agitating the whole time to get a Physical Training College started, feeling sure that there was an urgent need of one in London, the centre of most (good) things. I had my scheme all ready, and Mr Wells, the Battersea Principal, was in favour, but the Governing Body failed to consent, though approached several times on the matter. I was so eager to train teachers that, when three or four girls with special abilities for the profession asked for my help, I arranged a course for them at Battersea, that is to say, I helped them to choose the right theory subjects and coached them in practical gymnastics myself, every spare moment I could find. Perhaps it is only fair to myself to add that I did so without any fee, merely for the love of the work.

This was an early example of the quality of service that characterized Dorette's attitude to her chosen profession throughout her life. 'My heart was always in the training work'. On a later occasion she said, 'We are engaged . . . in the work of teaching the teachers for, unless the teacher has herself been taught, how can she teach others?'

After Dorette Wilke had qualified at Stempel's, she became, by invitation, a member of the British College of Physical Education and the National Society of Physical Education, founded in 1891 and 1897 respectively. Before admission to the Gymnastic Teachers' Institute she had, however, to sit the certificate examinations which, much to the delight of her students, she passed with flying colours.

Numerous accounts from students, staff, members of evening classes and visitors, all support the view that Dorette Wilke was a beautiful and graceful gymnast and a brilliant teacher whose enthusiasm for her chosen profession was infectious. Teaching prospective teachers to teach without destroying the individual's personal confidence is a gift. Dorette Wilke was blessed with this faculty and she used it wisely to develop individual talents and styles of presentation. Professional integrity, pioneering service and a missionary-like spirit were characteristic traits of this talented, vivacious, dynamic, outspoken, wise and generous individual who, nevertheless, had a charm of manner that endeared her to staff, governors, students, parents and visitors alike. As Ethel Adair Impey (née Adair Roberts), a member of staff from 1902 to 1905, said in later life:

Dorette Wilke was a great personality but quite the opposite of Madame Österberg in temperament; she was friendly and charming, open-minded and treated those above her and the most humble of her pupils alike.

... she consulted constantly with her staff, encouraged them to develop their own ideas and never took credit for what her staff had done.

In the early days, as was typical of many individuals of her generation, either a pet parrot, 'Polly', or later, a Pekinese was her constant companion. The first dog was called Peter Pan, the second Ting-Ling. Old students recalled taking Peter Pan or Ting-Ling to the surrounds of the net ball court for 'walkies'; when the Pekinese had obliged, they returned him to his basket in Dorette Wilke's room. The role of Head Mistress did not mask her 'love of life' nor her appreciation of the artistic atmosphere of Chelsea and the surrounding district. 'She frequently lengthened the daily walk to College by going via the Embankment'. She loved the river and was fascinated by its changing moods and the constant activity up and down the Thames. Her circle of friends was wide and varied and included Cecil Sharp, Evelyn Sharp, Herbert Tomlinson, Harry Bird Harper, Dame Ellen Terry, Dorothy Scott (Minto) and Alice Meynell. Typical of the customs of the day she was, on Sunday afternoons, 'At Home' to friends and any Chelsea Old Student who cared to visit her. She was there to chat, to discuss, to advise, to sympathize, to scold or to console — whatever action, in her estimation, was required.

When Dorette Wilke moved from Battersea Polytechnic to the South Western Polytechnic in 1896, she was accompanied by at least two of her students, Maud Jenkyn and Ethel de B Colinette, to complete their training. The first College Record Book dates from September 1898 and shows that five students were recruited into that first cohort, namely, Ethel Cartwright, Helen Ironside, Ethel Mary Dibden, Elizabeth Reed and Dora Smith. Anna Coltman, from Queen Alexandra's Gymnasium, joined the group for one term in January 1899. Reports in the magazines of the Chelsea Old Students' Association record Ethel Cartwright as a student from Battersea; she completed her training and left the South Western Polytechnic in December 1899 and was awarded a College Diploma with Distinction. Helen Ironside and Dora Smith were awarded College Diplomas after two years' study, the former with two terms interruption because of illness, so leaving in March 1901, and the latter with Distinction in July 1900. Ethel Mary Dibden and Elizabeth Reed completed one year only and did not qualify for the College award. Nevertheless on leaving College, they both taught the former at a private school in Exmouth, the latter at Mr Moss' Gymnasium, Eastbourne. Although Maud Jenkyn and Ethel de B Colinette did not receive College awards, leaving before the Chelsea College was inaugurated, they were invited by Miss Hughes, who trained at Chelsea from 1899 to 1902 (member), seconded by Miss Cartwright (Chairman), to become members of the Old Students' Association when it was founded on 28 May 1904.

The following vignettes of four of the first students illustrate the pioneering sense of service and dedication which was implicit in their training as teachers.

Maud Ann Jenkyn, born on 4 December 1878, was educated at Clapham Modern School (Girls' Public Day School Company) for eight years. After completing her training at the South Western Polytechnic and teaching for a short while in England, she became a missionary and served as Sister Maud in Nyasaland (1900 to 1913) with the UMCA Missions. She was confirmed on 1 January 1914 by Bishop Fisher of Nyasaland and professed on 12 February 1916 by Bishop Ridgeway of Sarum into the Anglican Sisterhood of St Denys. At this time, the chief work of the Convent was abroad and Sister Maud worked in India from 1920 to 1938 and at the All Saints Mission, Kalfania, Africa. Elected on 14 December 1944 and Installed on 9 February 1945 as Mother Superior, St Denys, Warminster, Wiltshire, she served for 13 years, in this capacity, until she resigned on 8 December 1957. (Mother Maud RIP 16 September 1961.)

Ethel Mary Cartwright, born on 1 October 1880 and educated at Clapham Modern School for eight years, was the senior student of her year. She taught at the Northern Polytechnic from September 1899 to July 1901 and Clapham Modern School from September 1901 to July 1903. From 1903 to 1904, she taught at private schools in the county of Kent and Beckenham. At the same time as holding the latter posts, she was also a member of staff (Assistant Mistress) at the Physical Training College, South Western Polytechnic from September 1901 to July 1904. In September 1904 she travelled to Canada to the Ladies' College, Halifax, serving on the staff from September 1904 to July 1906. She was then appointed to the staff of the Royal Victoria College, McGill University, Montreal. Here she founded the McGill School of Physical Education in 1912 and later the School of Physiotherapy. During 1915–16 she had leave of absence to return to the United Kingdom as Director of Physiotherapy in a military hospital. When she left McGill in 1927, she started chicken farming in Canada. In 1930 she became Professor of Physical Education at Saskatchewan University until her second retirement in 1943 when she returned to chicken farming. Ethel Cartwright, who died on 18 September 1955, was honoured in 1948 by the Canadian Association for Health, Physical Education and Recreation when she received the R Tait McKenzie Award of Honour. She was elected a member of the Saskatchewan Sports Hall of Fame and posthumously made a member of McGill Sports Hall of Fame in 1996. The June 1948 Bulletin of the Canadian Association for Health, Physical Education and Recreation reported,

> Ethel Cartwright is one of Canada's pioneers in our profession, a woman of great courage, ability and vision, a pathfinder in the establishment of sound professional principles and high ideals, a friendly human interest in people, an abounding enthusiasm in the complete education of the individual, respected and loved by generations of students and teachers, her name and her contribution to the cause of health, physical education and recreation, will live long in our memories.

When the Chelsea students gave gymnastic displays, Dora Smith 'was the leader in "figure-marching" because of her splendid presence crowned with a head of fuzzy red hair'; she was nicknamed 'Copper Top' by the cheeky London street urchins who played outside the Polytechnic buildings. On leaving College, she taught at a number of schools, including Mortimer House, Clifton Private School in

Richmond and St James, West Malvern from September 1900 to 1914. Her war effort included work with the Almeric Paget Massage Corps at various military hospitals, such as Sutton Veny, Salisbury Plain, Knowsley, and Oxford and with the British Expeditionary Force, Etaples. From 1919, she was appointed first to the Ministry of Pensions Hospital, Shepherd's Bush and later, in 1923, to Knotty Ash.

Helen Ironside taught at Streatham Hill High School from 1901 to 1917 and during the war went to the front during vacations. Later she became a welfare worker, with the post of superintendent at the munitions works in Croydon and, from April 1921, returned to teaching at Weymouth Secondary School until 1922, when she moved to the Central Secondary School, Sheffield.

All applications for teaching posts, made by the students, were supported by personally orientated testimonials handwritten by the Head Mistress. For example, 'Miss Mabel Salisbury has been a student at this College for two years. I consider her to be a teacher of exceptional power and ability which, combined with great moral strength, enthusiasm for her work and charm of manner, would make her a desirable member of any school staff. Dorette Wilke, 1906'.

This assessment was confirmed by Miss Ethel Trew, Head Mistress of Queenswood School Clapham in 1913 when she wrote:

> Dear Fräulein Wilke,
> I shall be requiring a new Physical Culture Mistress in January next and should much like to have one of your students. The best mistress I ever had was Miss Salisbury, who came to me direct from you, and I very much wish you could give me another student as good as she was.

During the first years of the College's foundation, students studied for various lengths of time depending on their initial qualifications, if any, their health or their previous and ongoing experiences. Several became visiting mistresses in or near London, while still being students at the College. Students therefore qualified after one, two or even three years at College. Many were recruited and rejected after one, two, three or four terms, or left because of lack of finance or to be married. 216 students were recruited to the first 12 cohorts, 1898 to 1909, and entered College; 158 qualified with the award of the College Diploma at the end of their training, including 42 with Distinction grading.

The first course of training, for a fee of 72 guineas, had three main strands, namely: Practical Studies, Theoretical Studies and Teaching Practice. This structure with certain modifications and changes in terminology, has stood the test of time in the training of physical educationists at Chelsea. Students also paid a library sub-scription of 1/6 per year and a games club subscription of 10/6 per year. They were advised that the cost of examination fees, books, and expenses connected with games during the training should not exceed £10. (See Figure 2.1.)

Examinations taken by the early students whilst at College included: the School Teachers' Certificate of the British College of Physical Education, the Certificate of the Gymnastic Teachers' Institute (including membership of these two organiza-tions), the Certificate of the National Society of Physical Education; the St John's

Figure 2.1: The first curriculum

The components of each strand were:

Practical subjects: *Gymnastics*   —   English, German, Swedish, Medical and
                                                    Vaulting.
                          Games   —   Cricket, Tennis, Hockey, Net Ball (from
                                                    1902 played in the gymnasium and 1906
                                                    outside) and Lacrosse (from 1905).
                          Dancing   —   Ballroom, English Folk and Morris
                                                    (from 1907).
                          Fencing
                          Swimming and Diving

Theoretical subjects: Anatomy, Physiology, Hygiene, Chemistry, Theory of
                          Movements, Elementary Science.

Teaching Practice: Individual classes   —   German system
                                               —   Swedish system

Other subjects: Ambulance First Aid, Massage, Life Saving, Sick Nursing,
                          Elocution, Voice Production, Singing, Criticism lessons and
                          a lecture in the final year.

Ambulance Medallion, First Aid and Sick Nursing Certificates; the Board of
Education, South Kensington, Elementary and Advanced Hygiene, Elementary and
Advanced Physiology and Elementary Science; the Certificate and Membership of
the Society of Trained Masseuses, which had been founded in 1894 and became the
Incorporated Society of Trained Masseuses in 1900, as well as the Chelsea College
Diploma.

Figure 2.2: Awards in 1902

The British College of Physical Education

8 students qualified for membership
13 students qualified for membership in Swedish gymnastics

The National Society of Physical Education

13 certificates awarded

The Gymnastic Teachers' Institute

10 first class certificates awarded

The Incorporated Society of Trained Masseuses

12 certificates awarded

In those early days, no educational entrance standard was set, but 'intelligence, refinement, observation, a cheerful disposition, combined with enthusiasm, good health, a well formed figure and a good general education' were desirable. 'My students must have brains; a healthy active body is not enough', said Dorette Wilke, when addressing visitors to the College. Many students entered the College with no formal school qualifications; they had been educated at home. Others, however, held varying awards ranging from the South Kensington Certificates, Certificates from the Royal Academy of Music, Trinity College, London, the Royal Drawing Society and the College of Preceptors, to Junior and/or Senior Awards from Cambridge, Oxford, London, Aberdeen and Queen's universities. A few had attended secondary schools but had not taken or gained external examinations. To assist girls to obtain an appropriate level of education prior to the College course, the Polytechnic had designed and provided, from 1901, a preparatory year for those whose parents could afford the additional fees of eight guineas per term for 12 weeks with 25 hours study per week, or £21 per session of three terms. The curriculum included the following: English, history, grammar, literature, foreign languages, elocution, hygiene, elementary science, arithmetic and gymnastics. By 1910, students were prepared for the London Matriculation Examinations in the non-professional course and by 1913 matriculation of a recognized university was the accepted standard for admission.

Gradually, students were recruited from a wide range of schools, including the Polytechnic's Day School, many schools of the Girls' Public Day School Company and a number of private schools. Candidates had to provide a medical certificate, from their own doctor, prior to entry: 'Miss Mabel Salisbury is in good health and of sound constitution — she is a fit subject to undergo a course of Physical Culture' (M Burgess and Dr Ford, 3 June 1904), or be examined by the College Medical Adviser, for which a fee of five shillings was charged.

All students were also medically examined at the beginning of each session by the Woman Medical Officer of the College and records, including anthropometric measurements, were kept. The measurements were sent to Professor Georges Dreyer, CBE, MA, MD, Professor of Pathology, University of Oxford, who was collecting statistics in connection with research work on physical fitness. In 1921, students were again subjects for tests of general efficiency, conducted by Dr Flack, who was working at Mount Vernon with Dr Cripps and Professor Leonard Hill. It is interesting to note that, prior to 1909, when the three-year course was introduced, the occupation of the student's father was written in longhand in the College Record Books, but in brackets, and only for those who were the daughters of doctors, clergymen, solicitors, service officers, artists or scientists. From 1909, however, all occupations were recorded and included merchants, architects, auctioneers, manufacturers, brewers, and later, farmers, engineers, tailors, chemists, journalists, teachers, shopkeepers and explorers.

After qualification, students were appointed to an even wider range of schools than they had attended as girls, both at home and abroad, including posts in Australia, Canada, China, South Africa, London County Council secondary schools, Girls' Public Day School Company schools, private schools, private gymnasia, polytechnics and training colleges. A few became county organizers, one or two His Majesty's Inspectors, some undertook further study and qualified, for example, as doctors, scientists, artists or physiologists. Many married and brought up their families. As one Old Student, trained from 1910 to 1913 wrote in 1936, 'This is my eleventh year organising in Nottingham. The beauty of a city organising post is that there is always something fresh to tackle. Camping, swimming, sports days, are now well established, and we are pegging away at nursery schools and keep fit classes'. A second Old Student from the same group commented, 'I am still finding life as a doctor most interesting. I think physical training made an excellent training for the medical profession — it gave one a wider knowledge of the human race, and made an anatomical examination far easier'. A third Old Student, trained from 1905 to 1907, helped in 1930 to wipe out a £12,000 debt, owed by the Derowen Cripple Training College, run in conjunction with Shropshire Orthopaedic Hospital and Dame Agnes Hunt's Surgical Home to train cripple boys and girls to earn their living, instead of being a burden to themselves and the state. The first 'free studentship' for a postgraduate student, was held as early as 1905–06 by Winifred Gladys Martyn, BSc, Kings College, London, Birkbeck Institute. She came primarily to do experimental work on 'fatigue' and had an individual timetable, but also received a College Diploma at the end of the year. In 1911 she became a member of staff lecturing in and with responsibility for psychology after she had completed her DSc at Bedford College, London. By this time, she had also married and become Dr Halsey.

Many Old Students actively supported the Women's Suffrage Movement participating in marches and/or became officers of the various branches of the organization throughout the country. One, Miss Dorothy Evans, who trained from 1906 to 1908, was summoned at Batley for riotous behaviour during a meeting held by Mr Runciman. Her father paid the fine to keep her from imprisonment. She resigned her school post and was appointed as permanent organizer of the Women's Suffrage work in the Midlands with her headquarters in Birmingham. This particular Old Student was, from 1917, a very active member of the Women's Suffrage Movement. She went to prison many times and was force fed, but she continued to fight, first, for the emancipation of women and, secondly, at the League of Nations in Geneva, for equal compensation for women who had suffered war injuries. Further examples of service to the community and the physical education profession include: Leila Rendel (Chelsea, 1902 to 1904); Evelyn M Perry (Chelsea, 1903 to 1905); and C Monica Hawkes (Chelsea, 1922 to 1925).

Leila Rendel was the first woman inspector of physical training (HMI PT) to be appointed by the Board of Education in 1908. She was also a co-founder of the resident Caldecott Community in 1911 (a charity supported by the Chelsea Students for many years). The aim of the Community was:

> to attempt to integrate the whole life of a child who, in a world of conflicting standards is so frequently unco-ordinated in mind and emotions.

The boys and girls of working men and women, were in some way deprived and/or emotionally unstable but basically of sound temperament, in fact, often of superior intelligence, once the behaviour difficulties were overcome.

Evelyn Perry was appointed as an Assistant at the Carnegie Gymnasium, Dunfermline on leaving College. Her experience included teaching in schools, in pupil teachers centres and in colleges in London. In 1916–17, she was appointed by the War Office to HM Munitions Factory, Gretna Green, as organizer of physical education. In February 1918, she became an HMI PT and later the Senior Woman Inspector. She served as the Chelsea Old Students' Association representative on the first Governing Body of the College from 1947 to 1952.

Monica Hawkes was Senior Commandant, ATS, in charge of physical training from 1941 to 1945 and an HMI from 1945 to 1967.

From its inception, the College has been staffed by well qualified women and men. (See Figure 2.3.)

'You see', Dorette Wilke said to her visitors in 1899, 'the chief point about our College is that we have a special teacher for every subject, practical and theoretical, so that the girls have the very best training it is possible to give them in every single branch of the work. This, of course, is a result that can be more easily attained in a College of this sort than in many others, for it is situated in an institute that provides excellent teachers for all subjects'. The Gymnastic Teachers' Training College was inspected by members of the Academic Board of the University of London, midsummer 1903. The Board aimed to promote the Extension of University Teaching and the Senior Inspector, Mr W A Osborne, MB, DSc, wrote of the Head Mistress, 'not only the physical and mental aptitudes, but the idiosyncrasies, habits, ideas and details of private life of each of her pupils were known to her (Dorette Wilke) and enabled her to modify, if necessary, the instruction given to each'. As one would expect, as student numbers increased additional and/or replacement staff for those who had left were appointed, although the staff:student ratio was perhaps the most favourable during the first few years of the College's existence. By 1913, staff averaged 23 sessions of teaching and supervising students per week with additional teaching practice and criticism sessions. The length of sessions varied according to the subject taught; for example, anatomy — one hour, advanced hygiene — $1\frac{1}{2}$ hours, singing — $\frac{1}{2}$ hour, gymnastics — one hour and hockey — $1\frac{1}{2}$ hours.

Dorette Wilke extended her own experience when in 1907, with support from Colonel Fox, HMI Physical Training, Herbert Tomlinson, FRS, former Principal of the South Western Polytechnic, and Sidney Skinner, Principal of the South Western Polytechnic, she became an examiner in physical training under the London County Council, for teachers in elementary schools trained by the London County Council organizers. In one of her reports she commented, 'Some of the candidates had had experience in teaching the subject and did fairly well, others were intelligent and sympathetic and did well on that account, but there was evident throughout, a great lack of real knowledge of the subject, due to insufficient training'. On this occasion, 12 students were examined and seven passed at the 55 per cent pass mark. Specific comments were made covering the following categories — carriage, voice, manner,

Figure 2.3: *The first staff of the College*

Eight were appointed specifically for their physical education expertise:

Froken Adolphsen (Diploma — Copenhagen)	— Swedish and Medical Gymnastics, Massage and Anatomy
Sergeant Jones (Grenadier Guards)	— English Gymnastics and Vaulting (also took boys' and men's classes)
Mr McPherson and *M Volland*	— Fencing
Mr John Hewke	— Games
Miss Beauchamp	— Ballroom Dance
Dorette Wilke	— Lectures in Class Teaching, Theory of Movements, 'Commanding', supervised Criticism Lessons and German Gymnastics
Miss Daly (was on the staff of Chelsea Swimming Baths)	— Swimming

and five from other departments of the Polytechnic:

H B Lacey	— Physiology
A G Maslen	— Hygiene
Dr Mary Coghill-Hawkes (College Medical Officer)	— First Aid and Sick Nursing
Miss Fanny Heywood (late Prima Donna of the Crystal Palace Opera Company and Lyceum Theatre)	— Voice Production and Elocution
Mr Seymoor Dicker (late organ scholar of Christ's College, Cambridge)	— Singing

Students, such as Ethel Cartwright, also coached their peers at Games (for example, Cricket).

---

answers to questions and corrections. Colonel Fox saw her as '. . . a practical worker' one 'thoroughly versed in hygiene and the theory of physical training'. Sidney Skinner said she was '. . . well known for her extensive and broad knowledge of the subject'. Herbert Tomlinson, in commenting on her experience and achievements wrote, '. . . this success was evidently due to her combined kindness and firmness, together with her profound and scientific knowledge of the various methods of physical culture adopted in England and abroad'. He continued, '. . . she is possessed of really wonderful energy and zeal and whatever she undertakes will be done thoroughly'.

Dorette Wilke had visited Cheltenham Ladies College to examine kindergarten students and there met the Headmistress, Miss Dorothea Beale. Miss Beale and Miss Buss, founder and Headmistress of the North London Collegiate School for Ladies in 1850, supported the professional training of young ladies to become qualified teachers and the inclusion of gymnastics, dancing and other physical activities in their schools' curricula. Dorette Wilke had also been to Scotland to examine men students and visited various centres of the Froebel Society to examine kindergarten students.

By 1908, Dorette Wilke realized that she would find it easier to carry out her duties as an examiner in physical training in Great Britain if she were granted British status for then she would have equal rights and capacities as those of a natural born British Subject. Her formal application form, completed on 29 February 1908, and considered in March 1908, was supported by a favourable report from the Chief Constable, on behalf of the Assistant Commissioner, F S Bullock, together with further support from four respectable and responsible persons — Mary Coghill-Hawkes MD, Gwendoline Alice Polgreen, Harry Bird Harper and Edward Hugh Pritchard. The first two were members of the College staff, the third, Secretary of the South Western Polytechnic and the fourth, a schoolmaster in Middlesex. The memorialist was described by Edward Parker (Sergeant) and W Bascombe (Acting Superintendent), as a

> Professor of Physical Culture, a respectable woman who intends to remain permanently in the United Kingdom, and seeks to obtain the rights and capacities of a natural born British Subject. She can speak, read and write the English language well.

After Dorette Wilke was registered as a naturalized British subject on 1 May 1908, she refused to be called 'Fräulein' and was universally known as 'Domina'; her surname Wilke was changed to Wilkie by the same Deed Poll, although in the official Polytechnic publications, it was not changed until 1914, for example, in the brochure of the Physical Training College for Women of that year.

At first, students not resident in London were expected to live in a boarding house attached to the College under the Head Mistress' supervision. Later, private accommodation was provided in Glebe Place, Trafalgar Square, Paulton Square and Sidney Street, prior to the opening of a boarding house in Oakley Street in 1902 by Mrs May. In 1905 the pioneer hostel, Cadogan Lodge for 14 to 20 students of the Gymnastic Teachers' Training College was opened at 11 Carlyle Square with Miss Wahlers as Warden. In succeeding years various changes were made to residential accommodation, but always extra places were provided. From 1914 to 1924, Miss Crowdy was Warden of the hostel called 'The House'; she treated students like grown-up people but, nevertheless, read interesting books to them on Sunday evenings 'with charm and understanding'. Each hostel developed its own traditions, including carol singing, when money was raised for a charity, such as the Children's Hospital in Tite Street, theatre visits, concerts and parties.

On 1 December 1900, Dorette Wilke had moved to a flat at 7 Elin Park Mansions, Chelsea and, on 15 December 1906, she moved again to live at 31

Beaufort-Mansions, Chelsea, where she remained in residence until her retirement in 1929. 'In 1914, she bought a cottage in Barley-Mow Hill, Headley, Bordon, Hampshire.' This was to be her home in retirement, during the holidays and occasional weekends in term time; she gardened and made improvements to her home 'until it became delightfully colourful and characteristic of herself'. Staff and students were welcomed to the cottage and third year outings by 'chara' (charabanc) to Domina's cottage 'were one of the things one looks back on with enjoyment' said an Old Student, whilst reminiscing.

When the College first opened within the South Western Polytechnic, accommodation was limited and primitive for the women physical training students and staff. There was only one gymnasium, which they shared with the men's and boys' classes taken by Sergeant Jones. The gymnasium had fixed and portable equipment, including vaulting horse, parallel bars, rings, ropes for climbing, coconut mats, dumb-bells, wands and Indian clubs. A new giant stride (a piece of gymnastic apparatus) was added in 1899. Part of the gallery of the gymnasium was curtained-off to form a cloakroom for the women students and the remainder of the gallery was used by them as a common room during their 'free' time. A chest of drawers served as locker space and one row of pegs was provided as hanging space. The students also shared a rest room with women students from other departments of the Polytechnic. The principle of sharing extended to Dorette Wilke and Sergeant Jones, who had one small dressing room for their use.

Sessions in anatomy and physiology took place in one of the Polytechnic's main laboratories and any available room was used for lectures in hygiene, class teaching, theory of movements and 'commanding'. Facilities for swimming were poor with the students initially using the small bath adjoining Chelsea Town Hall and nicknamed 'The Soap Dish'. 'The deep end was shallow enough for the students to stand and 12 boxes were provided along the sides of the bath for changing'. Later, students bicycled or were taken by horse-brake to Walham Baths until 1906, when the Chelsea (Municipal) Bath was rebuilt.

Considerable time was spent travelling to and from games fields; initially hockey and cricket were played in Battersea Park and tennis in Trafalgar Square, Chelsea, adjacent to Manresa Road (later renamed Chelsea Square). Subsequently, fields were available in Burntwood Lane, Wandsworth Common and at the Butchers Alms Houses Ground at Walham Green.

Gradually, between 1898 and 1929, through Dorette Wilke's continual requests and perseverance, accommodation was both increased and improved. This was particularly true, following the critical report of the London County Council inspectors in 1917.

> The most pressing problem in connection with the buildings is the provision of adequate accommodation for the work of the Physical Training College for Women . . . Hitherto, the Council has not aided this Department of the Polytechnic by equipment grants and it has been regarded as a branch that should practically support itself by the fees charged for the instruction. In view of the increasing importance which will be attached to physical training in the future, and of the need for a strong and well-managed training college for London students, we think

that the time has come when more formal recognition should be given to the excellent work that the College has done and is doing, and that it should receive more generous treatment in the way of maintenance and equipment grants. It should, we think, be looked upon by the Council as the London training college in this subject and given the opportunity and facilities to develop its work.

By 1929, the College had its own playing fields at Merton Abbey, new apparatus, refurbished and additional lecture rooms, a new gymnasium and extended hostel accommodation. A student, trained from 1909 to 1912, and writing in 1972 said, 'We worked in the Chelsea Polytechnic and had none of the amenities of present day colleges. No showers, no hot baths. We cycled to and from the games field and even cycled at night to teach in the clubs and the various youth movements which were just being started'.

As well as having permanent appointments Dorette Wilke, with the help of her students as teachers, always taught many private classes, tutored medical students as a special group and during 1900, she was one of Mr Sandow's lady instructors. A series of classes often culminated in a demonstration of gymnastics for the public or the children's parents. For example, on 6 April 1888 at Stempel's Gymnasium, the women's programme consisted of marching, mass exercises with light wooden bar-bells totalling 40 consecutive movements to music, maze, Indian clubs, rope climbing and storming board. The press commented the next day, the students '. . . emulate the correct and splendid style of their talented instructress' and, when reporting on her 'solo' performance, 'Fräulein Wilke distinguished herself by her grace and precision'. At Croydon in 1892 she stood with a '. . . bouquet held aloft while the little ones circled round her in a labyrinth of movements'. Work in unison lent itself to spectacle. The performers, irrespective of size and shape or speed of movement, were expected to keep in time and to work as one person.

Dorette Wilke's work extended in 1902 to establishing a Saturday games afternoon in Battersea Park for 'deprived' children in the districts of Battersea and Chelsea and to the London Working Girls Clubs. For the former, the notice to the Board Schools read, 'The time for fairyland is half past two till four pm and the only condition of entrance is a desire to play and be happy'. Many boys, as well as girls, arrived at the appointed time and place, and the former asked to play football. It is recorded, their teachers (the students) were equal to the occasion and quickly won the respect of the boys as worthy 'opponents'. As Dorette Wilke said, 'I . . . attempt to put a little brightness into their (the children's) lives, though they may know little enough of the higher aims of Physical Education'. Other charitable events included the annual Christmas party for local children, for which money had been raised, by the students, so that each child had a present from Father Christmas, as well as tea prepared by students of the Polytechnic's Domestic Economy School; the Chelsea College students provided the entertainment. College had contributed generously to various charities during the First World War. For example, £40 had been raised in aid of war funds from a demonstration of ancient and modern dance given at the Polytechnic. After contributions to war charities were no longer necessary, from 1918, the Chelsea Students, both past and present, together with students from Anstey, Bedford and Bergman Österberg Colleges of Physical Training endowed a bed in the Elizabeth Garrett Anderson Hospital. The Chelsea students subscribed £295 towards the initial £1000 required for endowment. The endowment fund was completed and the bed in use by 1922. For the purposes of identification, a small stained-glass window depicting 'Diana the Huntress' by Christopher Webb was placed at the head of the bed. Students from the four colleges continued to support this Charity well into the 1950s.

Of the Working Girls' Clubs, for factory girls, whose main employment was manual labour, it was said that Dorette Wilke has '. . . done more to help and encourage their efforts than anyone in the profession. For years she devoted much free time to judging competitions and her wise advice and enthusiastic bearing on these occasions must have inspired and helped many teachers and workers'. She also contributed to the work of the Clubs' committees and wrote a pamphlet on 'girls' hygienic clothing' which was published in one of Harmsworth's papers and in Dr Mortimers' book on *Home Nursing*. By request, she had 1000 copies of this pamphlet printed and circulated 'free' to poor mothers. She was appalled at the ignorance of matters of personal hygiene and the lack of responsibility on the part of parents, for the welfare of their children.

In her lecture in 1916 to the National Organisation of Girls' Clubs, on *The Best Form of Physical Education for Girls' Clubs* she advocated the Swedish system of gymnastics. '. . . here each exercise has a definite aim and is carefully graded according to its effects especially on circulation and respiration whilst in other so called systems, the exercises are often put together without the slightest knowledge or consideration as to their physiological effects'.

Teaching at the London Working Girls' Clubs was always part of the students' College teaching experience. The Old Students' magazine of 1929 records the following comments, Domina sent her students to these clubs 'not only to gain teaching experience, but to learn more of human nature and to see something of the lives of the less fortunate of the world's workers. It is impossible to forget her advice to bring a "missionary spirit" into one's work, for she herself has retained this spirit and fosters an interest in club work in her students'. The article continued, 'Volunteers from among third year students are still (in 1929) called for regularly to judge competitions and to help in other suitable ways, while every second year student is responsible for a club once a week throughout the winter. This is the outcome of Domina's own early work'.

Dorette Wilke lectured to many eminent audiences, including the New Victorian Club on 3 December 1901, of which she was made an Honorary Member; to delegates at the English Educational Exhibition, Imperial Institute, London on 27 January 1900; the West Ham and District Educational Conference on Physical Training on 5 December 1902; the West Riding County Council Educational Conference, Shipley on 12 May 1906; the Sussex course in 1906; Rotherham on 23 January 1909; the Japan British Exhibition Women's Congress, Earls Court 9 July 1910; the National Organisation of Girls' Clubs on 15 October 1912; and many other organizations, both at home and overseas. Contained in her texts are such comments as:

Children need at least twenty minutes exercise each day, under the supervision of well-trained teachers.

All observers of children notice their great desire for movement, every teacher knows how difficult it is to keep a healthy child still . . .

Plato says, 'The aim of Physical Training is to create a perfect harmony between body and soul' — what could be more beautiful?

A body as hard as steel, to work hard, to work well and bear up against our main difficulties. A mind as clear as crystal, to see and understand all that is good and noble and beautiful in the world, and also to distinguish the true from the false. A heart as warm as sunshine, so that we may feel and sympathise with the joys and troubles of our fellow creatures.

This is the mission of Physical Training.

She also taught many classes of ladies and children German gymnastics within the Polytechnic and at external venues, for example, at the Church Institute, Croydon and Queen's College. As one participant wrote, 'Only those who were privileged to attend her classes can in any way realise what a sweet and amazingly vital personality she had, which vivified all classes the moment she appeared, making it always a great joy to work for and with her', or 'Miss Wilkie was a brilliant teacher of gymnastics . . . Her vitality and her genius for teaching would have made anyone a gymnast'.

Although the College course had many components in the *Practical Studies Strand*, there can be no doubt that gymnastics formed the core (48 per cent) during the first era. 'Every morning, from ten to twelve, the girls do practical gymnastics under my tuition; besides this, there are two or three extra classes every week at which they take it in turn to be teacher, their lesson being criticised afterwards by the others'. The criticism lesson was a time of 'real ordeal' and yet it often served to strengthen the student's belief in herself and in her personal observations. At the end of the lesson, the 'College' adjourned to the Head Mistress's room where the 'victim' was first criticised by Dorette Wilke and then by her peers. 'Happy was the student who found a "*" at the end of her crit, for this meant distinction'.

Students loved Dorette Wilke's classes, 'they were our greatest joy'. She was unconventional and wore a scarlet gymnastics dress and sash, which reflected her colourful personality and her tall, well proportioned figure made for an impressive, dignified entrance. Her presence was felt by the students and she insisted on tidiness of hair, tunic and stockings and on punctuality; anyone who was late had to miss the class, a great penalty. Remember, she said, '. . . punctuality (is) a good habit . . . have it yourself first'. She had a great enthusiasm and sense of humour and the constant impression of 'being alive', which was infectious, was never far away.

The students also participated in the ordinary gymnastic classes held at the Polytechnic for older women students and, 'Every senior student, too, is required to invent a figure mass every week; and we have just been doing some pretty work with the wands that you might like to see', said Dorette Wilke to the visitors, as she took them around the College in 1899.

Some idea of the content of German gymnastics can be extracted from the programmes of displays of work given by pupils and students under Dorette Wilke's direction in 1901. 'Extension exercises, squad practice involving rings and jumping, low rings, parallel bars, inclined ladder, rope climbing, ornamental marching combined with mass exercises using flags, further squad practice with storming board, balancing poles and vaulting horse'. Or from a quotation from a letter written by a student, Alice Gardner, for her old school's magazine (South Hampstead High School) in 1900. 'We have half an hour of callisthenics which consists of marching, mass exercises with dumb-bells, bar-bells, clubs or free movements and one hour directed to vaulting, parallel rings, bars and other pieces of large apparatus'. At the turn of the century, Anstey and Bergman Österberg students concentrated on Swedish gymnastics, while Liverpool students concentrated on musical drill with some Swedish gymnastics to music.

In 1900, the *Model Course of Physical Training* based on the Army Red Book with military overtones and suitable for older boys and girls was launched by the Board of Education and was complemented in 1902 by the *Syllabus of Physical Exercises for Elementary Schools*. 'The object of training is not display, but the setting-up of scholars by the development of their muscles and activity, the quickening of their intelligence and the formation of the habit of obedience'. In the elementary schools, 'As a general rule, physical training should be carried on by the teachers forming the ordinary school staff, rather than by outside instructors, and this for reasons which all leaders will appreciate they must, however, first *learn* to instruct. For this purpose, groups of schools can combine to secure the services of a qualified instructor who should, if possible, have been trained in the Army gymnastic course'. Members of the Ling Association concerned that the Swedish system of gymnastics would be abandoned for unscientific drill based lessons, presented the Board of Education with a Memorial *Women Teachers for Women*. The Memorial was signed by 1400 people, including members of the Ling Association, doctors, teachers and people of standing. The trained women physical educationists did not want Army drill sergeants taking girls for physical education. Their efforts were rewarded; between 1902 and 1904 a new *Syllabus of Physical Exercises* was issued by the Board of Education. Colonel Fox had visited the Gymnastic Teachers' Training College for Women and had many discussions with Dorette Wilke (German gymnastic) and Ethel Adair-Roberts, appointed in 1902 to take Swedish gymnastics, medical gymnastics, anatomy and dancing. He used the Gymnastic Teachers' Training College students to test exercises and tables. The influence of the two women was clear for recognition was given in the new syllabus to forms of exercise other than military drill.

> Girls' Schools and those Boys' Schools in which it is not desired to undertake military drill, may make use of the great variety of free gymnastic exercises (including gymnastics, dancing and skipping for girls, Swedish drill, swimming drill, exercises with dumb-bells, bars, bar-bells, Indian Clubs, etc,) which are to be found in the numerous well-known textbooks of Physical Exercises now used in schools under the larger School Boards.

In speaking about the syllabus Colonel Fox quoted, 'The primary object of any course of physical exercises in schools is to maintain and, if possible, improve the health and physique of the children. This may be described as its *physical* effect'. He continued, 'but the exercises which conduce to this result may, if rightly conducted, have an effect scarcely less important in developing in the scholars' qualities of alertness, decision, concentration and perfect control of mind over body. This may be styled the *educational* effect'.

Although students, at the Gymnastic Teachers' Training College for Women studied both German and Swedish gymnastics, during 1906, the following question was hotly debated in both press and gymnastic circles, 'Should the system of Physical Training adopted in England be pure Swedish?' Swedish lessons were conducted by word of command; there was no musical accompaniment to the exercises as with German gymnastics. An alternative question was also considered, namely, 'Should music be retained as an accompaniment to exercises worked out on Swedish principles?' To facilitate discussion, Dorette initiated an interesting course, at the College, which was known as 'The Experimental Physical Training Class'.

> Many medical men and women, officers and inspectors of the London County Council, teachers and others interested in physical training attended this class, trying for themselves Swedish exercises with and without music, for children and for adults, and contrasting them with the German system.

Discussions of a scientific nature followed the practical class, but the trend of their findings was not recorded. After attending a demonstration of the Ling Swedish System at Anstey Physical Training College circa 1907–08, during the return train journey, just outside Paddington Station, Dorette suddenly turned to her companion, an Old Student of Chelsea, and 'out of the blue' said, 'It must go . . . the German system . . . it must go'. This event was prior to the introduction in the House of Lords by Viscount Hill of the Education (Physical Training) Bill and the publication of a new edition of the Board of Education *Syllabus of Physical Training for Schools*, based on the Swedish system in 1909.

'Go' the German system did, with all the rapidity and thoroughness so characteristic of Domina, until it was replaced by Austrian gymnastics following a visit by Peggy Oldland (a member of the Chelsea staff) to Vienna in 1923–24, where she studied under Dr Margarete Streicher and Dr Gaulhofer at the University of Vienna. Austrian gymnastics was to remain a hallmark of the training received by Chelsea students well into the 1940s. In 1913, an annual Swedish gymnastics competition for schools had been organized at Chelsea with a trophy 'The Daily News Shield for Gymnastics' awarded that year to the winners, the Grey Coat Hospital School.

Gymnastics in this era always included medical gymnastics. Dorette Wilke had commented in an interview circa 1899, 'We are going to make a special point of medical gymnastics in our course of training — not only are we going to give this branch particular prominence, but we are also going to inaugurate an examination for it'. The concern for 'health' was evident from this approach to gymnastics. Students had daily practice under supervision in the gymnastic method of treating the most common bodily deformities of school children. By 1911, Domina said, 'I am hoping to make great improvements in our medical work by putting it under the supervision of Dr Dobbie (College Medical Officer). I shall hope to begin with the thin edge of the wedge next term', which she did. Practice was supported by theory covering all physical deformities, examination of patients, treatments and the 696 hours of study culminated in sitting from 1920 the Conjoint Examination of the Chartered Society for Massage and Medical Gymnastics (previously the Incorporated Society of Trained Masseuses) and later, in 1944, the Chartered Society of Physiotherapists.

Until 1907, when Morris dancing was introduced by Miss Warren, a teacher from Miss Neal's Esperance Club, only ballroom dancing, The Lancers, Barn Dance, Waltz, etc; had featured on the curriculum. Miss Neal was working with Mr Cecil Sharp. For a whole week, students zealously practised Bean Setting, Laudnum Bunches and many other elementary dances. By the end of the week, they had discovered the adverse effects on the calf muscles of undiluted Morris dancing! Dorette Wilke had previously said, 'Dancing is in the widest sense beneficial, it encourages lightness, rhythm, grace and it should also cultivate graciousness of manner'. After Domina had met Cecil Sharp, she appreciated the value of his gospel as, accompanied by William Kimber (fiddle), he instructed both staff and students in Morris and Folk dancing. Outlining his views on the educational value of folk songs and dances, Sharp stated, '. . . I attach greater importance to their influence in training and refining the musical taste of the rising generation. As regards the dances, the Morris dances are an almost ideal instrument of physical education. Miss Wilke, the physical instructor at the Chelsea Polytechnic and Training College for Teachers, told me that the Morris dances were the very things she had been longing for. If they are danced properly, they exercise the whole body and, as everyone knows, exercise which is combined with enjoyment is worth far more than exercise which is merely taken for the sake of the exercise'.

As A H Fox Strangeways (1923) said in his biography of 'Cecil Sharp':

> It had not originally been Sharp's intention to play an active part in the teaching of the dances, but he had underrated the difficulties and dangers of popularisation. He now realised that satisfactory results would not be obtained unless first hand instruction was given by himself and he had direct control over his teachers. In the Physical Training Department of the South Western Polytechnic (now the Chelsea Physical Training College) he found an organisation which met his requirements and, in September (27th) 1909, a School of Morris Dancing was established in connection with the College, with Sharp as Director. Its object was: (a) to form classes in Morris Dancing, (b) to train, examine and grant certificates to teachers of Morris Dancing; and (c) to keep a register of certified teachers, lecturers and classes and to give advice and disseminate information respecting folk dances, folk songs, children's singing games and classes.

Domina was co-opted onto the Provisional Committee of the English Folk Dance Society in December 1911 and her cooperation, encouragement and sympathy were of real help to Sharp. On Tuesday evenings, Sharp held an 'experimental class' at the Chelsea Polytechnic '. . . where he tested any dance that he had just collected, or had deciphered from Playford'. Following a visit to Chelsea, in an article in *The Daily Telegraph* in December 1910, the correspondent wrote,

> . . . I was astounded at the brilliant entertainment provided by members of the various classes. I was given to understand that those who were performing, were either taking a course of instruction, had taken one, or were themselves teachers. In any case all concerned were wonderfully adept, and what they accomplished in something under two hours was full of grace, a splendid vigour and an immensely refreshing vitality.
>
> From what I saw, I am convinced that any reasonable person must realise the immense practical use that these dances may be put to. The dances have vastly more interest than that usually associated with folk-lore or antiquarian matters. They are full of a real grace nearly always; they have a rare rhythmic swing, are essentially typically British, and they provide a means of obtaining healthy exercise of the most fascinating character . . .

Sharp also travelled throughout Great Britain lecturing and took students from Chelsea Physical Training College to give practical demonstrations of dancing and singing games. The first team of English Morris and Country dancers was comprised of Chelsea second year students in 1909. As one member commented, in 1949, 'A very good time was had on those journeys and Chelsea was justly proud of this pioneer work'. The skill, vitality, grace and brilliant entertainment provided by the Chelsea students, who '. . . sang and danced their ways into the hearts of an enthusiastic band of sightseers . . .', was much appreciated. For example, 1909–10 was a very busy year for Sharp and the students, and included single sessions at Retford, Huddersfield, Taunton and Paris, and five sessions in London.

By 1928–29, dancing at Chelsea was, 'studied from an artistic and educational point of view. Aesthetic, national, ballroom and English Folk dancing' were also taught. The students studied dance composition and the history of dance and, during the second and third years of their training, they had 'experience in teaching all types of dance to children and adults'.

The Head Mistress was always planning for the future and 'Domina had a marvellous foresight as to the trend of affairs in professional matters, as exemplified by her early decision that three full years of training should be given, thus bringing it into line with a university education; by her decision that Matriculation should be aimed at as the entrance examination to the training, and by her early determination that her students should have a sound scientific background for their work, should know something of Chemistry, Physics, Mechanics and have the best Physiology and Psychology obtainable'. The aim of the third year of study was the application of knowledge gained in the first two years, as well as the new aspects of the curriculum such as principles of teaching and psychology.

From the early days 'theoretical subjects were studied so that students understood the reasons for giving specific exercises to children'. 'I have only been showing you the theoretical side first, because we Germans lay so much more stress upon it than you do', said Dorette Wilke showing a party of visitors round the

College in 1899. The content of theory in the first era was technical rather than philosophical. The syllabus for anatomy included in year I the general structure of the body — bones, joints, muscles — and, in year II, the systems — circulatory, digestive, nervous, excretory. Students visited hospitals or medical schools for dissection demonstrations. In physiology, there was a practical emphasis with students examining tissues and organs under the microscope, carrying out experiments, conducting analyses and tests and dissecting rabbits or frogs. The hygiene lectures were open to other students of the Polytechnic and included topics, such as: air, water, food, housing, disposal of sewage, prevention of disease, personal and school hygiene. General properties of matter formed the basis of the experimental mechanics course, while household science provided scientific training for students with no previous experience in measurement, constituents of common substances or the chemical constitution of food. As one Old Student, trained from 1907 to 1910 commented in 1949, 'We believed passionately in science — as we understood it — and we struggled to connect the sound background of anatomy which we were taught to the movements which we performed'.

Domina's desire to increase her own scientific knowledge of the various methods of physical culture in general, and of the various systems of gymnastics, in particular, taught in the schools in mainland European countries led her, during vacations, to travel abroad and visit schools in Switzerland, Germany, Denmark and Sweden. Her early teaching experiences soon convinced her that psychological knowledge was an essential part of a teacher's background. For three years, she attended Professor Adams' lectures, became a member of the Child Study Society and introduced psychology into the third year of the students' course in 1911–12 when she had lengthened it to a three-year training from 1909. The syllabus of 10 lectures per term for three terms covered definition of terms, pedagogical implications, concepts of major factors, adolescence and childhood and was taught by Dr Halsey.

Practical gymnastics was supported by theory of movements where students studied related topics including the history of gymnastics, construction and progression of gymnastic tables, methods of instruction and class management, as well as the physical effects of exercise and applied mechanics.

Practical games were also supported by the appropriate theoretical components related to each game and included specific skills, tactics, umpiring, teaching and coaching. College teams were fielded in each game and, for example, during the 1905–06 hockey season, the first XI:

Played	21	Goals	
Won	20	For	117
Drawn	1	Against	30
Lost	0		

Their opponents were local hockey clubs, such as Chiswick, Tulse Hill, Sydenham Hill, Highgate, Notting Hill, Ealing, Isleworth and Sandersted, Bedford College, Princess Helena College and the Chelsea Old Students' Association.

Dorette Wilke had a great gift for shaping raw and unpromising material and producing well qualified, observant teachers. She introduced students to teaching through practice on each other to gain confidence in the use of the voice. She counselled them, '. . . when you lose your temper you always lose your dignity as well . . .'. In parallel, they experienced observing individuals moving before being confronted with numbers of children and class management. Students had regular instruction and practice in teaching gymnastics and games including arrangement of lessons with and without hand apparatus. By 1902, '. . . two schools, the Secondary School and a Domestic Training School, were housed in the Polytechnic and the gymnastic classes for these girls provided the teaching practice, although the students also (attended and) helped with Dorette Wilke's (external) classes . . .'.

> The Hall was occupied by a series of classes . . . three or four classes were taught simultaneously from 12.00 to 12.30 and 1.45 to 2.15 and from 2.15 to 4.00 daily. When one third or fourth of the Hall and apparatus was one's portion, the possessor of the most interesting personality and biggest voice came off best.
>
> Fräulein Wilke laid great emphasis on the fact that she attaches the greatest importance to breathing exercises, to which especial attention is given during the College training. A lady teacher, who is herself both a trained actress and singer (Fanny Heywood), gives a lesson once a week on the art of lecturing. The posture of the body, every gesture, is carefully studied and the student is trained not to shout. The art of criticism is also carefully developed in the future teacher. The students are expected to freely criticise every class, and to criticise each other. Thus they are gradually trained to take first a small class, then a larger class and, lastly, a grown-up class. Much of their experience is gained by teaching in the Board School, which is attached to the Polytechnic.

Teaching was also available, under supervision, in local schools, such as the Servite School, Park Walk, Cook's Ground Board (Elementary) School (where Domina had organized a 20 minute per day experiment in physical training for the London County Council, with good results, in 1909), St Mary Bolton's and St Luke's Church Schools and the Royal Victoria Patriotic School on Wandsworth Common. By 1912, classes from local elementary schools came to the College gymnasium to be taken by the students. Of the experiment Domina said, when lecturing to the Women's Congress, 'The School Doctor picked out 25 delicate children (some of each class) and we have been at work for six months. I fully hoped to bring the children here this afternoon to show you our work. Alas, the London County Council refused permission! Perhaps they are afraid I might convert you all to the daily 20 minutes drill scheme!'

Professional or teaching practice studies included 'commanding' and 'the art as well as the science of teaching'. In the former, students were encouraged to 'Let your voice "ring out" the commands'; students had to go up and down the scale saying, 'I can speak on this note, I can also sing on this note'. With such training and the instruction 'keep your heads up', they developed the ability to pitch their voices at just the right level. 'Commanding' was treated as an art, but it had to be learnt. There was to be no movement of the class until a 'command' had been given and then an instantaneous and uniform response was expected, indeed precision was necessary for the correct conduct of the class. In the latter, kindergarten principles as expounded by Froebel, were also encouraged. The 'teacher must graft all his instruction upon the spontaneous activity of the child. The work of a teacher was not to give knowledge, but to supply material means and opportunities in a rational and harmonious order for the child's mind spontaneously to work upon'. Students also spent time on observation of movement, learnt how to make contact with the individual child and how to encourage pupils to participate, practice and improve their physical skills.

The strictness that was part of everyday routine extended to applications for teaching posts and, as one Old Student said, 'Before we were given a testimonial for an interview, we had to present ourselves to Domina in our interviewing costume, hat and gloves — a somewhat intimidating experience'.

There can be no question that the Head Mistress wanted a liberal education for her students.

> Perhaps here mention should be made of the many ways in which Domina ensured that her students should always be kept in touch with all that was helpfully new. There is every evidence that, in these early days, and all through the College life, if Domina knew that the students needed certain work which was not obtainable through the ordinary channels, she would pay for this out of her own purse, rather than the students be without it.

Domina also generously donated a sum of money to ensure the launch of the *Journal of Scientific Physical Training* in the autumn of 1908. This venture had been brought about by cooperation of the South Western Polytechnic Physical Training College, the newly formed Scottish League of Organisers and Teachers of Swedish Gymnastics and other interested parties. The first edition was issued free of charge to all the members of those colleges who expressed sympathy with the effort, but funds had to be raised by contribution before the publication of subsequent editions. The second edition was published in the spring of 1909 and continued to be issued termly, three times a year, until 1922, when it was renamed *The Journal of School Hygiene and Physical Training*. This publication helped to create a closer liaison between members of the profession, as well as making provision for dissemination of information and relevant articles, so contributing to the national development of physical education.

Students attended University of London Extension lectures given within the Polytechnic where they were introduced to, and informed about, such topics as The League of Nations, The British Fascisti, Dr Barnado's Homes, physiological issues, the National Playing Fields Association and physical training in Sunderland for children under 7 years. There were lectures in college about citizenship, Madam Bertrand's new system of physical training, English folk dance and songs of Europe. There were also visits to the Royal College of Surgeons' Museum, South Kensington Museum, to schools for the blind, deaf and mentally handicapped, educational centres, nursery schools and public swimming baths where they watched the London County Council experts teaching elementary school children. Dorette Wilke also made sure her students had knowledge of the production of equipment. 'I am going to take the students to as many gymnastic depots as possible . . . in order to teach them how everything we use is made; for I mean my girls to know every detail of their craft. I shall take them to several gymnasiums too, so that they may see the bad as well as the good. That is another advantage of placing our college in a large town'. The Head Mistress saw the College as a 'centre of progress' for physical training; in practice, this meant knowledge and appreciation of other systems of gymnastics and physical training, as well as the understanding of current systems in vogue in Great Britain.

In the Easter holidays of 1903, Dorette Wilke took a small party of students to Denmark and Sweden. The characteristic hospitality of the Danes and the Swedes enabled the students to see work in various schools and institutions and many friendly relationships were established. In July of the same year, Dorette took a team of 24 students to the Turnfest at Nuremburg. The students were boarded out with German families to see more of real German conditions in preference to staying in a hotel. Demonstrations of free-standing exercises and marching were given, both at the Festival and at private schools. One student, Fay Brackenbury, returned to Germany in 1904 as gymnastics mistress at the Institute, Lohmann, Rollnetsrasse 15, Nuremburg until 1914, the beginning of the First World War, when she had to return to England. During the Easter holidays of 1908, there was a four week visit to Hamburg, Altana, Copenhagen and Stockholm to visit schools, training colleges and voluntary evening clubs and to meet Herr Muller, Herr Knudsen and Colonel Balck of the German, Danish and Swedish institutes, respectively.

Old Students were often invited to join these educational visits as, for example, in 1910 when Domina wrote on 1 June to Mabel Salisbury (1904–06) 'Have you heard that we are going to take part in the Paris Hygiene Congress? Do come and join us, it will be such fun! We are doing a free standing table (which you practice by yourself), Net Ball and some dancing. Date: August 2–7 Cost £5 5s 0d. Do come, we want some old girls — Miss Turton (1905–07) is coming. We alone are representing England, so I want it to be a great success and covered with International Honours — the French are going to do all in their power to make our stay pleasant — *do come*. Let me know soon. Yours affectionately, (DW)'.

The visit was '. . . an extremely successful and memorable occasion'. Cecil Sharp spoke at great length on the values of his branch of physical education when introducing the dance programme given by the Chelsea students. His comments included the sentence, 'Educationists have not been slow to perceive the value of these discoveries and, in response to a recommendation recently issued by the Board of Education, our folk dances are now being taught in the Elementary Schools throughout the country'. Miss Lloyd, student from 1899 to 1902 and assistant to Dr Mary C Hawkes, the College Medical Officer, read a paper on 'Medical Gymnastics'.

The free-standing exercises, shown by the Chelsea students were introduced by Domina in the following way, 'The exercises in use in English Schools are based on the Swedish system of Educational gymnastics with the exercises so chosen as to be suitable for children of school age (5–14) and capable of being effectively carried out without the use of special apparatus. The gymnastic table, which will be presented, is a sample of a type of work in use in many English schools. Besides formal drill and gymnastics, organised games are an essential part of the scheme of instruction and, in girls' schools dance movements play a prominent part'.

There was a distinct emphasis on health as a benefit of participation in physical training lessons, but all was not 'sweetness and light' following this Third International Hygiene Congress. On 18 October 1910, Dr George Newman (Chief Medical Officer) wrote to Domina on black edged paper,

Dear Madam,

Certain statements have recently been made to me respecting the character of the demonstrations given by some of your students at the late Paris Congress on School Hygiene. I have received these reports with a good deal of concern, and I am anxious to obtain from you full and authentic particulars before reporting on the matter to the Board (of Education).

Will you therefore kindly let me know what demonstrations your Students gave in Paris, and whether it is a fact that they gave a display at a Casino. If so, can you let me have particulars as to its character and the conditions under which the display was given? Was the demonstration given before the Congress and the display given at the Casino according to your wishes and representative of your teaching?

I am, dear Madam,

Yours very truly,

The students had given two demonstrations of their work in Paris; the first at the Grand Palais before the Congress. The second at the Conversatzione given by the Society of Medical Inspectors of Schools of the City of Paris and the Department of the Seine in the Municipal Theatre at Englien, for the members of the Congress, who had been unable to be present because of other duties, at the first demonstration. The students had not been invited to the dinner, given by the Society, at the casino.

Domina was supported by a personal letter from Lauder Brunton dated 24 October 1910 to Dr Newman, who, with his daughter, had attended the dinner and the second private demonstration; no further action was taken.

The first annual display in July 1901 was given by the following nine students: Misses Wintle, Gardner, Ironside, Butcher, Coltman, Smith, Hughes, Reed and Skelton. The work included rings and jumping, balls, parallel bars, vaulting horse, high rings, Swedish exercises, Indian club exercises, skipping, high jump and the German wand exercise — 'Stabreigen'.

At the Ling Association Demonstration in the Royal Albert Hall in 1917, second and third year students from Chelsea College showed Swedish gymnastics taught by Miss Anderson.

... the only unrehearsed event was a terrific thunderstorm which took place during Chelsea's gymnastics. The climax was reached during the balance on high beams, when the roof of the Albert Hall was struck and Chelsea's fame in balance established, as the gymnasts remained unshaken throughout the episode.

As well as their annual displays, Chelsea students were often invited to give demonstrations of gymnastics and dance. For example:

27 January	1900	The English Education Exhibition, Imperial Institute, London
	1900	Great Exhibition of Paris
	1911	Physical training course for teachers at the Albert Hall
14 and 15 May	1920	Headmistresses, doctors and others interested in physical education
May	1921	The Ling Association
November	1922	The London County Council at the Albert Hall.

Domina always emphasized, with her students, the '. . . need for quick eyes . . .' and the necessity to be '. . . all the time on the alert, and it would be strange', she said, 'if her (the student's) powers of observation and perception did not receive a stimulus. Stranger still if technical study and the long series of elaborate exercises which she goes through with unfaltering precision failed to strengthen her memory'. For Domina '. . . discipline in any shape or form was held to be an educative agent'. Students worked hard, extremely hard 'under the eagle eye of Fräulein Dorette Wilke' but were happy. One Old Student said, 'Our Head Mistress, Fräulein Dorette Wilke was a martinet and woe betide any student who deviated in any way from perfection in work, punctuality, politeness, scrupulous neatness, good appearance and hard work'.

Domina always made a point of speaking to the leaving students and, in addition, to saying, 'I will answer any urgent enquiry by return of post to help you', emphasized social service, adherence to principles, the wonderful opportunities offered in teaching to influence young people to help them to develop and the moral responsibility they had towards their pupils. In her talk given to the third year students during the First World War years she said, 'We are glad that teaching is a social service. Our men die for their country, we must live for our country, live to the fullest capacity, live with an aim and object in life, live to be of real help and service to our fellow creatures'. She deplored 'poor carriage', 'sloppy dress' and 'bad manners'. Of the latter, she said, 'The present day rush of life ignores this, yet when you come to analyse manner, you find that good manner is nothing more or less than having consideration for others'. For Domina, physical education teachers were 'the cornerstone of the school'.

During the last year of the Great War (1918) food was very scarce in London. The students worked under great stress, were very jaded, and at great disadvantage. They could be found, together with the staff, queuing at 1 o'clock for bowls of soup and slabs of unappetizing grey-looking suet pudding at the Chelsea community kitchen in Manor Street. Rations were further supplemented by Glaxo. 'Glaxo Duty' for the staff consisted of putting on an enormous kettle to boil in the kitchen of the Domestic Economy Department, of whisking bowls of Glaxo until it frothed and of having mugs of hot Glaxo ready for hungry students at 10.30 am. The influenza epidemic affected the students during the summer term and yet, in spite of all the difficult events of the year, Domina managed to hold a luncheon party for the leaving third year students, which hostess and guests enjoyed.

Chelsea students, Old Students and staff contributed to the war effort in many ways, including working on farms, in the Forestry Corps, as fruit pickers, in hospitals, the ambulance service, munitions factories, teaching morris dancing to soldiers in France under the auspices of the YMCA, VAD nurses in Serbia and the Almeric Paget Massage Corps. During the summer vacation of 1918, 30 students and three members of staff, Misses Fountain, Read and Clark (Commandant), joined the Women's National Land Service Corps and went into camp with 150 other women workers at Ilchester, Somerset. They were there for periods of time varying from three to eight weeks, lived under canvas, worked eight hours a day and frequently put in overtime pulling flax. The Flax Camp was put on the official government record as work undertaken by the College.

The 'communal joys of camp' were further developed when the 7th Chelsea Girl Guide camp was held at Nutfield, Surrey in 1922. The formation of the College Camping Society took place in 1923 with Miss Ruth Clark as President and students paid a three shillings per year subscription. The programme arranged by the students included weekend and week or longer camps in Kent, Surrey, Dorset, Devon and Sussex.

During the 1920s, other societies were formed, such as the Debating Society (1923), Choral Society (1922), Dramatic Society (1927), an Orchestral Society (1921), Musical Society (1920) and Students' Christian Movement (1928). On 15 January 1921, the first College dance was held with jazz band accompaniment; 100 tickets were sold. The Games Council was established in 1924. 'Cricket Tea', when the College was entertained by year II students was a highlight of the summer term.

Initially, the Chelsea Old Students' Association was informally organized by the first students of the College '. . . with the idea of keeping in touch with one another'. It was formally founded at the inaugural meeting, held on 28 May 1904, when Miss E M Cartwright was invited to take the chair, even though she was leaving England to travel and work in Canada in September of that year. Twelve people were present: Misses Cartwright, Davy, Gardner, Hughes, Ironside, Kelley, Lambert, Polgreen, Skelton and Sky held College Diplomas (a condition of membership) and Misses Colinette and Jenkyn who were trained by Dorette Wilke before Chelsea was founded. A Committee of seven was elected with five members as a quorum and the aims were:

1　To bind together old students of the College.
2　To enable old students teaching in London to meet for practice and discussion; country members to receive reports of meetings.
3　To endeavour to forward the cause of Physical Education in England.

London members (a radius of 15, later reduced to eight, miles from Sloane Square) paid £1 1s 0d per annum, (later reduced to 17/6) whilst country members who had a postal vote for election of officers and members of committees, paid 10/6 (and later 7/6). Associates (members who had retired from the profession) paid 2/6 and a life subscription in 1913 was £1 1s 0d. There were weekly meetings of the Association, a week long holiday meeting or course covering gymnastics, dancing, medical and cultural lectures and lectures from Fräulein Wilke on current gymnastic topics once a month. Miss Polgreen was elected Deputy Chairman and Miss Skelton became the Honorary Secretary and Treasurer, a post she held intermittently until 1909. Dorette Wilke accepted the President's office and Mr Skinner the Vice-President's position.

From time to time, the objects were changed. For example, in 1913, they were amended to:

A To form an organised and independent body of trained gymnastic teachers.
B To keep in touch with educational development by means of weekly meetings and lectures.
C To forward the cause of Physical Training in England.

A competition was held for the design of an Old Students' badge, which was won by Miss G Herbert and depicted two Grecian women and a child circumscribed by the motto 'Mens Sana In Corpore Sano' — 'A Healthy Mind in a Healthy Body'.

Initially, the Association met weekly and the Old Students' programme of work for the Lent term 1905 consisted of:

3 February	— Gymnastic Class — Miss M A Hughes
10 February	— Discussion — re mass exercises
17 February	— Dancing — Miss E A Roberts
24 February	— Anthroprometric instruments, Research work and Registration — The Principal (of the Polytechnic)
3 March	— Gymnastics class — Miss E Newton
10, 17, 24, 31 March and 7 April	— Practice for the College Display Figure Mass with free exercises
Leaders	— Winifred Sky and Ruth F Skelton
Dress	— Reform tunic and girdle, white nun's veiling blouses, straight neckband and cuffs with double row blue feather stitching on both. Black shoes and stockings.

During the autumn term of 1905, the 12 week programme showed that Miss Gertzell took two Practical Swedish Classes; Miss Hankinson and Miss Baker, three lectures on Theory of Movements; Sir Lauder Brunton, a lecture on Physical

Education to which the current students were invited; Mr Oberholyer, a German Gymnastic Apparatus Class; Mr C H Moss, a Physical Drill Demonstration; Miss Cooper Coles and Miss MacEwan took the Dancing evening; Miss Nylen lectured on Anthropometrical Instruments and testing for physical deficiencies; and Fräulein Wilke gave a lecture and took a practical German Mass Drill and discussion session. The programme for the 1912 holiday course for 50 members of the Association included:

Gymnastics	—	Miss Welin (Central Institute, Stockholm)
Vaulting	—	Miss Bulau (Dartford PTC)
Miss Nellie Chaplin's ancient dances	—	Mrs Lake Taylor (Chelsea PTC)
Ballroom dancing	—	Miss Jenkinson (Assistant to Miss Hutton Moss)
Medical lectures	—	Dr Elmslie (St Bartholomew's Hospital)
Psychology lectures	—	Miss Gladys Martyn, DSc
Introducing teaching sex hygiene in the school curriculum	—	Miss Norah March (Clapham Day Training College)
Treatment of patients by suggestion	—	Dr Constance Long.

In 1914, the Old Students' Association formed a Registration Sub-committee, under the Chairmanship of Miss Ruth Skelton. This reported to the Advisory Committee in Physical Training which, in turn, reported to the Teachers' Registration Committee to meet the requirements of the Registration Act of 1914. Old Students were '. . . urged to take advantage of this opportunity of securing professional unity'.

In 1905, the Old Students' Association had started a library with £2 2s 0d set aside for the purchase of books, and with the following rules:

- No book shall be kept more than one week.
- It may be renewed for a fortnight, if not required by another member.
- Books kept beyond a week, without renewing, will have a fine on them 1d a day.
- Books should be kept in a cupboard at the South Western Polytechnic by kind permission of the authorities.
- All books must be covered and, when sent to country members, must have postage paid by them.
- Books which are damaged, must be replaced.
- New and second hand books accepted.

Miss R Clark was appointed Librarian.

The Chelsea Physical Training College Old Students' Association produced an Annual Report for its members containing information on, for example:

- Officers for 1913–14
- Constitution of Association
- Further information for members
- Minutes of General Meeting
- Annual holiday course
- Children's welfare exhibition
- College news
- Names and addresses of members.

An annual leaflet was used as a means of communication from 1908 until 1920 when the first magazine was produced. When the first leaflet was produced, Dorette wrote,

Dear Students,

I feel I must write you a short letter just to welcome the new venture and to wish the magazine every success.

I hope it will be the means of binding us all more strongly together. Let 'Progress' always be our watchword, for we must fully realise that there is still much to be done.

We must do our best to improve physical training and, above all, to improve the conditions under which work is carried on . . .

We have a great work to do; let us strive to do it well, always realising that we are only at the beginning of things, and that progress depends on the earnestness and effort of each one of us. The College has done well. I am proud of my Old Girls.

Always yours affectionately,

Dorette Wilke

At the later time, Domina's letter said

My Dear Children All,

My best congratulations to your new venture! May the new journal prosper and thrive. May it form another strong new link between present and past students — may it carry on successfully the old well loved Chelsea traditions.

This is my wish
Yours with fond love,
Domina 1920

In 1913, '. . . the OSA founded the College Fund, a fund by which voluntary subscriptions should ultimately form the capital for a College Scholarship', to help students in training at Chelsea. The proposal was made by Miss Cecily Williams and seconded by Miss Adine de Tiel at the General Meeting and passed with only two dissentients. Members knew that the

> building up of this fund will be a work of patience through many years, but the important point is that it should be *begun*, and that the Old Students should remember it is there, and in their prosperity or otherwise send so much as will increase its amount even by a little.
>
> Subscriptions will be received at any time by the Secretary whether they take the form of twelve penny stamps or a five pound note.

The original Trust Deed was signed in 1916; there were always and continued to be three Trustees. The first Trustees had to raise the capital to £150 before the first scholarship of 36 guineas could be awarded. The name was changed to the Dorette Wilkie Fund, at the Annual General Meeting in January 1930 to commemorate the work of Domina.

From the foundation of the College, students were expected to buy and wear the College uniform which changed periodically as fashions changed. In the early days, the College colours were blue, white and red, the colours of the Earl of Cadogan, a member of the Governing Body of the Polytechnic and on whose land the institution was built.

In 1898, the College costume consisted of a navy serge shirt blouse, with turned down collar, white pique tie, white belt and white canvas shoes, navy serge knickers buttoned on to the blouse and a circular navy skirt which was removed for apparatus work. Gowns were always worn except in the gymnasium and woebetide the student who ever put her nose outside the gymnasium door, which had to be kept carefully closed, minus her gown. For games, the costume was a white flannel blouse and a navy skirt about three or four inches from the ground. College hats — a white boater, with navy blue band and the College band (white with GTTC in blue) were compulsory, winter and summer. The College badge consisted of the coat of arms of Earl Cadogan with GTTC and SWP above and below, respectively. Miss Bartel, the College dressmaker, made the uniforms from 1898 to 1902. 1903 saw the introduction of the tunic designed and made by Walter Clemo, the College tailor, with a second tunic for games, of the same pattern, but eight inches from the ground. The cost of the necessary outfit amounted to about £10 and the tailor and shoemaker attended at the beginning of each session to take measurements.

The College was initially for women students who intended to teach physical training in secondary schools. From September 1908, however, Chelsea provided a one-year course for men students, who had previously qualified as teachers from training colleges or were university graduates, under the direction of Lieutenant Braae Hansen, formerly of the Danish State Teachers and Gymnastics colleges, Copenhagen. The course with a 55 per cent pass mark in teaching gymnastics and a 55 per cent total in all subjects included Swedish gymnastics, gymnasium games, allied theoretical subjects, gymnastics theory, hygiene, anatomy, physiology, commands and teaching. The students had six hours gymnastics, seven-and-a-half hours anatomy, physiology and hygiene, four hours gymnastics theory and seven hours teaching, including commanding, weekly. Women staff of the Chelsea Physical Training College and Polytechnic staff from other departments contributed to the work of the Men's College of Hygiene and Physical Education. The Board of Education sanctioned students' attendance and provided a grant of £40 per annum: £15 for the Institute's fee and £25 for maintenance. Colonel Fox presented 24 scholarships of £10 each to the students for expenses. These students had to show physical fitness for gymnastic exercises, as well as general and elementary scientific knowledge at interview. The Board of Education, in 1909, had acknowledged that the teaching of hygiene and physical exercises to pupils, in both primary and secondary schools, was of equal importance to their education in other branches of knowledge. During their course, the students taught gymnastics to the pupils of the Secondary School for Boys attached to the Polytechnic and arrangements were made for them to have teaching experience in local elementary schools.

The course, however, in spite of being the only one-year 'specialist' course for men in England, was not popular and closed in 1912. The first students did, however, form the Chelsea Men's Old Students' Association.

By 1922, recognition had been given to the College at national level when, 'By changing the name to Chelsea Polytechnic, the Borough proclaimed to the world that, within its boundary, were a School of Science and Technology, a School of Art, and a School of Physical Education where the lovers of learning could bring their knowledge to a University standing'. This action followed the conferment of Royal Status on the Borough.

During the early part of 1929, Domina became seriously ill; she retired to her cottage and did not return to College in an active way again. In a letter to the staff, she wrote 'You will all have to work harder and take on extra responsibilities during my absence, but I know you will do this cheerfully. I thank you all with all my heart for your devoted work. You have all done so much in making the College what it is and I am so proud of having a staff who, at all times, have always put the welfare and interest of the College first'.

In a second letter, dated 6 May 1929, she thanked the staff for the gifts they had so generously sent her. 'I wish you could have been here when that wonderful surprise basket of yours was opened! . . . there was food for the body and food for the soul and food for contemplation — there was raiment for my poor old body and there were scents and snaps and smokes and the joys of future beauty in the garden . . . and last, but not least, that wonderful basket was cram jammed full of loving thoughts peeping out from every corner and parcel and coloured label . . . and for all these wonderful gifts, I can only say thank you with all my heart'.

On Good Friday 1929, she wrote to the 68 Old Students attending the holiday course when Miss Andersen was taking gymnastics. In her letter she made several references to 'The quiet of the cottage . . . the message of Spring . . . the voices of the birds . . . the great future of the College . . . and . . . when the pain does come, it is too dreadful to contemplate . . .'. She said, 'Dear Children, I am very tired now, writing is an awful effort. Remember it is my right shoulder, arm, elbow and hand that are affected, hence the difficulty in writing . . .'. 'Now goodbye to you all. I feel quite cheerful and very hopeful to be up and well quite soon. My fondest love to you all'.

At the end of the College session on 12 July 1929, Dr Harlow sent the following telegram to Domina, 'We, Principal, Staff and Students, assembled at the close of session, send our affectionate greetings to our beloved Domina, and express heartfelt sympathy in her prolonged illness. We deeply miss her genial presence, and wish to comfort her with assurance that she is constantly in our thoughts, and that we are determined to attain the high ideals with which she has always inspired us'.

After great physical suffering, Domina died peacefully, her spirit released, during the morning of Sunday 19 January 1930 aged 62 years. The funeral service on Wednesday 22 January 1930 was taken by the Rev Michael Ridley, Rector of Headley; the College closed for the day. The service was attended by personal friends, the Principal and representatives of Chelsea Polytechnic, the staff of the College and representative past and present students.

Domina was buried in Headley Churchyard. The inscription on the headstone, made from grey Forest of Dean stone reads:

> In grateful memory
> of the life and work of
> DORETTE WILKIE
> Born June 14, 1867
> Died January 19, 1930
> Founder and for 31 years
> Head Mistress of Chelsea
> College of Physical Education

Above the lettering was carved a simple design of a rising sun, and a simple curb surrounded the green turf. As one Old Student wrote after visiting Headley, 'It is dignified and in harmony with the beautiful surroundings which Domina herself selected for her resting place'.

The memorial service for her was conducted by the Ven Archdeacon Bevan, Rector of Chelsea Old Church (All Saints), Cheyne Walk and member of the Governing Body of the Polytechnic on Saturday 25 January 1930. It was attended by staff and students of the College, former members of the staff and Old Students from all parts of the country, representatives of the Governing Body, Dr Harlow (Principal), Heads of Department of Chelsea Polytechnic, evening class students, representatives from Anstey, Bedford and Dartford Physical Training Colleges, the Ling Association, the British College of Physical Education, the English Folk Dance Society, the Chartered Society of Massage and Medical Gymnastics, the National Federation of Working Girls' Clubs, and personal friends of Domina.

From the preceding account, it is clear that, while there were many advantages for the staff and for the students of the College in being an integral part of a Polytechnic, there were also limitations and restrictions. Specialist physical training facilities on site were limited, valuable time was lost in travelling to and from playing fields and students' energy used in bicycling across London. In spite of these problems, Chelsea College of Physical Education was established and flourished. The course was directed towards a 'sound Education in Physical Training' and developed from two to three years with university status, one of Domina's treasured ideals unfulfilled until after her death. The acknowledged success of the first 31 years says much for the pioneer determination of the staff and students who overcame all difficulties and attained a high standard of professional training. Domina's vision had been achieved.

The democratic and progressive social unit of staff and students had been ably led by their Head Mistress whose 'magnificent courage and loyalty to her ideals . . . had brought the College to its present status'. Her strong, good, steadfast and colourful personality influenced everyone with whom she came into contact.

Many tributes were paid by Old Students in memory of Domina, and include:

> The spirit of College was born of Domina's great love, dedicated to her children and fulfilled by them. In a world corrupt, confused and devoid of direction, she created, nurtured and inspired with infinite care, and infinite patience, all that is eternal, and beyond man's understanding.

> It was her own gift of service which had built the College up in a very few years, under the difficulties of lack of space and equipment into an institution with its own personality and characteristics and one which was always just ahead of the moment. It was her own unique mixture of independence and adaptability that enabled her to do this within the framework of the Chelsea Polytechnic where perforce every new step had to be taken in collaboration with the Principal. That collaboration was always won and, in retrospect, one realises that this, in itself, was a tribute to the soundness of judgement that characterised all Fräulein's plans for the future.

> During her illness, even when she was physically weak and in pain, her interest in College and professional matters never waned. She pondered over and discussed future developments and, to the end of her life maintained the vision, judgement and open mind that characterised her planning in the early days and, after 31 years of courageous work, left a College with sound educational principles and fine traditions.

She was a spontaneous and everlasting inspiration. **'To know her is a liberal education.'**

3 Transition: 1929–1958

May Fountain
Headmistress (1929–45)
Principal (1945–50)

'Essentially modest, without thought of self and always ready to give credit to others.'

The appointment of Miss May Fountain as her successor, brought Domina great happiness. May Fountain was born on 3 May 1888, the fifth daughter of Joseph Septimus and Margaret, three years after Dorette Wilke had arrived in England.

She was educated at Wynand House, Bowes Park School for Girls, a private school with places for 100–150 pupils in Greenwich, as her father was 'anxious that all his five daughters should have a recognized training which would enable them to earn a living'. May Fountain passed both the Senior Cambridge and the London Matriculation 1st Division examinations and felt that 'the school gave much beyond preparation for examination'.

The school staff would have liked her to go to a university, but they did acknowledge her intense interest in physical education. The staff also realized that the training available at the specialist colleges, Anstey, Bedford, Chelsea, Dartford, Dunfermline and Liverpool offered 'a new profession' for women. May Fountain had carefully studied all the prospectuses and selected Chelsea, 'as the range of work available within the Polytechnic context appealed to her'.

She was accepted for training in the Gymnastic Teachers' Training College, South Western Polytechnic and started her two-year course in September 1906. Miss Fountain had persuaded her parents of the advantages of attending the Gymnastic Teachers' Training College, but respected their conditions of her attendance. As recorded in 1981, in the *Chelsea News*,

The modern student would probably dissolve in mirth at the thought of the problems of an Edwardian young lady who had first to overcome parental opposition at the mere thought of going to such an establishment, and then having struck a bargain with them, stick faithfully to it. Their bargain was that she must live in lodgings as close to the College as possible, and be accompanied everywhere by her personal maid! So even the short trip from Glebe Place (200 yards) across the perilous horse-bus-ridden King's Road (to Manresa Road) was made always keeping that rule.

Miss Fountain thoroughly enjoyed her student days, but it is typical of her foresight, intelligence and wisdom that the outstanding impression of her time as a student was 'An awakening to the enormous potentialities of Physical Education in general education and medicine'. Throughout her professional life, she retained an awareness of the potentialities of physical education and directed her efforts towards the fulfilment of these early ideals.

Miss Fountain was an extremely able student in both practical and theoretical studies; she was the second student at Chelsea to be awarded the King's Prize for Physiology and she gained the College Diploma with Distinction in July 1908.

Her first appointment, in September 1908, was as a lecturer on the staff of the Diocesan Training College, Truro, where she stayed until 1910. She commented in later life, 'The Board of Education must have approved of my qualification, although there was no official "recognition" in those days'. During these two years, as well as lecturing to students on all aspects of physical education, Miss Fountain completed the Chartered Society of Massage and Medical Gymnastics Teachers' Certificate and later took courses, for this organization, in England, Denmark and Sweden. From September 1910, in pursuit of further knowledge, she joined the Royal Central Institute of Gymnastics in Stockholm as 'an extra student' for one year and then moved to Dr Arvedson's Gymnastic Institute, Stockholm for a year where she received the Medical Gymnastics' Diploma at the end of her course. During this time, she became proficient in Swedish and translated a number of difficult technical works. September 1912 saw Miss Fountain back at Chelsea Physical Training College as a member of staff (senior lecturer) with special responsibility for massage and medical gymnastics and to lecture in anatomy. The students said, 'she was an excellent teacher of this subject'.

The summer of 1921 was spent, during her sabbatical term of leave, in Denmark, Sweden and Finland visiting schools and colleges. She was particularly impressed by the teaching of Fröken Elli Björkstén, who had brought a 'new look' for women to the stereotyped form that had universally been developed in Swedish gymnastics. Björkstén's work was characterized by suppleness, ease, grace, simplicity and rhythm; she created a joyous atmosphere in the gymnasium which appealed to Miss Fountain.

Miss Fountain was a very loyal and hardworking member of staff who co-operated more and more closely with Domina in the late 1920s. Her professional integrity was respected by her colleagues and by the students. The qualities of leadership that she possessed and demonstrated so easily destined her to become Headmistress of the College on Domina's retirement. Frequently, on the retirement of the leader of an establishment, several members of staff who have served a college for many years also decide to leave. This was not the case when Miss Fountain was appointed to succeed Dorette Wilkie; that staff remained could be seen as ready acceptance and public recognition of the ability of a colleague to lead the College. As one Old Student said, 'We can still go back to Chelsea and feel that it will be "ours" the same as ever, not having passed into strange hands and ways unknown to us'. This rather familiar attitude for the known did not deflect Miss Fountain from taking Chelsea forward with innovative schemes, progressive ideas and new developments, as she saw appropriate, for the 1930s onwards. In her own words, 'there is a Chelsea feeling which has, all through expressed itself in open-mindedness, inquiry and willingness to learn'.

Miss Fountain took up her new office on 1 September 1929; the College was inspected by the London County Council on 30 November 1929. The Report to the London County Council Education Committee, Higher Education Sub-committee expressed confidence in the new regime. 'The present Headmistress was for many years a member of the staff and one may rest assured that, under her leadership, backed by a band of enthusiastic lecturers, the College will maintain its position and carry out new developments. The members of staff are all highly qualified in the subjects for which they are responsible'. There were six full-time members mainly responsible for all practical aspects of the course, that is: gymnastics, games, dancing, class teaching, supervision of students' teaching practice and theory of movements. The eight part-time members were Polytechnic lecturers in other departments and contributed to anatomy, physiology, mechanics, theory of treatments, first-aid, home nursing, hygiene, physics, chemistry, psychology, methods of education and class singing. The College Medical Officer was also a key member of staff. The number of staff with medical qualifications was indicative of the emphasis placed on this aspect of the course and the importance of practical work was underlined by the number of Chelsea Old Students appointed to the staff. Miss Fountain's 'vision' for Chelsea, and for physical education, was always converted into practical solutions and her 'rightness' in judgment was proved on so many occasions.

The first major innovation which Miss Fountain initiated was the One-Year Course for Certified Teachers run in conjunction with Whitelands College. Whitelands was already providing third year courses in other subjects for which the Board of Education allowed a £40 grant per annum (Board and Residence £10; Fees £30). Miss Fountain felt that it was '. . . important for the future of the College of Physical Education that we show that we wish to keep up with the demands of the educational schemes of the day and are willing to co-operate'. Negotiations took place during 1929–30 with Miss Mercier (Principal, Whitelands), Miss Monkhouse (Chief Inspector, Women's Training Colleges, Board of Education), Miss Ash (HMI PT) and Miss Perry (HMI PT, Chelsea 1903–05). The outcome of discussions led to the establishment of the course for certified teachers, who wished to specialize in physical training in 1930–31.

Miss Fountain justified the course on the following grounds:

> The raising of the school leaving age to fifteen years; (a recommendation not implemented in 1932) and the scheme for the reorganisation of Elementary Schools

involving the formation of an increasingly large number of Senior Schools providing post-primary education for children 11–14 plus calls not only for a large increase in the total number of teachers required, but also demands that these teachers shall hold still better qualifications for this work.

With the increase in the number of teachers required we are not concerned. There is no intention of appointing Physical Training experts in the New Senior Schools. But there is certainly need for a number of teachers from the Elementary Training Colleges holding an additional qualification in Physical Training.

Miss Katherine M Richardson (Chelsea 1923–26) was appointed to the staff to be in charge of the course. Eight students were admitted to the first cohort and the course was inspected by Miss N Palmer (HMI) and Miss E M Perry (HMI).

Figure 3.1: Members of the first one-year course for certified teachers

Name	College	Appointment
N G Bland	Stockwell	Nottingham Education Authority
A Gray	Leeds	Liverpool Education Authority
G A Harris	University College Southampton	Manchester Education Authority
P Hoyland	Bingley	West Ham Education Authority
E Hulbard	Homerton	Kent Education Authority
M E Hunt	Whitelands	Birmingham Education Authority
B Smith	Homerton	Bury Education Authority
K Sutton	Avery Hill	Cumberland Education Authority

These students worked with year I for gymnastics and folk dance, with years I, II, III, for games and theory of games and had other lectures, such as theory of movements and class teaching as a separate group.

By the time the course closed for the duration of the Second World War, 75 students from 28 colleges and 19 local education authorities had successfully pursued the course.

During 1929, Miss Fountain served on the Advisory Sub-committee, planning the syllabuses for the University of London Diploma in Theory and Practice of Physical Education. Her breadth of knowledge and insight into the comprehensive nature of physical education were invaluable in discussions and meetings. A Committee, led by Principal Sidney Skinner (Chelsea Polytechnic) and with membership of Eva Lett (Dartford), Margaret Stansfeld (Bedford), Dorette Wilkie (Chelsea), Marion Squire (Anstey) and J Honora Wicksteed (Ling Association) had prepared a *Memorial* in 1926. It was circulated and signed by 1400 persons during 1927 and presented to the Senate of the University of London on 26 January 1928.

We, the undersigned, beg the Senate of the University of London to institute a Diploma in the Theory and Practice of Physical Education. The importance of scientific Physical Education has been recognised by its inclusion in the ordinary curriculum of all public secondary and primary schools in this country. The study and the teaching of the subject have become highly organised, and there already exists a large body of trained teachers, to which over 100 new members are added each year, who devote their whole time to the work, and many of them have prepared for this branch of the teaching profession by following a three years' course of study at a training college specially devoted to the subject.

In view of the great value of this side of education, in a country whose population is mainly urban, we believe that the time has come when the profession should be put on a satisfactory basis.

At present, the teachers receive Diplomas from their own Colleges, and we consider it of the utmost importance that a Diploma shall be granted by some Central Authority to represent a definite standard of training and accomplishment, and to give the profession the dignity it deserves.

The position that the University of London holds in the country suggests that it is the best body for this purpose, and we therefore petition the Senate to extend its interest in the furtherance of Health and Education and to institute a Diploma in Physical Education.

The University had agreed that: 'The object of this Diploma is to testify that the holder has successfully undergone a course of training for Physical Education, including the practice of teaching, together with scientific studies appropriate to such training'. This object remained constant from July 1930, when the Diploma was instituted, until 1952 when, with the formation of the various University Institutes or Schools of Education, it was superseded. The specific objectives of the course in the first two years were to provide students with factual knowledge and experience of all aspects of physical education and the allied sciences. 'During the third year, the knowledge gained in the first and second years is applied and the Art as well as the Science of teaching is considered'.

Chelsea was the first college to be recognized in 1930–31 with nine students successfully completing the Part II examinations in 1933 (Part I had been taken in 1932).

Figure 3.2: Results: London Diploma in the Theory and Practice of Physical Education, 1933

21 candidates entered for Part I in June 1932: 10 successful; 11 failed.
6 resat Part I November 1932: 4 successful; 2 failed.
13 candidates entered for Part II May 1933: 9 successful: (Winsome Bach, Doris Evelyn Gray, Ada Margaret Jarvis, Marjorie Nellie Lord, Jessie Lyle Murchison, Evelyn Margaret Stanley, Dorothy Edith Stevens, Joy Kathleen Warwick and Doris Ruth West).
16 exceptional merits were awarded.
3 referred: (Beatrix May Brookes, Marjory Higgs and Eileen Ashton Stray) successful in 1934.
1 failed.

Part I consisted of anatomy and physiology and was taken during the summer term of the students' second year in College. Part II comprised examinations in hygiene, principles and processes of education, theory of gymnastics, teaching and practical subjects, with written papers taken in the summer term of year III. The first Presentation Ceremony, attended by Miss Fountain, Miss Clark and Dr Halsey, was held at the Albert Hall on 10 May 1934 when J L Murchison and J K Warwick were present to receive their diplomas. It was not compulsory for students to sit the London Diploma and, from known records, at no time was a full cohort entered for these examinations.

Between 1933 and 1952, 403 candidates from Chelsea were awarded the London Diploma; they achieved 55 distinctions and 473 credits.

The College was third in the 'league' table of six, ie:

Figure 3.3: The London Diploma: Overall positions

First	Second	Third	Fourth	Fifth	Sixth
Dartford	Bedford	Chelsea	Anstey	Liverpool	Nonington
(15 years)	(16 years)	(20 years)	(16 years)	(16 years)	(11 years)
(Number of years each institution offered the course.)					

No men's college of physical education ever applied to take the London Diploma course.

The Chelsea College Diploma course, incorporating the London Diploma course, was very comprehensive and covered the following subjects, which were all examined and marked:

Figure 3.4: The Chelsea College Diploma Course

Year I	Year II	Year III
Anatomy	⇨	Psychology
Physiology	⇨	Theory of Movements — Lecturing
Hygiene	⇨	Hygiene Lecturing
Physics	Medical Gymnastics	⇨ Theory Practice
Chemistry	Theory of Treatments	⇨
Massage	Home Nursing	
Child Study	First Aid	Teaching Dancing
Theory of Educational		
Gymnastics	⇨	⇨
Theory of Games	⇨	⇨
Theory of Movements	⇨	⇨
Teaching (Class)	Teaching	⇨
Gymnastics	⇨	⇨
Dancing	⇨	⇨
Folk Dancing	⇨	⇨
Hockey	⇨	⇨ Practical Coaching and Umpiring
Lacrosse	⇨	⇨ " " " "
Netball	⇨	⇨ " " " "
Organised Games	⇨	⇨ " " " "
		Games Lecturing
Rounders	⇨	⇨ Practical Coaching and Umpiring
Cricket	⇨	⇨ " " " "
Tennis	⇨	⇨ " " " "
Swimming	⇨	⇨

From scrutiny of the examination mark book of 1928 to 1948, it was evident that, while students had to pass practical subjects, these marks were not credited towards the final grade of the College Diploma.

Miss Fountain was always ready to 'seize an opportunity' and turn it to an advantage. From 27 June to 9 July 1931, she took (and led) the whole College (90 students and 10 staff) to Minnis Bay, near Birchington, Kent, to camp. Miss Fountain, Miss Clark, Miss Richards and ten students formed the advance party; the camp was laid out, tents pitched, palliasses filled and provisions put in place. The main party arrived on Monday 30 June, in three charabancs. 'Staff and students learnt together the art of camping, the chief instructors being members of the College Camping Society and the students who had camped as Guides during their school life'. The camp was such a success that the venture was repeated in 1934 and 1939 to 'provide experience of an organised camp and interdependent community life, and to give opportunity for practical professional work under unusual conditions'. At 6.30 each morning, the 16 third year orderlies were summoned by the signal of a bell rung enthusiastically by Miss Appleton. The campers' programme started with breakfast at 8.00, included a variety of physical education and camping activities each day and finished with 'roll call' at 9.30 in the evening. 'All were in bed and quiet by 10.15 pm'.

Teaching practice, in a variety of schools, as well as at the Polytechnic, work in girls' clubs and the College Clinic continued to be important aspects of the Diploma course. First year students collected the classes at the front door of the Polytechnic, enveloped in their large black gowns, and escorted the children to the gymnasium. This practice was known as 'Bobbying' and '. . . was a contact with the young whom I thought rather like London sparrows', recalled an Old Student.

The College Clinic patients' records for the spring and summer terms of 1939 show that 30 children, seven boys, 22 girls and one by surname only, with ages ranging from 15 months to 14 years attended the clinics for treatment of postural deformities. The majority, 23, had defects of feet and legs with nine suffering from spinal or postural abnormalities and two miscellaneous; four children had multiple problems. Six were referred by St George's Hospital, 15 by school doctors, six by headteachers and three by local doctors.

Miss Fountain, always keen to keep the College in the vanguard of professional developments, had made the following projections circa 1936 as aims and objectives for the College:

(a) improvement in the efficiency of the Diploma Course;
(b) extension of the One Year Course for trained certificated teachers;
(c) establishment of a post-degree course in Physical Education for graduates in other subjects; and
(d) extension of evening courses of training for Club Leaders, and teachers of 'keep fit' classes.

She declared,

> The training (at Chelsea) is thus a basic one in the subject of Physical Education, and should lead to such an understanding of Physical Education that, those who

have taken it, are able to organise suitable schemes of work and carry them out in any type of institution, be the primary aim educational, recreational, social or remedial. By this it is not meant that every individual qualified is necessarily suitable for every one of these four avenues of work, but that, if her temperament and personality are suitable, she is equipped.

In 1933, The Board of Education had produced a completely new publication, *The Syllabus of Physical Training for Schools*, in which the Scandinavian influence was marked. Chelsea staff and students had again contributed to the preparation of what became known as the 'Physical Educationists' Bible', although it was produced primarily for the class teachers of children up to 11 or 12 years of age at 'all age schools'; it was reprinted annually until at least 1947. 'The object of Physical Education and Training, is to help in the production and maintenance of health in body and mind'. Correct or good posture was essential for complete physical development.

Nationally, there was emphasis on physical fitness resulting in growth in the demand for physical recreation. Under the leadership of Phyllis Colson and Phyllis Spafford, and with the combined cooperation of the National Association of Organizers of Physical Education and the Ling Association of Teachers of Swedish Gymnastics, the Central Council of Recreative Physical Training was launched in 1935 under royal patronage.

During the autumn term of 1935, Chelsea contributed to work for recreative clubs by holding on Tuesday evenings between 7.15 and 9.00 pm, a course of Recreative Physical Training for club leaders and others interested in developing the physical activities in social organisations. The course had been arranged in connection with the Central Council of Recreative Physical Training. The content included recreational gymnastics (keep fit work), dancing, skipping, indoor games, elementary theory and teaching practice. Further courses were mounted during succeeding years, including those based on the books *Folk Dances from Many Lands, Scandinavian Dances* and *Recreation and Physical Fitness for Girls and Women*.

By 1936–37, 'keep fit' classes, together with gymnastics, national and English country dance were a regular feature of the College's programme for club leaders and others interested in recreational physical activities. In 1937, with government grants available and 'in response to the demand for more leaders of recreational physical training, a course for club leaders was organized by College in conjunction with the Central Council of Recreative Physical Training. This course consisted of thirty weekly sessions of two hours each and was taken by Miss K M Richardson'. In February 1936, Mr Geoffrey Shakespeare MP, Parliamentary Secretary to the Board of Education, had visited Chelsea to learn more about the training of women physical educationists.

On Saturday 3 July 1937, Chelsea students, together with students from Anstey, Bedford and Dartford gave a display of gymnastic exercises and apparatus work as part of the 'Festival of Youth' at Wembley Stadium, in front of King George VI and Queen Elizabeth, in celebration of their coronation year. Chelsea Old Students acted as stewards. Early detachments marched past the royal couple and the

Princess Elizabeth. There was community singing with the Band of the Welsh Guards and 1500 participants performed a programme of 'keep fit' to music. Field games, including handball, shinty, netball, stoolball and rounders were demonstrated by members of all kinds of clubs, sports organizations and associations engaged in social work. The boys and girls gave exhibitions of gymnastics, boxing, wrestling or fencing. 1500 members of the Boys Brigade performed to music by their own bands and 1500 Girl Guides gave a display of maypole dancing. Members of the English Folk Dance and Song Society, both adults and children, performed English country dances.

During January 1935, the British Medical Association appointed a Physical Education Committee, 'to consider and report upon the necessity for the cultivation of the physical development of the civilian population and the methods to be pursued for this object'. On 3 December 1935, members visited Chelsea; they received a summary of the students' training and watched children's classes and games in the playground, the treatment of patients, a gymnastics class for children, a practical physiology lecture, a hygiene lecture, first, second and third year students' gymnastics classes, dancing demonstrations by second and third year students and recreational classes for children in the College gymnasia. The British Medical Association Report of the Physical Education Committee was published April 1936.

When Miss Fountain was appointed as Headmistress, the demand for instruction within the Chelsea College of Physical Education had outgrown the premises and facilities available within the Polytechnic. The accommodation occupied by the College was scattered throughout the Polytechnic building and the facilities for social activities were limited. In 1934, Miss Fountain stressed the desirability of the College having exclusive use of the physical education accommodation and of the need for extended facilities. She said, 'In putting forward these points, I should like to make clear that I fully realise the difficulties under which all departments of the Polytechnic are at present working through lack of accommodation, but I consider that the environment in which students of Physical Education work is of the utmost importance and, unless a high standard is maintained, the work of the College cannot be carried on efficiently, nor the right type of student attracted to take her training here'.

During 1936 a National College of Physical Training and Recreation was discussed, a site opposite the Polytechnic was proposed by the governors as suitable, but it was considered too expensive by the London County Council, who proposed use of the athletic ground at Merton or one of the large sites which the Council hoped to acquire for the purpose of sending out every elementary school child for one day each week for organized games. Lengthy negotiations followed, with the governors seeing the advantages of keeping the College within the Polytechnic outweighing those of a separate institution on a remote site, despite the inadequacies of the accommodation.

National events, however, cut short the debate on 'new premises for the College'. During the Munich Crisis of September 1938, structural alterations were started to the Polytechnic to convert it into premises for Civil Defence purposes. Arrangements were made for everyone to go home when the situation became extreme. All trunks were packed and labelled at hostels, equipment was stored at College, books were parcelled-up and rooms were cleared. College was recalled a week later to unpack, sort, replace equipment and goods and get down to work.

The College celebrated its 'fortieth birthday' on 8 October 1938. During the afternoon, Old Students, from the first to the fortieth year, watched, '. . . many year I students clad in backless "bathing dresses" who, quite filled the hall, and showed, under Miss Clark's direction, Austrian gymnastics. This type of work is informal, and is an excellent preparation for movement of any kind, dancing, or games, or athletics'. At this time, year I students spent the gymnastics periods of their first half term at College practising the Austrian system. The year II students, under Miss Partridge, demonstrated Swedish gymnastics and the year III students, appropriately dressed in national costume, presented dance studies which had been sent from Holland to the College and had been translated by Van Kralingen, a year III student in 1937–38.

During February and March 1939, tentative arrangements were made, in case war was declared, for the College to be evacuated to Loughborough. '. . . on the basis that women's colleges in evacuation areas would proceed to men's colleges in reception areas'. Dartford, Dunfermline and Nonington Colleges also made 'evacuation' plans. Dartford was housed in three hotels in Newquay, Cornwall; Dunfermline was transferred to the Teachers' Training College, Aberdeen; and accommodation was found for Nonington in Bromsgrove for the duration of the war. By August 1939, it was clear that Loughborough College would be unable to provide facilities for Chelsea. Miss Fountain made it her personal duty to visit Miss Perry (HMI Senior Woman Physical Education Inspector for the Board of Education). Miss Perry instructed Miss Annie Rogers (Senior Woman HMI for Wales and an Old Student of the College from 1913 to 1916, later to become Principal from 1954–1958) to 'Make Miss Fountain and your College your job until you have got them housed'.

Miss Rogers and Miss Fountain set off, by car, for Wales. They had been warmly received in Aberystwyth with offers of teaching practice classes and use of the gymnasium at Ardwyn School and lecturers' services from the University, but no accommodation was available in this town to house the College. They drove eight miles north along the coast to Borth and arrived in sunshine at low tide. 'Miss Fountain's fertile imagination immediately envisaged College games in progress on the four mile stretch of hard sand'. The Grand Hotel, where they lunched, provided suitable accommodation for staff and students and had three hard tennis courts. The proprietor, Mr Bennett, agreed to the exclusive use of the hotel by the College, if a minimum of 60 persons was guaranteed. Miss Fountain returned to London; her 'mission had been accomplished' and Miss Perry's instruction had been carried out. The billiard room became the medical gymnasium, the ballroom was suitable for indoor work, and the dining room was used for lectures.

On the declaration of war, 3 September 1939, the College was prepared for evacuation to Borth, never to return to London. Attention was given to every detail of the move from listing and packing equipment, to sending red labels, to be worn, to all new entrants to the College, so that they might recognize each other at Paddington Station! 'Preparations to leave were complete, but a move could not be made until the LCC had given sanction'. Seven days elapsed between presenting the evacuation scheme and formal approval of the plans. Domina's portrait was stored, for the duration of the war, in a specially prepared room at the Polytechnic, together with valuable science apparatus. The charcoal sketch of Domina, from which the artist worked, was taken to Borth.

'That night (21 September 1939) the pile of equipment was packed into two College games buses, from which the seats had been removed. With Miss Legg and Miss Cater as passengers, who would supervise the unpacking in Borth, the buses drove away from the Polytechnic at 4 am'. The College assembled: Misses Fountain, Cater, Clark, Davis, Gairdner, Hermes, Legg, Parkinson, Partridge and Powell took up residence; year III arrived on 28 September, year II on 29 September and year I were received on 1 October; within 10 days, the whole operation had been completed. 'Reliability' and 'adaptability' became the key characteristics every student was expected to show, no matter how varied their individual talents during their stay in Borth.

Miss Fountain's efficient administration and organization enabled the College to settle in its environment with the minimum of fuss and in the minimum of time, 'How thankful . . . we were to have learnt . . . the possibilities of working and living under unconventional conditions' (reference to camp), she was heard to say, whilst surveying Chelsea's new home.

Tuition fees remained at 16 guineas per term, with a games club membership fee of 7s 6d per term and fees for residence were £33 per term. Age of entry regulations were changed to 17 years 6 months on 1 October of year of entry, and not more than 18 years 6 months on the same date. Even with these regulations, some students were 'conscripted' and had their three-year training interrupted. Miss Fountain had always made the possibility of conscription during the course very clear to new entrants.

> I am pleased to confirm my offer to you of a place in the College next September, and I hope it will prove possible for you to complete your training.
>
> From the copy of the regulations which I sent you in my last letter, you understand that you are taking a risk. In the event of your being called-up in the middle of a term, it would not be possible to refund tuition fees: a proportion of the fee for residence would be refunded.
>
> No Certificate is given until the Three Year Course has been completed. In the event of your Course being interrupted, you must undertake to accept the decision of the College authorities as to the stage at which you are allowed to re-enter.
>
> In your reply, please state definitely if you are willing to accept the offer of a place under the conditions as stated. 3 June 1943.

M . . . , together with other students, accepted a place, but in September 1944 had to intermit her training; she was 'called-up'. Miss Fountain had fought to keep the students for the whole of the first year and, in this, she was successful. The students should have been 'called-up for work of national importance' in February 1944. For a few students, the call-up period was of short duration, and they did various teaching practices during the remainder of 1944–45 before returning to

Chelsea, September 1945 to complete a further two years training. 'I do not know how the other girls were affected by having a year out of College, but it did me a lot of good. I matured a lot in that year and returned to College with much more self-assurance and with more reason to settle down to hard study. I think this applied to the others too, and helped to persuade Miss Fountain that the taking of mature students would be a good thing'.

The urban environment of Chelsea had been exchanged for the rural environment of Borth; the College hostels for bedrooms in the Grand Hotel with the added luxury of hot and cold water; baths in four inches of water (maximum) and 10 minutes per person supervised by Miss Parkinson, and the bus ride to Merton for the coach ride to Aberystwyth. Gymnastics took place in Ardwyn School at the end of the school day; the sands of Borth served as the Chelsea playing fields with the sea of Cardigan Bay for swimming and life saving with the Royal Life Saving Society Bronze Examination taken between two moored boats and the local residents and soldiers as spectators. One Old Student reminisced, 'if it had not been for the shouted encouragement of a soldier, I do not think I would have passed'. End of term meant carrying all the portable gymnastic apparatus from the village hall to the hotel and packing it with the rest of College possessions in the medical gym.

Staff and students adapted to their 'new' conditions; 'The surrounding country is very beautiful and unspoilt and, at present, we seem to be removed from the tension of the towns, so that concentrated work is possible'. 'May we all face the future with courage and an unswerving belief that the results of good work are not wasted, though they may not always be visible to us'.

In contrast, they also 'saw the conditions under which the miners and their families lived with their blackened houses all huddled together and slag heaps close by; it was not a pretty sight'. In her report, for the session 1940–41, Miss Fountain said, '. . . my warmest thanks to the full-time staff for their adaptability and resource in our new conditions of work and play, and for this unfailing co-operation in the life of the College as a whole, which is making our sojourn in Borth a valuable experience in the history of the College'.

Old Students remembered receiving a 1s and 6d boxful of coal weekly with more in their boxes if they went to chapel, gathering driftwood from the shore and picking up additional coal from the station yard for Sunday evening fires in their rooms.

Numerous were the memories of students swimming in the sea with a hot water bottle inside their swim suits to keep warm in the freezing cold water, of staff on the beach giving 'unheard' instructions through a megaphone and watching their efforts through binoculars even when, as beginners (non-swimmers), they had their 'feet on the bottom and feigned breast-stroke'. Many remember learning to sing the Welsh national anthem with Dr Jones. When they had trouble with the language, they substituted 'My hen laid a haddock high up in a tree, I had it for supper, I had it for tea!'. Those that mastered the Welsh language joined the St Matthew's Church Choir. Pleasures and leisure were self-made and simple like 'skimming pebbles on the sea', but a positive approach was a helpful attitude to adopt. 'Miss Fountain and her staff made it clear to us, at the beginning, that there would be obstacles to life in Borth, but these were there only to be overcome and successfully so, too'.

All students had to report to the Headmistress at the beginning of each term and no student was allowed to absent herself from College lectures without previous permission from the Headmistress, except in the case of illness or sudden emergency. House rules at Borth strictly adhered to the well established code of conduct of the College and domestic arrangements were carefully detailed. Punctuality, courtesy and emphasis on taking personal responsibility in the adherence of regulations, especially under war-time restrictions, featured prominently in the house rules. The College experienced difficulties in engaging domestic and maintenance staff. The students cleaned their own rooms and, under Miss Partridge's supervision, undertook the dragging, watering and rolling of the hard tennis courts.

The timetable at Borth was flexible and varied with the tide, which was 'an excellent groundsman'. At low tide, rostered students moved backwards to mark out the sand using a cricket stump held between the legs, with pegs and string to draw lines and circles for netball, hockey and lacrosse. Netball goal posts were held in place by buckets filled with stones; oil drums, also filled with stones, were used to ensure goal posts for hockey and lacrosse stayed erect. 'When the War Ministry were putting metal spikes in the Borth beach to prevent German aircraft from landing, she (Miss Partridge) was adamant that they were not placed in the area where games were played'. When asked what if the enemy invaded, 'The Bird' assured the men from the Ministry that her students would be there with hockey sticks frightening them away! She won — no metal spikes were embedded!

Teaching practice took place in local and surrounding village schools and on the local beach. The 'Chelsea Buns' were the despair of the bus conductors when they wedged the gangways with bags of balls or lassoed unwary passengers with hoops, small, medium or large, as they travelled on the village buses to and from teaching practice. The Log Book of Borth County Primary School has many entries related to the work of the College. For example:

29/09/39 Miss Legg of the Chelsea Physical Training College, visited the school today to ask permission for her students to take a class in physical training.

4/10/39 Miss Powell, Chelsea Physical Training College, visited school today to make arrangements for dancing lessons for the pupils on Saturday.

To augment this rather limited practice, 'Through the kind cooperation of the Head Masters and Head Mistresses of a number of Public High and Secondary Schools each Third Year Student had a fortnight's intensive teaching, coaching practice and observation in a Secondary School at the end of the Autumn or Lent Terms'. If possible, students were allocated to schools in their home towns, or en route to their homes or within the vicinity or in towns where they had relatives or friends with whom they could stay. Clinics were set up for local children in Aberystwyth and Borth, keep fit classes for the Borth Social Club and Women's Institute became regular features of village life, and voluntary dance classes for children were established. As Cardiganshire was a reception area, the school population increased and opportunities for helping with out of school activities for evacuated children were freely available.

Students who entered for the Conjoint Examination of the Chartered Society of Massage and Medical Gymnastics also finished the Lent term with a fortnight's experience in the Massage Department of a large hospital which was again near or en route for students' homes. In 1947 the renamed Chartered Society of Physiotherapy extended the course from two to three years and included electrical work. Chelsea students ceased to take this examination, although they continued to study and practise remedial gymnastics. 'Experiment with Austrian gymnastics for school children did not get very far until the war years when Miss Connie Powell had the unique opportunity of supervising the whole of the gymnastic work taught by third year students at Ardwyn School, Aberystwyth. Six consecutive years of work in a grammar school convinced staff that the type of gymnastics that the girls had practised was on the right lines'. This style of gymnastics demanded great powers of observation and discrimination in selecting and developing material. Chelsea students demonstrated this work at the Ling Association Annual Conference in 1947; the programme included contributions from students at Anstey, Bedford, I M Marsh and Nonington Colleges of Physical Education.

In London, students had benefited from lectures from Fräulein Maria Ebner, from Vienna on Dr Streicher's natural Austrian gymnastics and athletics in 1932; Miss Chameir on revived Greek dance in 1933–34; Margaret Morris on the Margaret Morris movement; Mr Matthias Alexander on the Alexander method of retraining posture; Miss Karpeles on English folk dance in 1935; and Phyllis Colson on the Central Council of Recreative Physical Training. In spite of the difficulties of travel, the policy of inviting eminent speakers to the College continued during the war. Some lectures had direct relevance to the students' professional work, such as those from Rudolf Von Laban and Lisa Ullmann who took modern dance classes with the students and local school girls. Kurt Hahn, Head Master of Gordonstoun School, also evacuated to Wales, spoke on 'his ideas in education and the work of his school'. Mr Douglas Kennedy took the students for English folk dance and made an annual visit to Borth and Miss Diana Jordan lectured on central European dance (forerunner of modern educational dance) in 1940–41. Miss Ebner took the students for athletics from 1942 onwards and Miss Kirschner lectured on physical awareness and body control in 1944, 1946 and 1948.

Figure 3.5: Cultural lectures

Other lectures had a broader cultural significance and included:	
Dr Percy Scholes	— 'History of Music' and 'An Introduction to Modern Music' — illustrated by gramophone records.
Dr McAllister Brew	— Educational Adviser, National Association of Girls' Clubs
Dr Harlow	— Principal, Chelsea Polytechnic
Miss P Whateley	— 'Save the Children Fund'
Miss Leila Rendel	— 'Caldecott Community'
Mr S H Wood	— Education (Ministry of Education)
Dr E E Watkins	— 'Eugenics' and 'Evolution'.

Staff and students were invited by the Joint Debating Society of University College, Wales and University College London, to hear Mr Jan Musaryk speak, and to the lectures given by Miss Vera Brittain on 'The Shape of the Future' and Professor Joad, 'What is at Stake?'. In 1941, the debate, 'The evacuation of slum children into higher social circles would prove beneficial to the community' was successfully carried by two Chelsea students. Chelsea students were also successful in carrying their motions in 1942 and 1943.

In 1943 22 students were examined and passed the tests qualifying them to act as members of the Civil Defence Services in the capacity of air raid wardens. Unfortunately, no vacancies existed in Borth, therefore the students could not be enrolled by the Cardiganshire Civil Defence Committee or be issued with uniforms and equipment. They could, however, offer their services to the Senior Warden, take part in exercises, help in any emergency and state in any application for professional employment that they had qualified as air raid wardens.

Students attended and continued to give demonstrations of their work, particularly dance and gymnastics to a variety of audiences and for many organizations, including the Central Council of Recreative Physical Training. For example, they attended the demonstration of recreative gymnastics by British and Swedish teams, organized by the Ling Physical Education Association, the Central Council of Recreative Physical Training, the National Swedish Gymnastic Association, in conjunction with the National Fitness Council and the Anglo-Swedish Society, at the Albert Hall, on 26 March 1938. Students had demonstrated medicine ball work at the Ling Association holiday course held in January, 1938. They participated in the physical fitness display at Chelsea Town Hall, on Thursday 17 November 1938, showed keep fit work for members of the Borth Social Club and Women's Institute in 1939 and took part in the University of Wales Inter-Collegiate week functions in 1940 when they demonstrated dancing.

Throughout the nine years stay at Borth, Miss Fountain was in residence with the students. Possibly 90 keen, energetic, high spirited and youthful physical education students under one roof who were mainly dependent on their own resources for entertainment, while responsible as individuals for their own behaviour and conduct, needed a 'mature' word of advice periodically! It was indicative of Miss Fountain's expectations of each individual that she made students responsible for maintaining discipline, although she was in *loco parentis*, but also in character that she felt she should be 'in residence'. 'It was difficult to creep up the stairs without getting caught by Miss Fountain, whose hearing was acute, if one was later than the 10.00 pm limit!'

Food was strictly rationed with each student having a weekly limited supply of butter, sugar, jam and bread, although rural fare for main meals was nutritious. Students lucky enough to be in a 'plum' school for teaching practice (a convent) received a chocolate biscuit and milk at break. Other luxuries were coffee and cake at the village café and making toast on Sunday afternoons over the fire, in your own room. On Aberystwyth day (Friday), lunch often consisted of a packet of cheese and kipper sandwiches, a large slab of fruit cake and NAMCO (National Dried Milk Powder and Cocoa) to be mixed with boiling water. Memories were very mixed; as one Old Student recalled, 'A winter day and night, probably on Sunday; we sat round the fireplace in our bedroom, huddled over a small fire wearing coats, hats and gloves. The wind howled past us up the chimney or out through the door. The coal and wood was collected by walking along the railway line and, apparently, we were stealing from railway property!' In contrast, another Old Student wrote, 'I remember glorious summer days when we danced on the beach. I also remember cycling to Talybont for fresh boiled eggs and homemade scones; a real treat in those days of rationing'.

Throughout the war years, Miss Fountain travelled regularly to London to attend meetings. While in the capital, she also arranged to interview candidates and many Chelsea students were accepted after meeting Miss Fountain at Victoria, Paddington or Euston stations, in one of the city's hotels or in the small basement office from which the Principal of the Polytechnic worked during the war. In spite of these difficulties, the College intake was kept at approximately 30 students per year.

One of the most important meetings attended by Miss Fountain was held on 11 August 1942 when the Committee for the Training of Teachers raised and considered the following issues:

- the restricted nature of the course at the Women's Specialist Colleges of Physical Education;
- recognition from the Board of Education if students qualified in more than one subject;
- the place of the physical education specialist in primary schools;
- the possibility of a four-year course; and
- the University of London Diploma in the Theory and Practice of Physical Education to rank as a degree.

These issues were to have far reaching effects when implemented which was often many years ahead within the third and fourth eras.

Talks about the future of the College had been ongoing and a second very important meeting/conference was held at Chelsea Polytechnic on Tuesday 16 November 1943. It was recognized that the work of the College was national in character and therefore the institution should be developed as a National Centre for Physical Education in a densely populated area as a corporate part of a larger educational institution. Formal approval by the Board of Education, the London County Council and the governors of the Polytechnic was necessary before any scheme could be implemented. Following the conference and over the next few years, various sites in London and surrounding counties were investigated again and various trusts were approached for financial assistance.

The advantages of remaining within the Polytechnic environment, as different from the other specialist women's physical education colleges which were private, separate autonomous institutions, were seen specifically in terms of:

- mutual contact of staff;
- educational value of Polytechnic functions for students;
- centralized administration;
- opportunities for experimentation;
- the 'spiritual bond' experienced as a constituent part of a larger institution.

One site, Ranelagh Club, was of particular interest for here the development of recreative physical activities, including training in camping for children drawn from the thickly populated areas of Fulham, Chelsea, Putney, Hammersmith and Barnes, as well as facilities for the College, was possible.

Chelsea College was visited by Miss E Oakden HMI and Miss E M Perry HMI, during 1943. They represented the Physical Education Sub-committee of the McNair Committee and were collecting information for a report on the future training of teachers and youth leaders. The McNair Committee had been appointed '. . . to investigate the present sources of supply and the methods of recruitment and training of teachers and youth leaders and to report what principles should guide the Board in these matters in the future'. The Report, published in 1944, recommended far reaching changes in provision for the training of teachers and, in particular, two substantial constitutional changes; first the establishment of a Central Training Council and, secondly, clear integration of all training institutions. The women's physical education colleges were mentioned as providing the schools with three-year trained teachers, but were not recognized by the Board of Education. As the Report stated, 'that specialists in physical education are trained in separate colleges, does not mean that they differ in significance from specialists in any other subjects'. The Report also mentioned that the specialist colleges were not part of the grant-aided system of education. Fees were high and, therefore, the profession was 'not freely open to talent, regardless of financial circumstances'. The recommendation that colleges concerned with this work should be brought into closer association with one another and with the universities was, in the long term, to alter radically the training of teachers of physical education. It was, therefore, clear that the work of the specialist women's colleges of physical education was, at this time, of particular interest, as it was outside the 'recognized' system. Miss Ambrose, Headmistress of Dudley High School, said in a paper given at the Ling Association holiday course in 1945, 'I think the great hope for the future lies in the proposal dimly foreshadowed by the McNair Report and, under discussion by some Universities, of a degree in Physical Education, which would have the same high standard as an Honours Degree with a subsidiary academic subject'.

At the end of hostilities in May 1945, the College was unable to be reaccommodated in the Chelsea Polytechnic. By 24 November 1945, the Principal, Dr Harlow, had written to Miss Fountain in the following terms, '. . . it is difficult to get anything done for the College in the London area. . . . What do you think of the idea of Loughborough?' Over the next two years, there was an unending stream of correspondence between the Principal and the Headmistress. The Principal, 'desperate' to proceed with planning and expansion, was prepared to use the 'threat to close the College in order to get something done' and confident that this would not ultimately happen. 'They will never let us do that in view of the dire national need'. The College was now under 'real threat of closure'; crisis point had been reached.

From 1945–47, Miss Fountain continued 'the fight' to keep Chelsea College of Physical Education open. As Domina had remarked to an anxious Old Student, towards the end of her own life, 'Fount is a good fighter, dear child'. When it was absolutely clear that the College could no longer remain as part of Chelsea

Polytechnic, every possible avenue was explored simultaneously with provincial local education authorities, including Eastbourne. It was also clear that the Carnegie, Nuffield and Pilgrim Trusts were not likely to support requests for funding when money was available for provision for teacher training through public funds. Miss Fountain attended numerous meetings, wrote many detailed memoranda and personal letters and explored every avenue open to her. The first goal was to get the College back to London and, only when it was clear 'that the LCC could do nothing for the College', did she set out to find a new and permanent home for the College with a 'sympathetic' education authority.

A second 'crisis' point was reached in 1946 when Dr Harlow telephoned Miss Fountain to say that prospective students for September must be withdrawn. The Principals of Anstey, Bedford, Dartford and Liverpool Colleges of Physical Education were approached by Miss Fountain and each agreed to take five or six of Chelsea's new intake students. The students were notified and none withdrew their applications for admission to Chelsea or in the event of closure, to attend one of the other specialist colleges of physical education. The drastic action, advocated by the Principal, had been avoided.

During its time of crisis, the College was ably supported by the Old Students' Association, the Head Mistresses' Association and the Ling Physical Education Association. In a letter to the *Times Education Supplement* dated 5 March 1946, Miss Cater, Chairman of the Old Students' Association, set out the consequences of the potential loss of a well-established but forward-looking institution at a time of teacher shortage, as well as the achievements of the College.

Reprieve for the College came when the Ministry of Education said, 'This College must go on'. A very important change in the status of the College took place after fairly lengthy negotiations with the Ministry of Education and the College. The first of the specialist women's colleges of physical education was recognized, from 1 April 1945, as a Training College for Teachers under the Regulations for the Training of Teachers for the time being in force.

From 1929, prior to grant aid being available, the Governing Body of the Polytechnic had granted a 'free place' once every three years to a student, entering the College, as a memorial to Domina. Three students held the Dorette Wilkie Scholarship: Evelyn Stanley from 1930 to 1933; Elizabeth M Kirby from 1933 to 1936; and Honor Fry from 1936 to 1939. The Old Students' Association had also offered a £15 bursary annually from the College fund, either to one of the above students or to another student who required financial assistance. Students who were in receipt of a London County Council Senior County Teaching Scholarship had to train at a City institution as a condition of their award. This regulation, under the Further Education and Training Scheme, was relaxed when the College moved to Borth in 1939. From 1939, some local authorities had been paying part or full tuition fees (up to £50 8s 0d per annum) and grant aiding students towards the cost of residence (£10–£50 per annum). Many societies, such as the Society for Promoting Training for Women, the London Bequest Fund (City and Guilds) and the Royal Patriotic Fund supported students. Individual schools awarded scholarships to their pupils. The sums of money involved again ranged from £10–£50 per annum.

Some students borrowed loans from local education authorities, individual schools' funds, the Central Employment Bureau or the Thames Wall loan scheme, for sums of money ranging from £25–£100 per annum. From 1945, when the College was recognized, students received 'free' tuition and a local authority grant, based on the means-tested parental income, towards residence, uniform, equipment and travelling expenses. Students were now, in 1945, 'recognized' or 'private' and many who had previously lacked financial support, had access to funding under the 'recognized' status scheme. Responsibility for the College had been formally accepted in 1946 by the London County Council through the Chelsea Polytechnic governors, until the time arrived for the transfer of the College to its 'new' home.

In 1946, the Eastbourne Education Authority was directly approached by the Ministry of Education with regard to the future of the Chelsea College of Physical Education. Its future was bleak without the support of a sympathetic and interested authority. It would be true to say that the Chief Education Officer, Mr John Aspden, played a significant role in the acquisition and transfer of the College from the London County Council to the Eastbourne Education Authority. Between 21 January 1946 and 1 April 1947, many visits were made, letters exchanged, meetings held and negotiations conducted between the Ministry of Education, Eastbourne Borough Council, through the Secondary and Further Education Sub-committee and Education Committee of the Eastbourne Education Authority and the College. When, in 1946, the town's officials left for Wales to discuss the question of removing the College to Eastbourne, they were given their instructions in two words, 'get it'.

From the College's point of view,

> Eastbourne became a reality when, on 3 December 1946, the Chief Education Officer for Eastbourne, Mr John C Aspden, the Town Clerk, Mr F H Busby, and the Borough Treasurer, Mr I Cowan, came with Dr Harlow to Borth for negotiations. Two days spent in Borth and Aberystwyth discussing business and administration, as well as meeting staff and students, gave the College confidence in the impending changes. The friendliness and obvious interest in College shown by the visitors and their surprise and some amusement at our village life made this important occasion a very pleasurable one.

In 1947, the editor of the Old Students' magazine wrote, 'It is inevitable that some Old Students will regret a certain change of character that may possibly result. We can, however, be fully confident that there will be no deviation from the high standards and aims which have characterised Chelsea training in the past. The same nucleus of staff who guided the College so successfully through its first crisis eight years ago, will in the same way set the seal on this new venture'.

With the above changes, came a third and a fourth change; Miss Fountain ceased to be the Headmistress and was appointed as the first Principal of Chelsea College of Physical Education. The standing of the College and, by implication, teacher training in physical education was recognized when it became a constituent college of the newly enlarged Institute of Education of the University of London; the Inauguration Ceremony was held on 19 December 1949. Miss Fountain had planned to retire at the end of the 1945–46 session but with the Polytechnic Principal's encouragement, she led the College until August 1950 when it was 'safely' in Eastbourne.

Although the Minister of Education, Ellen Wilkinson, approved the transfer to Eastbourne and approved the proposal that the Eastbourne Local Education Authority should become responsible for the Chelsea College of Physical Education as a 'provided' college under the provisions of Grant Regulations No 7, 1946, the Admiralty was unable to vacate the two buildings occupied by HMS Marlborough, Hillbrow and St Winifred's, until the summer of 1948. The three buildings, Granville Crest, St Winifred's and Hillbrow were inspected and purchased for £52,919, then adapted and fitted out for a further £64,179. Six acres of playing fields at Hindsland were acquired, in addition to the 11 acres already owned, and laid out with six full-sized hockey pitches and two cricket squares. A pavilion and groundsman's cottage were erected by 1952–53 and 1957, respectively. The conversion of the chapel at Hillbrow to a laboratory by the Eastbourne County Borough direct labour force and J G Robinsons, was approved by the Ministry of Health on 21 October 1947. The chapel was, therefore, deemed de-dedicated, that is, it was 'no longer dedicated to the service of Almighty God'. The very impressive brass lectern was moved to All Saints Chapel, The Meads, Eastbourne, where it was still in use in 1998.

The administration of the College was formally transferred from Chelsea Polytechnic (London County Council) to the Eastbourne Local Education Authority on 1 April 1947. At the same time, the Principal and full-time members of the teaching staff were offered appointments '. . . their status . . . remaining as at present . . .' under the Eastbourne Education Authority.

The 'bare necessities' which had left the Polytechnic in 1939 had multiplied, and a 'colossal packing-up' was completed by staff and students and all equipment was transferred to Eastbourne. In spite of workmen still busy on the various premises, by 8 October 1948, the College was ready to receive the third year students. Second years arrived on 12 October and first years on 15 October. Within one week, the College, in spite of its unfinished appearance, was in its permanent buildings, was buzzing and alive, a hive of activity; the College had been saved and its immediate future was safeguarded.

Victory in Europe Day on 7 May 1945 had been celebrated by Chelsea staff and students in Borth with an impromptu Victory Tea Party for 200 local children, followed by sports on the beach. A few years later, an Old Student remembered, 'The fact that rain drove the competitors and onlookers into the hall, in no way dampened spirits on this happy occasion'.

When the College closed down at Borth on 2 July 1948, the people of the village presented the College with a parchment

To the Staff and Students of Chelsea College of Physical Education — We, the residents of Borth, gratefully remember your sojourn in our midst during the years 1939 to 1948. By going about your activities blithely, you did much to ease the strain of these years and your many courtesies and kindnesses have been greatly appreciated. As strangers you came, you leave as friends.

The Trustees of the Public Hall, Borth, the Cardiganshire Local Education Authority, the Headmaster and staff of the Ardwyn County School, Aberystwyth, as well as the proprietor and staff of the Grand Hotel (which had been purchased by the Welsh League of Youth and renamed Pantyfedwen) the vicar, the local doctors, the stationmaster, the postman, the policeman, the shopkeepers and the staff of the University of Aberystwyth, were formally thanked for the assistance they had given the College. A service of thanksgiving had been held at St Matthew's Church, Borth on 27 June 1948 for the hospitality offered and the welcome extended to College, in this village, at the outset of war and for the past nine years.

On Wednesday 19 July 1950, at Pantyfedwen, Borth, a slate tablet was unveiled by Sir Ifan ab Owen Edwards, to commemorate the stay of the College 1939–48.

This building named in turn CAMBRIAN HOTEL, GRAND HOTEL, PANTY-FEDWEN erected 1870 sheltered in times of emergency UPPINGHAM SCHOOL 1876–77, the students of ALEXANDRA HALL, UCW 1937 and the CHELSEA COLLEGE OF PHYSICAL EDUCATION, 1939–1948. It was presented to the WELSH LEAGUE OF YOUTH by D J JAMES, ESQ, as a Silver Jubilee Gift, 1947. This tablet was erected in grateful appreciation of the kindness and co-operation of the people of BORTH by the Staff and Students of the CHELSEA COLLEGE OF PHYSICAL EDUCATION on their departure to EASTBOURNE.

In her reply to the citizens of Borth, Miss Fountain said, 'When we were living here, we often thought of those, who in other times of emergency, had sheltered here before us, the boys of Uppingham School under the great Edward Thring, 300 boys in this building in the days of candles and lamps and the winds and draughts, just as they are now. We choose the words, "sheltered in times of emergency" advisedly. We had some discussion about the word "shelter" and looked it up in the Oxford Dictionary. "Shelter" — thing serving as a shield or barrier against attack — danger — heat — wind. Screen built to keep off wind and rain — a place of safety, and we felt it was the right word'.

The Commemorative plaque, kept in the coastguard's house following demolition of the hotel, was reset on the refurbished Town Hall, Borth on 13 September 1989, as part of the Aberystwyth and District, Liverpool and London (Lewisham and East Grinstead) Evacuees' Association 50th Anniversary Reunion. The ceremony was attended by Elizabeth Murdoch (Head of the Chelsea School), Joy McConachie-Smith (Deputy Head), Wendy Burrows (member of staff) and 19 Old Students, who had trained at Borth.

Following acceptance of the College by the Eastbourne Borough Council, the first independent Governing Body of Chelsea College of Physical Education was constituted with:

• Six members nominated by the Local Education Authority
• One member nominated by the University of London
• One member nominated by the Governors of Chelsea Polytechnic

- One member nominated by the Old Students' Association of the College
- One member nominated by the East Sussex Education Authority
- One member to be co-opted with interest or experience in Physical Education

The Principal, in spite of the views of the Senate of the University of London, was not an ex-officio full member of the Governing Body.

Figure 3.6:   Members of the First Governing Body of Chelsea College of Physical Education

---

The first members, with four changed LEA members during the first year in brackets were:

Mr Alderman A E Rush JP (Eastbourne Education Authority)
Councillor Bignell (Mr Alderman S N Caffyn) (Eastbourne Education Authority)
Councillor H A C Dingell MBE (Mr Councillor H Jowett) (Eastbourne Education
    Authority)
Councillor Sir Robert Dodd CSI (Eastbourne Education Authority)
Councillor Mrs W L Lee (Eastbourne Education Authority)
Councillor Mrs E Hamblin (Mrs D F Whitworth) (Eastbourne Education Authority)
Professor A B Appleton, MD MA LRCP MRCS (University of London)
Professor Winnifred Cullis, CBE MA DSc (Chelsea Polytechnic Governing Body)
Miss E M Perry, HMI (Chelsea Old Students' Association)
Mrs J Gow, MBE (Mrs B M Braithwaite) (East Sussex Education Committee)
Dr F J Harlow, MBE BSc FInst. PARCA DIC (Principal of Chelsea Polytechnic)
    (coopted member) (**Chairman**)
Chief Education Officer and Clerk to the Governing Body — J C Aspden MA

Although Miss Fountain was not a member of the Governing Body, she was always in close touch with the Chairman, the Governors and the Chief Education Officer and made a detailed report about the work and concerns of the College at each meeting; she was fully consulted on all matters.

On 31 October 1950, on the recommendation of the Ministry of Education, the Governing Body was appointed as a Sub-committee of the Education Committee in its own right, and reported to the Secondary and Further Education Sub-committee. The exercise of their functions with respect to the government of the College was delegated to the Governing Body 'except the powers to borrow money, to raise a vote, to grant or take a lease of land, to sell or acquire land, or to fix the number and salaries of the administrative staff, and subject to the condition that this Committee shall not expend without the approval of the Local Education Authority any monies in excess of the amounts specified in their annual estimates for the College'.

Organization and reorganization of rooms, as new buildings became available, was ongoing from the day the College opened at Eastbourne, and for many years to come. The original three buildings were frequently changed and supplemented over the next few years. The new gymnasium, approved by the Minister of Education in 1946, was built and completed by November 1948 on the Hillbrow site. The College gymnasium, '. . . was light, airy, spacious, with a good floor and was fully equipped, truly the finest in the land and an inspiration to teachers and taught'.

The official opening of the College on 28 January 1949 at 3.00 pm by the Minister of Education, the Right Honorable George Tomlinson, coincided with the Golden Jubilee celebrations of the College. The ceremony took place in front of an invited audience including: members of the Governing Body, HM Inspectors, heads of schools in the town, members of other training college staffs, the College staff and past and present students.

Figure 3.7: Official opening of the College at Eastbourne

The **Platform Party** consisted of:
Dr F J Harlow MBE (Chairman of Governors who presided)
Minister of Education and Mrs Tomlinson
The Mayor (Councillor Randolph E Richards) and Miss Richards
Mr C S Taylor (MP Eastbourne)
Councillor Sir Robert Dodd (Chairman, Education Committee)
Miss May Fountain (Principal)
Mr J C Aspden (Chief Education Officer)
Mr F H Busby (Town Clerk)
Rev L E Meredith (Vicar of Eastbourne)

The Order of Proceedings was:
Opening Hymn
Dedicatory Prayers
The Chairman of the Governors
The Principal
Official Opening
Vote of Thanks
The National Anthem

The Golden Jubilee Celebrations were held on 29 January 1949, when 174 Old Students and 48 guests: members of the Governing Body, past members of staff and local friends, sat down to lunch in the Gold Room at the Winter Garden, Eastbourne. Tables were arranged in 'years' with at least one representative from every year since 1902 to the present day. Alice Gardner was the oldest 'Old Student' at the celebrations and M Smith, Senior Student, and K B Woolf, year II, were invited to represent the 'present' students. Present students had been invited to hear the speeches and 80 of them sat on the platform above the hall during this part of the proceedings. Miss K McConnell, Chairman of the Old Students' Association, presented the College with a portrait of Miss Fountain as a gift from past and present students and staff. Dr Harlow, in accepting 'this magnificent gift', on behalf of the Governing Body, said,

> I must tell you the secret I have kept for 20 years.
> At the time of Dorette Wilkie's retirement, 'an illustrious giant in the world of Physical Education' I had wondered 'was there anyone who could possibly fill the post in so worthy a manner?' After consideration of the applications I had made up my own mind and decided to consult Dorette Wilkie who had taken no steps whatever to influence me or the governors. I was received, as always, with the utmost cordiality and much tail wagging on the part of her little dog. After a brief

discussion I said, 'I would value your opinion as to the choice of your successor'. Without the slightest hesitation she said, 'Why May Fountain, of course'. I knew then that my judgment was the right one. Time has proved without question that the choice of Miss Fountain as Domina's successor was the right one and your action today in making this gift not only sets a seal to that choice, but does a much deserved honour to Miss Fountain's distinguished career as Principal of the College.

Miss Fountain was always conscious of the College's inheritance and said in her talk to the leaving year III students in 1949, 'We must be careful not to lose amidst all this (new gymnasium and other facilities) our initiative and the gift for improvisation for which Chelsea is renowned'.

The students had an extended programme of external lectures in Eastbourne when, initially, the opportunity was taken to invite members of the local community to the College. John Lake, ARCA, FRSA, Curator of the Towner Art Gallery, gave a series of lectures covering art galleries and museums 'What is Art?', 'Art and Nature', 'Good Bad Taste', 'The British Scene' and 'Contemporary Art' in 1949–50. During 1950–51, Mr K C Harrison, MBE, Eastbourne Librarian and Mr Charles Taylor, MP addressed the students, the latter on Parliamentary procedure. In 1952–53, H K Bagnall Oakley, MA, MRFS, spoke about the flowers and fauna of Sussex. During 1953–54, different aspects of local government were covered by the officers who had played a major part in the successful transfer of the College to Eastbourne, Mr F H Busby (Town Clerk), Mr I Cowan (Borough Treasurer), Mr J C Aspden (Chief Education Officer) and Mr R Williams (Borough Engineer and Surveyor). Later, experts in various aspects of physical education, heads of a variety of institutions and well known authorities on a range of cultural topics were invited to contribute to the lecture programme. For example: in 1954–55, J Izon, BA gave a series of 10 lectures on modern drama; Len Goossens talked about the evolution of the oboe and gave a recital accompanied by Mabel Louveraine; and Sigmund Leeder lectured on modern dance with the students of his school giving a dance recital.

The College Library of pre-Second World War days was a specialized one, as books on all other subjects could be obtained from the Polytechnic Library and the next door Chelsea Public Library with its excellent Reference Section. With the increasing number of students at Eastbourne and the change in validation of courses, the specialized sections of the College Library had to be enlarged and, with the introduction of special fields of study, entirely new sections on music and literature had to be developed. Books on travel, civics, art and nature were bought in 1953. By 1958, the total stock was more than 5000. Initially, (even in Eastbourne) students were responsible for the Library but, when Miss Gough was appointed to the staff (in 1951), she acted as the College Librarian with a Student Librarian responsible for the organization of signing in and out of books. A Library Committee was formed by two representatives from each year, plus third and second year students responsible for each of the 14 sections of the Library, namely: anatomy, physiology, theory of movements, remedial gymnastics, health education, games, dancing, education, music, literature, art, travel, civics and nature.

Throughout the various eras, the College uniform has reflected social attitudes and customs and, even during the war years, as high a standard of uniformity as possible was expected. The students were allocated 20 'extra' clothing coupons in recognition of their special needs. Old Students were generous in returning College uniform for current students' use. The Polytechnic Secretary obtained a London County Council 'issue' of plimsolls and students hand-knitted gymnastic knickers in grey unrationed wool from Lerry Mills. The green Liberty silk dresses which were expensive, were patched and handed down, black wool bathing costumes with straps at the back (the forerunner of the leotard?) were worn for Austrian gymnastics, while 'Harrisons' — thick navy wool pants, were worn under shorts on cold days when, but only when Miss Partridge, 'The Bird', had written at the top of games lists 'Harrisons to be worn today'! By the 1940s, the tracksuit had temporarily replaced the gown.

In 1952, a new constitution was drawn up for the Students' Union. Its aims:

(a) The initiation, coordination and encouragement of such College activities as are not primarily the concern of the College authorities;

(b) the formation and expression of student opinion concerning all student organized activity in College;

(c) the representation of student opinion, when necessary, to the College authorities.

The committees of clubs and societies shall be appointed separately by the clubs and societies, and shall in all cases be Sub-committees of the Executive Committee. The clubs and societies shall be run by the students.

Students, and not members of staff, became Presidents of the individual clubs and societies. Attendance at general meetings was no longer compulsory *but* 'present students must be prepared to accept the responsibility of setting an example of public-spiritedness to all incoming students, so that this clause may remain as it now stands'.

After the College had moved to Eastbourne, the 1955 third year students wanted a College crest which linked London, Borth and Eastbourne. The cost of the grant, £157 10s 0d, was raised by various activities and a contribution from the Old Students' Association to purchase the Arms. The governors and the Town Clerk approved the request and the Mayor of Eastbourne signed the Memorial. Miss Gough and a representative group of students visited the College of Arms to discuss the design. The Arms were granted in 1957: 'Azure a Winged Bull Statant Argent horned and unguled and resting its dexter fore foot on a Sphere Or on a Chief also Or between two Sea Horses Vert the dexter legs raised a Pale Ermine thereon a Cross throughout Gules sermounted of an Open Book proper edged Gold'. Chelsea was represented by the Winged Bull of St Mark from the Chelsea Arms, Silver on Blue Field; Physical Education by the Sphere (Ball); Eastbourne by the sea horses, and the University of London by the open Book and Cross (red). The original motto, 'Mens Sana In Corpore Sano', was retained.

During the second era, the first term of the students' three-year course remained one of 'probation'. The governors also reserved 'the right on the recommendation of the Principal to require the withdrawal at any time of a student whose progress or conduct was considered to be unsatisfactory or if she was found to be unsuitable for the teaching profession'.

Students' and Old Students' achievements between 1930 and 1958 included representation at county, territorial, national and international levels in, for example, lacrosse, hockey, netball, athletics and swimming. Diane Coates (1950–53), as a year II student, represented Great Britain at the Helsinki Olympic Games in 1952 in javelin throwing. She threw 148 feet $9^1/2$ inches. Diane was presented to the Queen, Prince Philip and Princess Margaret on 9 July 1952 when the British athletic team was invited to a reception at Buckingham Palace. One Old Student, Marjorie Cadel (1931–34) was appointed as the first All England Women's Hockey Association National Coach from 1953 to 1955, while another, WT Barker (1929–32), became the Chief Superintendent of the London Women's Police (Metropolitan Police Force) in 1961. 'Her greatest headache (she said was) in dealing with the male who issues the most wonderful orders, without any reference to her, and then registers the utmost surprise when she says she is going against them as the ideas put forward just aren't suitable for women'.

Old Students were to be found both at home and overseas, giving local and national public service in their home or regional communities, contributing to the war effort by joining the Auxiliary Territorial Service (ATS), the Women's Auxiliary Air Force (WAAF) or the Women's Royal Naval Service (WRNS) or the civil and nursing services. Many joined the Air Raid Precaution (ARP) service as wardens, served in the Women's Voluntary Service (WVS), in the Women's Land Army, were firewatchers, ambulance drivers or members of the Red Cross or St John's Ambulance Service or acted, as one did, as Treasurer for the 'Local Jam Centre'. The majority, on leaving College, held a teaching post in a secondary school. Many progressed to lecturing in general and specialist colleges, or organizing or inspecting at county and national levels, respectively. Some contributed to outward bound centres and others held positions of responsibility in various organizations.

Elsie Palmer (1933–36) became an organizer on leaving College first, in Durham, secondly, in Manchester and thirdly, for Lancashire. She was Chairman of the Manchester Dance Circle for 25 years and, as the County Education Officer said, 'she will long be remembered for her breadth of interests and the relationships she could see between music, drama, movement and art and the integrated approach for young children'.

Maisie Mitchell (née Bomford 1935–38) was the Head of Department at Avery Hill College from 1960 to 1975 where one of the new eight 'wing' courses for women's physical education was provided in 1960. She was the first Chairman of the Association of Teachers in Colleges and Departments of Education (Physical Education section) from 1964 to 1967 and served as a member of the Governing Body of Chelsea College of Physical Education as the Chelsea Old Students' Association representative from 1960 to 1964.

After her retirement to Boscastle, in Cornwall in August 1950, Miss Fountain acted as an Assessor for the London University Diploma in the Theory and Practice of Physical Education until 1952 and as Examiner for the Institute of Education, University of London, until July 1955. She continued to attend the summer reunion of the Old Students' Association until at least 1977 and took a '. . . full part in the life of Boscastle . . .'. She was a member of the Church Parochial Council, the Women's Institute, the Cornish Society, the Chelsea Society, play and poetry reading groups and the Boscastle Art Society. She was seen, in 1970, joining in the Processional Furry Dance down the main street of Helston! Throughout her time as Headmistress and Principal, Miss Fountain was stalwartly supported by Miss Ruth Clark (Chelsea 1903–05), first as Senior Mistress and then as Deputy Principal. Ruth Clark was the first student to enter the preparatory course, designed by Dorette Wilke in 1902, for those candidates who were too young to enter the professional course, in order that they could continue their general education and study those practical and theoretical subjects which would be of use to them later. After qualifying and teaching in London and Montreal, she joined the staff of Chelsea in 1915 and organized educational visits for students, as well taking students for dance and training them as teachers. Following a year's leave of absence to organize physical education for women students at Queen's University, Kingston, Ontario, she developed gymnastics on Austrian lines, in keeping with the work of Dr Margarete Streicher at Vienna University. Miss Clark was 'a tower of strength' especially during the 'make do' problems encountered throughout the years in Borth. Her keen sense of humour lightened the load for everyone during both routine days and difficult times.

Gwyneth Cater
Principal (1950–53)

Miss Gwyneth Cater (Chelsea 1918–21) held the office of Principal from 1950 until she died suddenly and most unexpectedly on 2 December 1953. Miss Beryl Gough acted as Principal for the spring and summer terms 1954, until Miss Annie Rogers was appointed Principal, by invitation of the governors from September 1954.

Miss Cater, a keen folk dance teacher, had returned to the staff of the College in 1933 and served in London, Borth and Eastbourne. She had been in charge of the one-year course, from 1935 to 1939, made major contributions to the success of the College camps, taught gymnastics and dance to the students, made the initial contacts with schools in Eastbourne, and served on innumerable College and national committees.

During her short term of office as Principal, she was responsible for many College developments. Changes in the structure of the course were reflected in the content of the curriculum and in teaching practice experience. By the autumn term of 1951, the first group of students to be completely trained at Eastbourne were in their third year. This cohort was the last to take the London Diploma and College Diploma Examinations. The students recruited in 1950 were the first group to take 'The Examination for the Teachers' Certificate of the University of London, Institute of Education'.

The Teachers' Certificate at Chelsea (and Dartford and Nonington) validated by the University of London and inaugurated in 1950) had as its main aims:

1 The study of and practical experience in, all main branches of physical education.
2 The study of theoretical subjects necessary to an understanding and intelligent application of the practical work.
3 The training of the teacher; 'Physical Education was recognised as a subject of study'.

In the summer of 1952, third year students had spent two days observing routine school work in various grammar and independent schools in Sussex. In the Lent term of 1953, they spent three weeks on block teaching practice in grammar or independent schools. This arrangement became permanent and many students travelled to neighbouring counties where they resided locally for the period of school teaching practice. Miss Cater was also responsible for the intensive building programme which covered the purchase, adaptation and finishing of Ravelston, Bishopsbourne and the Welkin House. During her term of office, there was increased library provision with the purchase of 188 books in 1949, covering 22 main sections.

The initial special fields of study offered at Chelsea for the student's personal development, were advanced physiology, music and movement, and English and drama. Later biology and art and crafts were added to the options available.

From the first cohort to take this course, 42 students successfully completed the Teachers' Certificate gaining 10 distinction marks and 20 merit marks; there was one student who failed to qualify.

Figure 3.8: Results of the first Teachers' Certificate course

Distinctions		Merits
3	Special Physiology	3
1	Anatomy and Physiology	8
2	Education	
1	Practical Physical Education	4
1	English and Drama	3
2	Music and Movement	2

Another chapter had opened at a time of change; the Area Training Organisation, in which the College played its part as a constituent College of the University of London, Institute of Education, which had been reformed from 1 September 1949, involved the Principal and staff in heavier responsibilities as members of a team of colleges. The College was visited on 7 February 1949 by four members of the University's visiting panel: Miss D M E Dymes, Dr P V McKie, Professor A A Moncrieff and Miss D R Oldham. This panel also visited Dartford and Nonington Colleges of Physical Education in March 1949. The visitors were favourably impressed by the buildings and equipment, but suggested that a full-time 'lecturer in education' be appointed, rather than continuing with the practice of employing part-time staff, so that the 'principles and practice of education' occupied its proper place as the central core in the course of training. If organized research was to be undertaken, and they suggested it should be, the appointment of additional staff would need to be implemented. The visitors recommended that, 'the Chelsea College of Physical Education be continued as a constituent College of the Institute of Education for a further period of three years as from 1 October 1949'. Subsequent approvals followed until the College became a constituent member of the School of Education, University of Sussex in 1965.

On 24 October 1953, 18 Lombardy poplar trees were ceremoniously planted at Hindsland by the Mayor, Principal and Governors, to mark the Coronation of HM Queen Elizabeth II and 'to serve as a windbreak'. This was the last College function hosted by Miss Cater.

Miss Cater was a gifted individual, who unstintingly brought her expertise and interests into the service of the College, as Principal, following 20 years as a loyal and valued member of staff.

Beryl Gough
Acting Principal (January to August 1954)

Under Miss Gough, the College continued to move forward with purpose 'indicative of the unity . . . fostered' under her brief leadership. When Miss Rogers took office, Miss Gough remained as Deputy Principal until her retirement in July

1967 'to cultivate her garden'. She is perhaps best remembered as a '... tall, singularly impressive figure ...'. When she was appointed as lecturer in drama, 'The wind of change blew hard and we wondered what had hit us. ... the restricting limits of a physical education course were widened in a most refreshing way'. Miss Gough will also be remembered for the outstanding performance of 'Kalevala' on 30 June 1967 performed by 'The Production Club', under her direction, to mark the opening of the John Fulton Hall and as her 'farewell' to the College.

Annie Rogers
Principal (1954–58)

In 1912, Miss Rogers decided to apply to Chelsea as the one College offering a three-year course in physical education and with the attractions of London. Family, friends and school staff envisaged, '... life would be one long round of practical work'. For Miss Rogers, student days were a time of hard work but 'one of the best lessons I learned was that one could always go the extra mile; this has been invaluable advice during my lifetime'.

Miss Rogers was a 'motherly and jolly person' who had retired as Chief Woman Inspector for Wales July 1954 'with all the pleasure in the world'. She commented, 'It's been a good life, and I've enjoyed it enormously, but it will be nice to stand and stare a bit'. Miss Rogers was invited by the governors to lead the College, for at least two years, but held office until August 1958. 'Loyalty and gratitude to her old College prompted her to accept the invitation'. She was not to stand and stare.

'Her generous response to the governors' appeal was rewarded by the interest and pleasure she immediately found in the work and life of the College'. 'She also blew through the College life a fresh wind'. Her 'very personal, impulsive and intuitive approach' led to expansion of student numbers, new staff appointments and an increase in facilities. The College was inspected by seven HMIs including Miss R Foster, Miss J Lindsay and Mr J H Goldsmith from 14 to 19 November 1955. The governors received a confidential, but detailed oral report on 2 December 1955. The assessment covered the following areas: premises and equipment, catering, library, staff, students, programme, science, practical work, special fields of study and corporate life. The report included critical comments and positive suggestions and concluded that the College under the present Principal had entered upon a new lease of life.

In 1956–57, Miss Rogers reestablished the one-year course as the Supplementary Course under the leadership of Miss Jacqueline Langridge (Chelsea 1942 to 1945). Twenty-one students, who had completed courses of teacher training, were enrolled to receive specialist training in physical education, to meet the needs of the schools. Numbers were fairly consistent over the next five years, ranging from 13 to 31 with, in total, 137 enrolled and 134 successfully completing the course.

The new and converted buildings on the Welkin site were finished and the assembly hall, at Hillbrow, was officially opened on 20 May 1955 by Mr Robert Speight, MA, FRSL, Vice-President of the British Drama League. This new facility provided splendid accommodation for a performance of a Cantata, 'In Windsor Forest', and of a Masque 'The Bridal Day', both by Vaughan Williams who had collaborated with Miss Gough (producer, assisted by Miss Lawer, student), Miss Cartwright (choreographer) and Mr Davies (music director) in its production. Dr Vaughan Williams and his wife were present at the performances given at the opening ceremony.

1958 was marked by the Old Students' Association as the Diamond Jubilee of Chelsea College of Physical Education, and it heralded the next era in the history of this institution. On this occasion, 200 Old Students lunched in Eastbourne Town Hall, having been greeted by Misses Fountain, Clark and Rogers at the top of the steps. Following the toasts and speeches, they reassembled at Hillbrow for a programme of gymnastics and dancing given by the current students.

Miss Rogers was a caretaker Principal whose personal and intuitive approach had, nevertheless, prepared the way for her successor to discern the needs of the College in a quite different way.

For nearly three-quarters of the second era 'Chelsea' had been led by Miss Fountain at a time when 'the life of the College hung in the balance'. She had overcome superhuman difficulties, upheld the College tradition of experiment and development and, although a 'stickler for standards and discipline', she had never been 'a slave to stereotype'. She died on 6 February 1981, and her Memorial Service was held on 21 February 1981 in the beautiful old Forrabury church in Boscastle, where she had worshipped twice every Sunday for many years.

Miss Fountain, during her 21 years of office as Headmistress and Principal of Chelsea, had seen the College through two major crises. In so doing she, as Dorette Wilke had done before her, had exhibited a remarkable blend of firmness and tolerance, great courage and quiet dignity, resoluteness and charm of manner, sound leadership and inspirational foresight in the service of the College and the physical education profession. She had visited many countries to observe different methods of gymnastics and the training of students to teach physical education. Her knowledge was applied to the work of the Chelsea students and she had always insisted that the College should be flexible in its curriculum. Miss Fountain had held many offices during her professional life, including President of the Ling Association; a member of the Council of the Chartered Society of Massage and Medical

Gymnastics; a member of the Council and the Executive Committee of the Central Council of Recreative Physical Training; Chairman of the Physical Education Panel of the British Film Institute; Chairman of the Federation of Societies of Teachers of Physical Education; and a member of the Committee of the Fédération Internationale de Gymnastique Ling.

By nature, Miss Fountain was fearless, thoughtful, kind and generous and these personal qualities were appreciated by staff and students. Her faith never wavered, her vision never dimmed, her wisdom was widely respected, her persistence was rewarded. Her unobtrusive behaviour, good judgment, equanimity and personal tenacity had maintained a level of training, in very difficult circumstances, over a number of years. **'She led by example'.**

4   Expansion: 1958–1976

Audrey Bambra
Principal

'. . . a character in her own right'.

The appointment of Miss Audrey Bambra as Principal of Chelsea from 1 September 1958 changed the custom of employing a Chelsea Old Student to lead the institution, which had been the practice since its inception. Born on 13 July 1917, she was educated first at Bournemouth High School for Girls, later renamed Talbot Heath School (1926 to 1935) where she was influenced by an outstanding Head Mistress, Miss C F Stocks, MA. Secondly, she attended Anstey Physical Training College (1935 to 1938) when Miss Marion Squire was Principal. Miss Squire was a dedicated professional and a strict disciplinarian, but also a woman with a great sense of humour who set and expected high standards of work and conduct from her staff and from her students.

Many of Miss Bambra's educational convictions stemmed from her years in a school where understanding, inventiveness and originality, together with the acceptance of personal responsibility were valued above examination success. Therefore, she first appreciated the importance of the relationship of education and examination results as a personal guide. Secondly, that teaching pupils how to learn and the process of education, was for her more important than the actual information acquired which may soon be outmoded. Thirdly, inventiveness and originality should be prized rather than the ready acceptance of convention.

Right from the start of her course at Anstey, Miss Bambra was an exceptional student. Her reputation as a dancer preceded her and was maintained throughout her training. While she enjoyed all physical activity, she was no specialist games player, but an excellent umpire. She was good at both gymnastics, taught by Miss

Squire, and swimming; her teaching ability was outstanding. Significantly, it was 'strength of character that made her stand out from the crowd'. It was, therefore, no surprise to anyone when her peers unanimously elected her as their set representative and later, in her third year, she became an efficient and effective Head Student of the College. The students had recognized someone who could lead them, express their views clearly and establish a good relationship with the Principal. Her physical strength and determination contributed to her individual style of leadership and these characteristics were to be ever present and stand her in good stead throughout her professional career. Miss Bambra always acknowledged,

> The training I received at Anstey gave me a sound foundation on which to build my personal philosophy and practice. It has always provided a measure, for me, against which I evaluated new ideas. My career seemed to develop of its own accord as I took opportunities when they offered themselves, frequently with great regret for the work which I was leaving.

Between leaving Anstey and her appointment as Principal of Chelsea, on a commencing salary of £1160 per annum and with the status and title of lecturer in the Institute of Education, University of London, conferred by the Vice-Chancellor, Miss Bambra had two enjoyable years of teaching at Merchant Taylors' School, Crosby. This experience was followed by a lively and challenging year as a technical representative of the Central Council of Recreative Physical Training working in the Eastern counties. From there, it seemed natural to her to move into teacher education at Leeds Training College, at that time evacuated to Scarborough. Here she came under the influence of educators of high repute, including Helen Simpson, the Vice-Principal, who became the Secretary of the Association of Teachers in Colleges and Departments of Education and Dorothy Gardner, Head of the Primary Education Department, who became a member of staff of the Institute of Education, University of London. While at Leeds Training College, she said, 'I realised that the child and not the teacher was central to the education process. Students should lead children to the understanding of rather than the memorising of facts. It is often more important to know where to find the answer to a question than to know it. Movement is a facet of human capacity to be nurtured just as carefully as intellect and emotions'. At Leeds Miss Bambra also met, for the first time, Ruth Foster HMI, later to become Staff Inspector for Physical Education. She was a source of valuable advice to Chelsea, as were her successors in the post of Staff Inspector, Miss A Stephen and Miss E G Pollard. In September 1945, Miss Bambra moved to the Municipal Training College, Hull, for one year and was then invited by Miss Squire to join the staff of Anstey College. For three years she was responsible for the development of health education and basic movement, the forerunner of modern educational dance. In 1949, she was drawn again to general teacher training and moved with a friend, Miss Margaret Caudwell, who also trained at Anstey (1934 to 1937) and was on the Anstey staff at that time. Together with Miss A Elizabeth Cooper (later to join the Chelsea staff) they set up a new department in the recently established City of Coventry Training College under the Principalship of Miss J D Browne. Miss Bambra took responsibility for dance and welcomed the opportunity to explore integrated studies, especially through participation in a combined course, 'music, movement and drama'. It was from this post that she was tempted back into specialist training of women students as teachers of physical education. When Miss Bambra was interviewed about her career, she said,

> My conviction is that I have never been ambitious (contrary to her contemporaries' views), but that I very early decided that opportunities were for taking. There was no idea of a race to the summit, but a sense that challenges were always to be accepted.

As Miss Bambra walked into Chelsea and her office on the first morning of her new resident post and role in life, she was aware of the 'atmosphere' of the College and commented, 'I can feel the spirit of the place in the skirting boards'. She was also immediately aware of the general attitude of friendliness and of goodwill and kindness in abundance. Fresh from the open and stimulating style of the City of Coventry Training College, she quickly perceived a culture which was overprotective, even claustrophobic, and certainly lacking in the challenge and dissent appropriate to young adults in higher education. She remembers saying to a discussion group of student representatives in exasperation, 'I am the only rebel in this place'. Members of staff, many of whom had been at Chelsea for lengthy periods of time, must have questioned 'the wind of change' that blew in at gale force on her appointment. Her personal approach was analytical and intellectual in the search for sound principles on which to base the teaching of movement. She encouraged and inspired the staff to pursue the same thought processes. Her method was also pragmatic; it followed the order of systematic analysis of relevant factors, extrapolation of general principles and development of flexible plans for future progress.

The first staff meeting of the third era was held on Monday 29 September 1958, with all members of staff present when, from the Chair, 'Miss Bambra opened the meeting and informed the staff that staff meetings would be held each Monday at 5.00 pm and, as far as possible, would end at 6.00 pm'. The topics on the first agenda covered curriculum, professional, social and domestic matters. The meeting ended when 'Miss Bambra informed the staff that she will see the students and staff in their break 10.45–11.15 am and 1.45–2.10 pm, and that the staff should see Miss Mabey (her secretary) for appointments at other times'. The pattern, format and relationships had been set, but it was not long before meetings were held on a monthly rather than a weekly basis!

Her status as the Principal of the College was enhanced with a policy change by the Eastbourne Education Authority. On 1 April 1959, Miss Bambra was the first Principal to become an ex-officio member of the Governing Body of Chelsea, and this was 10 years ahead of the recommendations contained in the Weaver Report (1966) and implemented in July 1969. Her duties were set out in the Articles of Government dated 4 May 1959, as follows:

> The Principal shall control the internal organisation, management and discipline of the College, shall exercise supervision over the teaching, administrative and domestic staff and shall have the power of suspending students from attendance for

any cause which she considers is adequate but, on suspending any student, she shall forthwith report the case to the Governors.

She also had to notify the Chief Education Officer and governors of changes in the curriculum. Her regular termly reports to the governors were comprehensive and, during her tenure, included information about first, students: home and overseas, numbers on courses, applications, acceptances, withdrawals, teaching appointments, games honours and examination results; secondly, staff: conferences and courses attended, lectures given, courses tutored, publications, activities organized, academic awards, coaching sessions, coaching awards, resignations, retirements and appointments; and thirdly, College events, visitors, in-service education, outdoor pursuits courses, College gymnastics team, children's camp, student exchanges, workshop for young people, sports development, international links, research topics, All England Women's Hockey Association film featuring Chelsea students and Miss Burgum (a member of staff) and the National Keep Fit Festival.

Miss Bambra inherited the Teachers' Certificate Course validated by the Institute of Education, University of London and the quinquennial visits. The first and, as it was to transpire, the only London quinquennial visit for Miss Bambra was in 1963. The opportunity was taken by Miss Bambra and the staff to discuss work and problems with members of the visiting party:

Mr Boufler (Carnegie College)
Miss Casson (Lady Mabel College)
Miss Laidler (Domestic Science College, Battersea)
Dr Tenen (Furzedown College)
Professor Linnel (Dean of the School of Pharmacy)
Mr Elvin (Director, Institute of Education)
Miss Egan (Deputy Secretary, Institute of Education).

This course continued until 1967 when the group of students recruited in 1964 completed their training. The Teachers' Certificate course was constructed with the three main sections:

1 The study of, and practical experience in, all main branches of physical education.
2 The study of theoretical subjects necessary to an understanding and intelligent application of the practical work.
3 The training of the teacher.

proceeding concurrently. Students were required to pass examinations in the theory and practice of education, a special field of study and an examination in the theory and practice of physical education.

Each student selected, in her second year, one of the following subjects: physiology, biology, drama, music and movement or art and craft, as a special field of study for her own cultural development.

After one year as Principal, Miss Bambra introduced at the beginning of the autumn term 1959, a general introductory course for all incoming students who, for the first half term, were initiated into the broader aspects of physical education, the child and his interests, the body and its movement, the relationship of arts and physical education and the place of the environment in physical education. By 1968, year I students were introduced to the College and its work through an orientation week when all aspects of physical education featured on the time-table. Students also met all members of staff, explored Eastbourne and its surrounding environment and were introduced to the Students' Union and its various activities.

Thus began the quest both to broaden and to deepen the field of physical education and, as the editor of the Old Students' magazine wrote in 1961, 'Chelsea College of Physical Education is strong and very much alive to new ideas and the changing scene'. By 1960–61 able third year students had the opportunity to make additional study of one of the following specialisms: dance, youth leadership, science and movement, physical education for handicapped children or outdoor pursuits. These topics were later, by 1967, extended to include skill and movement, education, philosophy, assessment of human performance and physical education for children with special needs. As Miss Bambra said to the Old Students at their Annual General Meeting that year, 'no Old Students would wish a College to continue as it was when they were students; that would be no compliment to the far sighted founders of women's colleges, nor to the early students'.

By 1961–62, the title of the course had been changed to the art and science of movement or, as the students quickly dubbed it, 'art and sigh'.

With the establishment of the University of Sussex and, in particular, the School of Education, led by Professor Boris Ford and Professor A J Allen, came new opportunities for physical education, as Miss Bambra said in a paper to the Universities Conference in 1964, to be '. . . accepted as an appropriate high level study in a University which has already a reputation for lively and original thinking and for a non-traditional pattern of study'.

Following an opportunity to join discussions at the University on 'Universities and physical education', Miss Bambra in thanking the Vice-Chancellor, wrote, 'My long experience in training colleges has indicated that minimum standards may be preserved by detailed restrictions, but maximum standards are best sought in conditions of freedom'. The University of Sussex, School of Education Academic Committee produced a report from the Teachers' Certificate Working Party, of which Miss Kingston, Head of the Department of Art and Science of Movement, was a member, in 1968 entitled *Learning for Teaching*. Significantly, the School accepted '. . . that individual colleges should enjoy a generous measure of autonomy and the . . . learner orientated curriculum is a very great change indeed, making heavy demands on a teacher's patience and capacity for understanding of children'. While the University gave a certain level of freedom to the well established specialist College, nevertheless, it scrutinized thoroughly the content of syllabuses, the wording of examination papers and the standard of marking. As David Hencke later wrote in *The Reorganization of Teacher Training, 1971–77*,

Sussex University, as a new university, without the traditions of many older universities, took a liberal view of its job of validating teacher training courses in the college. Its area training organization was comparatively smaller than many others, taking in Brighton, Eastbourne, Chelsea, Seaford and Bishop Otter Colleges, the Brighton School of Art and the University Education Department. (Hencke, 1978)

The Certificate in Education course from 1965 onwards, as validated by the University of Sussex, School of Education, was reconstructed in the following way at Chelsea: art and science of movement, education, a liberal study, a further study (for some students), the practice of teaching and the activities courses.

The above sections were supported by practical work at a high level in all aspects of physical education, namely: dance, gymnastics, games, athletics, swimming and outdoor pursuits. Students taking the latter course, went on expeditions, usually at Easter, to experience mountain walking, rock climbing, orienteering and canoeing on rivers and lakes. They visited at least one of the following locations: the Isle of Skye, Loch Lomond, River Tay, Julian Alps, Snowdonia, Peak District, Lake District or Cornwall.

A basic course in anatomy and physiology supported the advanced course in the art and science of movement. There was a curriculum course in school remedial exercises, study of education with particular reference to the needs and interests of children and young persons and study of the principles of the curriculum in relation to physical education, special theory of physical education and health education. Teacher training was continuous throughout the three-year course and based on the work in education. Students had opportunities to teach all aspects of physical education at primary and secondary levels. The optional courses and special fields of study continued, but were not viewed as teaching subjects. Students remained in 'stable' groups throughout the three-year course for education, dance, gymnastics and theory of art and science of movement and for anatomy and physiology (two years), but formed heterogeneous groups for other subjects. One hundred and six students successfully completed the first Certificate in Education course in 1968; 92 in the art and science of movement, four in physical education, and 10 in dance, all at advanced level and supported by education and practical teaching. Twenty-seven students also passed a main level subject: nine in art, eight in music and movement, nine in social studies and one in the biology of man. Nine distinctions and 103 merits were awarded.

As Miss Bambra had said when giving her Annual Report to the Old Students' Association in 1961,

> In Physical Education, we have always, and rightly, been very much concerned with the training of the teacher and have not even tried to separate our material from method. In establishing the study of our subject, we have found a new title, which we hope also indicates the width of the work; that, in addition to techniques and skills with their background of anatomical analysis we consider very fully the more creative aspects of Dance, with the Laban movement analysis.

Theory and practice were to be intertwined and complementary in the Certificate in Education course. The 'professional orientation' was retained with emphasis on teaching and experience, rather than achievement of high personal standards of performance although these were encouraged. In practice, the latter were very important to the students who enjoyed the physical activities components of their course. After all this is 'what they were good at' before they entered Chelsea.

Miss Bambra believed,

> The curriculum of a specialist college of Physical Education has two complementary aims. Firstly, to offer a liberal higher education which will enable the student to realise her full potential and to develop the wide resources of knowledge which she will need as an educator; a liberal education in which her specialist interests are closely interwoven with a wide spread of related studies. And, secondly, to provide professional preparation based on an understanding of the educational needs of children and an appreciation of the vital part which movement plays in their growth and development, mental, physical, emotional and social.

The paramount qualities required by a potential teacher were therefore: knowledge of subject and children; understanding the way in which children learn and develop; combined with personal maturity and professional integrity.

Shortly, after her appointment, and during 1959, Miss Bambra had outlined the 'Place of the Specialist College of Physical Education' in terms of its function. Chelsea was to provide opportunities for 'the detailed study of (human) movement and physical activities in all their aspects and in relation to the education and recreation, of children and young people'. At this stage, the College was to provide not only for a three-year initial training, with the opportunity of a fourth year at degree level by 1967–68, but to continue to offer the supplementary course, which was opened to men in 1973 and to overseas students from the 1960s. Development of courses for postgraduate students, courses of advanced training in preparation for work in training colleges or as organizers and refresher courses proceeded and opportunities were provided for research by specially able students.

Under Miss Bambra's leadership, priority was given to the study of movement, the fundamental core content of the course, and to the study of children (to degree level), and not to the acquisition of personal skill (though this too would receive attention). Physical education was described by Miss Bambra as 'a worthwhile vehicle through which to educate the schoolchild'. It was to be viewed both as a series of subjects and as an aspect of education. The thinking, feeling, doing relationships were important aspects of the educative process.

The 'nomenclature' debate had begun and seismic changes had been signalled leading to a total reorganization of the College timetable in 1965 to allow greater flexibility and student choice. The restructuring of existing and the development of new courses, together with a complete rethink of aims, objectives, content, methodology and evaluation was in train. '. . . every hour of timetabled work (20) carried with it an equivalent period of student work, either practical or theoretical'.

In February 1966, Miss Bambra had prepared a brief paper in which she outlined a possible future of a 'Specialist College of Physical Education' as a 'Centre for the Study of Movement'. She envisaged the centre offering courses appropriate for men and women students in the following areas: education, recreation, therapy, industry, research, dance and movement. Summer schools would continue to be developed for lecturers, lower sixth form pupils, Old Students and local teachers.

As Miss Foster, the Staff Inspector for Physical Education said, 'the readiness (for change) stems from the enthusiastic lead given by the Principal in developing the curriculum and in changing the pattern of courses to be in line with modern ideas on a balanced education for teachers in training'.

From 1963–64 and in line with all the above changes, the College timetable and curriculum had been reconstructed to provide basic studies in year groups in the mornings and activities, science and liberal studies in heterogeneous groupings in the afternoon. The physical activities were sub-divided into four grades:

I   Basic techniques, skills, teaching
II   Advanced skills, tactical play, rules
III Technical skills, personal performance, theoretical knowledge
IV   Various positions of play, high standard in personal performance.

Advanced courses in coaching and umpiring prepared students to take the examinations of the appropriate National Governing Body of Sport. For example: Women's Amateur Athletic Association, Women's All England Hockey Association, All England Netball Association, Amateur Swimming Association and the All England Ladies' Lacrosse Association. In the evenings, students could choose courses in recreational activities, which enabled them to become competent coaches, officials and/or performers in individual sports such as golf, judo, archery, trampolining, canoeing, badminton, table tennis and sailing.

A fundamental principle in the design of the new Chelsea curriculum was, 'the student first masters basic areas of study which have a common focus and later develops aspects of the work to meet her own needs, interests and abilities'. In theory, no two students were to follow the same curriculum pattern; in practice, it was a very different story. Students were encouraged by the staff to make personal decisions to develop strengths, to concentrate on a few chosen activities and to master weaknesses. They were meant to build on previous experience and attainment. Nevertheless, while flexibility was the main advantage, certain elements had to be passed before progression could be achieved. Competent players were, in practice, reluctant to 'jump' grades in case they missed out on teaching points and 'mad was the scramble' to sign up for the course(s) on offer at the beginning of each half-term. Standards were set for the physical activities courses and students had personal choice and flexibility in the programmes they elected to follow.

Miss Bambra passionately believed physical education was an integral part of the process of education and equally education was an integral part of the process of physical education. The two were interdependent, yet they could be used independently as the method of delivering the educative process. There was more to the process than the mere acceptance of a title. The fields of study were now closely related to the academic disciplines of philosophy, psychology, history and sociology.

Figure 4.1: Interrelationship of disciplines

Discipline ⇨	Education ⇨	Physical Education
⇩	⇩	⇩
Philosophy ⇨		⇨
⇩	⇩	⇩
Psychology ⇨		⇨
⇩	⇩	⇩
History ⇨		⇨
⇩	⇩	⇩
Sociology ⇨		⇨

Within the space of less than 10 years, fundamental changes had been achieved in the concepts of physical education as a subject for study at higher education level and as a basic school curriculum subject at primary and secondary levels. Study of physical education and sport at further education colleges was to be substantially developed in the next era, although initiated in the late 1960s/early 1970s. Chelsea cooperated with the Eastbourne College of Arts and Technology in this development locally and with other Sussex and out of county colleges.

The editor of the Chelsea Old Students' Magazine had written in 1965,

> Change is usually mistrusted — we are conditioned into thinking it is all ultimately for the better. The general effort we must all feel is the increased pace of modern living, the increased materialism. In a world of labour-saving devices from the car to the washing machine, we all bemoan the lack of time to stand and stare. But we cannot halt progress and would not wish to for the wide effect is of great benefit to a great many — not least in the widening of opportunities for participation in so many activities in our own field.

In 1965, the Chief Education Officer reported (to the governors) that:

> . . . the establishment of an Academic Board to consider all matters relating to the academic policy of a College was in accordance with present trends. It was, however, necessary to bear in mind the importance of the relationship of the Academic Board with the Governing Body and, in this connection, the Secretary of State for Education and Science had himself set up a Working Party to consider matters relating to the government of Colleges of Education. It would, however, be some time before this Working Party was likely to report.

The Weaver Report (1966) established governing bodies of colleges of education as separate committees. No longer were they to be sub-committees of Education Committees. They were to be responsible for the general running of the College with membership from a wide range of interests, including the Principal, academic staff, the local education authority, the University, teacher training and specialist subjects. The Senior Administrative Officer became the Clerk to the Governors and was also responsible for general administration, maintenance and initiating the estimates of expenditure, the latter under the direction of the Principal. The Academic Board was to be responsible for the academic work of the College for student selection and for making arrangements for teaching practice.

The DES *Circular 2/67* led to the Education Bill, which became the Education (No 2) Act of 1968, '. . . to provide for the making by local education authorities of instruments of government of maintained colleges of education and to provide that the Colleges should be conducted in accordance with Articles of Government made by an order of the local education authority and approved by him'.

The Governing Body of Chelsea was reconstituted with the full participation of the Principal and representatives of the academic staff in the government of the College. The choice of Miss Barford and Miss Turner to represent the academic staff on the governing body reflected the confidence of staff in two senior colleagues that their views would be clearly and accurately presented. Miss Barford, appointed to Chelsea in September 1961, had proved to be a very wise, hard working and able colleague and, later from 1967, Deputy to Miss Bambra; she was generous with the amount of time she spent on college affairs; nothing was ever too much trouble for her; she had high professional standards and was warmly acknowledged by all members of staff as their 'personal tutor'. She had been outstandingly successful in ensuring the smooth running of the College through her unremitting attention to the maintenance of happy relationships between all members of the College. Miss Barford's selfless, good humoured and tireless service contributed greatly to the quality of the general life of the College as an educative force as important to the community as to the formal academic work of the approved courses. Miss Turner trained at Chelsea from 1932 to 1935, was appointed to the staff in 1949. She was a vital, energetic and fun loving person, who was a great friend and confidant to all who came into contact with her, but particularly to the students from overseas. She combined a calm serenity with a bubbling gaiety, a joyous love of life with wise counsel and sweeping generalizations with attention to detail. Staff knew both Miss Barford and Miss Turner would consult them before attending meetings to speak on their behalf.

The governors had always taken a keen interest in the affairs of the College, from attention to detail including the minutiae of staff and student progress in the early days, when all accidents and illnesses were reported by the Principal, to concern for the quality of education and training in the early 1960s, to discussion of the place and role of the College in the future during 1966–76. The 'Collier (Chairman) Sub-committee' had been set up within the College in October 1964, to draft a constitution for the proposed Academic Board. Initially, it recommended that: 'The purpose of the Academic Board shall be the formulation and expression of a corporate policy on academic matters'. From its inception, the Academic Board was to play a vital part in determining the academic philosophy and policies of the College.

The 21 clauses of the Constitution included provision for membership, as follows:

Principal	—	to take the chair
Deputy Principal		
Principal Lecturers	—	all
Staff representatives	—	equal in numbers to the Deputy Principal and Principal Lecturers to be elected by the Academic Council.

The Secretary to be elected from the members.

The constitution was approved on 30 November 1966 but, by 27 May 1968, eight amendments had been discussed and agreed by the Academic Board and approved by the governing body. An example of the changes can be gauged by reference to Clause 1. In 1966, it read:

> The purpose of the Academic Board shall be the formulation and expression of a corporate policy on academic matters as, for example, the planning and organisation of academic and professional studies; the selection of candidates for College courses; the evaluation of students' progress; the consideration of building plans and estimates, particularly where they bear on such items as the provision of teaching accommodation and equipment.

and by 1969,

> The Academic Board shall have the powers and duties set out in the current Articles of Government for the College, together with any further powers and duties delegated to it by the governors.

The powers and duties were defined as:

> The Academic Board shall, in consultation with the Area Training Organisation and subject to the approval of the governors:
> (a) prescribe a curriculum for use in the College which shall include a systematic study of the principles and practice of teaching;
> (b) make arrangements for the examination of the students of the College in the courses taken by them;
> (c) make arrangements by agreement with the authorities concerned for students to obtain practice in teaching under proper supervision in schools approved for that purpose.

The Board had the right to make representations to the governors on any academic matter and the Principal had to consult the Board on the regulation of admission of students. The Board could also recommend the suspension of students for unsatisfactory standard of work.

The first meeting of the Academic Board was held on 5 October 1966 when departmental reports were received, the Constitution of the Academic Board was clarified, and the BEd syllabuses were considered. Eleven meetings were held during 1966–67 when all major issues of academic importance were debated. For example, topics included the relationship of the Certificate of Education and the BEd courses; the function of the Board of Governors; and staff representation on the governing body.

College policy was therefore determined democratically before implementation.

Figure 4.2: The basic committee structure of the Academic Board

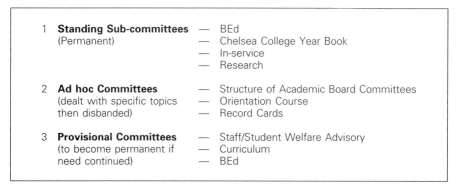

With the passing of the 'Representation of the People Act', the age of majority, in 1969, came a marked change in staff–student relationships and attitudes towards authority. Young people at 18 years of age were now legally adults, with the right to vote in political elections, enter into financial and legal contracts and take on adult responsibilities. They had personal independence and a right to privacy. The Principal and staff were no longer in *loco parentis*. For the students, acceptance of 'responsibility' had to accompany 'rights'; staff had to adjust to 'loss of' automatic authority; mutual respect had to be earned. These changes were, however, not easily acquired overnight by either side. As Miss Bambra said, 'Young people are now of age at 18 and it is increasingly evident that, notwithstanding the benevolence of the College's intentions, students are experiencing growing difficulty in accepting residential terms which have been agreed on their behalf by other parties'.

Student representation was granted on the Governing Body from 1969 with the President ex-officio and one other student in membership. In 1970, for the students 'liaison with the Academic Board had been through the Staff/Student Curriculum Advisory Committee, with the right to attend for the discussion of any items brought forward from this (Student Executive) Committee'. From 1973, 'three full-time registered students of the College to be appointed by the Students' Union' were members of the Academic Board.

The 'Harrison (Chairman) Sub-Committee', set up in June 1966, aimed to '. . . steer a middle course between the non-involvement of the many and the over-involvement of the few' in exploring the constitution and terms of reference of the Academic Council and the General Staff Meeting. All members of the teaching staff formed the Academic Council to hear accounts of the Academic Board's deliberations and to advise, after discussion at the Chairman's (the Principal) invitation and on general academic matters. All members of the teaching, administrative, domestic and technical staff formed the General Staff Meeting to hear and discuss, when necessary, items of a non-academic nature. There was, in practice, some repetition in reporting and discussion, but the structure prevailed until the end of the era.

Following the publication of the James Report, *Teacher Education and Training* in 1972 and the White Paper *Education — a framework for expansion* in 1973, the College Curriculum Development Committee held discussions which led to the development of diversified degrees in the College. Meantime, the Chelsea governors established a sub-committee to consider the implications of the James Report. '. . . they are of the opinion that Chelsea College of Physical Education should be maintained as a separate institution, and that plans should be made for its future development as a specialist centre in accordance with the terms of paragraph 17 of *Circular 7/73*'.

The Eastbourne Education Committee had established a sub-committee, 'to examine the Circular in relation to the two colleges (Chelsea College of Physical Education and Eastbourne College of Education) and further and higher education in general taking into account views expressed by each governing body'.

The Robbins Report, *Higher Education* published in October 1963, had recommended:

1   colleges should provide for 750 students with smaller colleges becoming the exception;

2   the three-year concurrent course to continue with four-year courses leading to a professional qualification and a new form of degree, the BEd, to be provided;

3   an in-service BEd be considered to enable practising teachers to gain graduate status on a part-time basis;

4   Teacher Training Colleges to be renamed Colleges of Education;

5   Colleges of Education and Institutes of Education (university based) to become Schools of Education responsible to the Senate of the University for the BEd degrees. The Schools to have their own Academic Board and Boards of Studies;

6   Local Education Authorities to be represented on the Governing Bodies of their colleges and the School of Education;

7   the Governing Bodies of Colleges of Education to be independent.

The first BEd (Hons) course of which physical education was a component, was validated by the University of Sussex and mounted in 1967–68 at Chelsea. It had a tripartite structure and was taken by the students as a fourth year of study. For Chelsea students, it was physical education — either aesthetic aspects originally titled 'movement', or scientific aspects, or social aspects (40 per cent); education — adolescence (40 per cent); and a linking study (20 per cent) — which grows from the two disciplines and stems from a topic of interest to the individual students. The case for physical education to be included was based on the following statement:

> Physical education as an academic discipline has scientific, social and aesthetic aspects, and among its contextual studies are anatomy, physiology, psychology and sociology. At the centre of these studies is kinesiology, as applied to the study and understanding of human movement. It is a study concerned with man as an individual and as a social being, engaging in the motor performances required by his daily life and in the physical activities which offer aesthetic, health-promoting and cultural satisfaction.
>
> Physical Education has developed its own areas of research, and its hitherto loosely integrated body of diverse materials is gradually becoming a systematically organised field of knowledge capable of being studied in a disciplined and scholarly way.

Of the first eight students, Dilys Beynan, Linda Black, Rosemary Campbell, Gillian Hollis, Diane Jamieson, Ruth Jessop, Margaret Moir and Marion Pudge, all of whom gained a BEd (Hons) degree (two upper seconds, two lower seconds, three thirds and one pass), three studied aesthetic aspects, one scientific aspects and four social aspects. Their linking studies were entitled: expressive movement as a means of communication; the educational value of dance; why do people dance?; balance in physical education environments; motivation and marathon events; bridging the Wolfenden gap in Stourbridge; leadership and physical skills; and the significance of physical ability in social group interaction. The first, first class BEd degree was awarded to Penny Crisfield in 1972.

A one-year postgraduate course was approved, originally for women students in 1962 and, by 1972, for men and women students who wished to take a teacher training course with subsidiary physical education. In 1963–64, one student, Pauline McCullough, BA, who had read English at McGill University, Canada, completed the course. Recruitment to this course was slow; four students arrived in 1964–65 from the universities of Reading, Durham, Birmingham and Queen's Belfast. By 1972–73, for example, 15 students were recruited, eight men and seven women, who had read mathematics, biology, chemistry, history, English or politics, successfully completed the course and became qualified teachers of their degree subject and physical education. Miss Bambra commented in her report to the Old Students' Association, 'when one of them marries a last year's third year in the summer (1973), we shall establish a new tradition with the first all-Chelsea matrimonial partnership'. At the end of 1973, students had been accepted from at least 39 universities and four polytechnics, with BA or BSc qualifications in a variety of arts and science subjects. The College had also started to '. . . build a really extensive collection of information about the development of physical education in all parts of the world . . .'. Second year students had opportunities for exchange visits on a *quid pro quo* basis with contemporaries at either universities or other specialist physical education institutes from either Dalhousie, New York State, Beer-Sheva, Wingate, Amsterdam, Köln, Munich, Madrid or Hungary. The Junior Year Abroad course originated in 1965 with a request from Springfield College, Massachusetts, for a programme to enable some of their undergraduate students majoring in physical education to study abroad for the third year of their four-year degree course. The Junior Year Abroad course was 'an experience not to be missed', and was firmly established by 1969 with the period of study assessed for credit purposes in the students' own institution. Subsequently, the programme was expanded to include students from at least 24 other universities in America and five in Canada. The overseas programme also expanded to cover, for example, 15 countries in 1974–75 and 25 countries in 1975–76. In 1975, an exchange programme for second year students included seven countries and eight students from the Danish State Institute of Physical Education in Copenhagen had spent eight days, 28 March to 4 April, in the homes of Chelsea students.

From the summer of 1970 to 1975, Chelsea and Anstey year II students exchanged residential locations. The courses were jointly staffed with Chelsea students studying aspects of education in an industrial setting (Birmingham) and Anstey students pursuing a concentrated swimming and sailing (on the sea) programme. The three specific aspects offered to Chelsea students were:

- the education of children of immigrant origin;
- education of slow learners;
- leisure facilities in an industrial city.

To prepare staff to cope with further expansion, changing circumstances and new ideas, in 1971 Miss Bambra invited Professor Ben Morris (Professor of Education at the University of Bristol) to lead a discussion on 'personal relationships in a college of education'. In the same year, staff also participated in a one-day conference on 'methods of Study' based on Jerome Bruner's book, *Towards a Theory of Instruction*, published in 1966–67. Bruner covered the dual themes of: how children learn and how they can best be helped to learn, in eight essays. His work was based on the nature of intellectual growth and its relation to theories of learning and methods of teaching. He saw instruction as the means of transmitting the tools and skills of a culture. His earlier book, *The Process of Education* (1960) reflected the outcomes of a searching discussion at the Woods Hole Conference to open new paths to learning and teaching. The content of this publication was dealt with more deeply in the later publication. Chelsea staff examined their own approaches to teaching and learning, in the light of Bruner's theory, for their own work, for their work with students and for students' work with pupils.

During 1971, the Staff/Student Curriculum Committee had considered the topic 'self-evaluation' based on a paper by a member of staff, J R Homer. His paper had five main aspects: self-evaluation as a vital part of education; self-evaluation and course planning; self-evaluation and assessment; self-evaluation and self-direction; and self-evaluation and practical considerations. During discussion, students' anxieties were clearly revealed and inconsistency in standards of marking students' work and projects was raised. At the same time, the Academic Board and the Academic Council held lengthy discussions on 'interdisciplinary studies for students of physical education'.

In keeping with current trends, during October 1972 the Physical Education Department supported the change of name from 'art and science of movement' to 'movement studies' as the title for the main course. When this suggestion was debated by the Academic Board in October 1973, it agreed to adopt the title 'human movement studies' in keeping with the title of the proposed new diversified BA degree which had been accepted by the University of Sussex for development. Chelsea was one of the first specialist physical education colleges to accept the subject of human movement to be studied in its own right.

The new degree aimed to:

  (i)   develop an understanding of the nature and significance of human movement through the establishment of principles and the examination of theories of movement;
 (ii)   examine the development of skill in sport and in every day life;
(iii)   review the contribution of movement study to man's health and social well-being;
 (iv)   consider the place of movement as a means of human communication;
  (v)   investigate the contribution of movement and physical activity to the child's development and education.

It was a joint degree, in that students pursued, initially, either human biology or sociology with their study of human movement. Seventeen candidates were offered provisional places for the first course in September 1975.

Movement was, therefore, studied in teacher education courses as an educational, recreational and remedial force in the lives of children and adults. Observation and analysis formed an important part of the study, and consideration was given to movement as a means of expression and communication. The development of skill in movement and the acquisition of techniques were studied in detail. The fundamental study of movement in the teacher training courses continued to be supported by work to a high level in the following aspects of physical education: dance, gymnastics, games, athletics, swimming and outdoor activities. Laban's XVI basic movement themes were used as the foundation for experience in the art of movement, the practical and theoretical study of 'modern educational dance'. In gymnastics, the body was trained in the functional aspects of movement, with the gymnast contributing her own ideas as she experimented and explored the many movement possibilities to answer the task set by the teacher or herself. In activity courses, students mastered basic and advanced techniques, tactics, rules, teaching and coaching methods and umpiring according to the level of the course and their abilities. In education, lectures in the teacher training courses covered the history and development of ideas, the critical examination of educational theory and practice and the knowledge requisite for the understanding of children and their learning.

Liberal studies remained an in-depth study of one topic of cultural or academic interest outside physical education, selected from art, biology, drama, music and social studies.

Further studies in youth leadership, advanced dance, physical education for handicapped children, outdoor pursuits or science and movement, continued to provide additional work for able students leading to independence of thought. During this era, additional subjects like assessment of human performance, education and philosophy became available. Science and movement became movement and skill and physical education for handicapped children was retitled physical education for children with special needs. For students not pursuing further studies, selective courses could be undertaken from: comparative physical education; creating electronic compositions; learning to philosophize; movement in water; muscle physiology; preparing tapes for teaching; study of human performance; teaching physical education as a science; the teacher and non-verbal communication; and visual communication. Technical courses were also available for students in athletics officiating, committee procedure, first aid, keep fit and dance, labanotation, lighting and sound effects, make-up, music for dance, oral communication, swimming officiating, technical aids, photography and closed circuit television. In the practice of teaching,

> The teacher's role is (now) less obtrusive (than previously) but her influence is no less important than before, since it is through the quality of her skill in movement observation and in her relationships with the class that she establishes the 'rapport' and the two-way flow of ideas which enables her pupils to work in partnership with her, to improve the quality and diversity of their work.

Year 1 students spent half a day per week on school experience, either with children at College or in the local primary schools. A short block primary school practice took place in the summer term. Year II students experienced a five week secondary block practice in the second half of the autumn term in Sussex or Surrey schools, preceded by a group practice, one day a week, in local schools in the first half of the autumn term. By 1968–69 'In accordance with the current trend, particularly in the University of Sussex School of Education, to involve teachers more directly in the training of teachers, it is hoped that the group practice may be a really cooperative effort between College and schools'. Year III students experienced a five or six weeks block practice in secondary schools in Berkshire, Buckinghamshire, Dorset, Hampshire, Bournemouth, Portsmouth, Southampton, Oxfordshire, Sussex or Wiltshire.

Supervising staff were advised, 'Careful consideration should be given to students' schemes of work (teaching practice) and emphasis placed on the maintenance of students' notebooks and the daily records of students' work'. A Joint Consultative Committee with teaching practice schools was established in 1965 to consider and resolve related issues. It was attended by members of the College staff, physical education teachers, headteachers and physical education advisers. Teaching practice conferences, as a follow-up to block practice, became a regular feature of the College calendar and were attended by College staff and students, physical education organizers in school practice areas and headteachers and physical educationists from the practice schools.

Throughout the era, first year students continued to attend camp at the end of the summer term, either in the New Forest or at Blacklands, East Grinstead. From 1960, second years took part in a recreational activities week, at the College, organized by the Central Council of Physical Recreation.

In 1960–61, three students from the London College of Dance and Drama formed an experimental group for a one-year course leading to the Teachers' Certificate. This course was transferred to Dartford College of Physical Education in 1965. During 1963, consultations had taken place between Miss Bambra and Miss Ruth Foster, and with the support of Lisa Ullmann, to establish an advanced course in dance with the Laban Art of Movement Centre at Addlestone. The course was approved for a September 1964 start. This three-year specialist course in dance, under the leadership of Miss Lorna Wilson, aimed to: develop an awareness of the quality of movement in a wide range of experiences; to appreciate dance as a communicative art; and to encourage confidence, originality and clarity in movement. Students spent years one and three at Chelsea and year two at the Centre. By 1972, a link with the Guildford School of Acting and Drama Dance Education Ltd had been approved by the Delegacy of the University of Sussex for a one-year course (fourth year for the students) leading to the Certificate in Education. J Browne, J Harding and C Kemp were the first students to complete the course.

The innovative in-service BEd (Hons) full-time and part-time was discussed in 1971–72. 'The characteristic of this in-service BEd, is that it has been developed as a regional scheme by a Management Group representing each of the colleges and the University'. It was a course specially designed to meet the needs of practising teachers returning to part or full-time study, as well as an integrated model for course design radically different from that of the initial BEd degree course. Additional complexities arose from the regional sharing of teachers and resources and the variation in levels of provision between and within institutions. Modifications arose from monitoring, evaluation and consolidation. At Chelsea, the specialist subject study was physical education or dance. Education development studies and interdisciplinary studies could be taken either at Chelsea or at one of the other constituent colleges or School of Education of the University of Sussex. Five students took the preparatory year in 1971–72 and the full-time year in 1972–73 at Chelsea. They attended either Chelsea, Eastbourne College of Education or Brighton College of Education for educational development and interdisciplinary studies. The results of the whole group were first class honours — three; upper seconds — 15; lower seconds — 35; thirds — four; passes — two. These results show the wide range of ability level of the students selected for this pilot course, but do not reflect the students' individual development, their general enthusiasm for the course nor the degree of cooperation and integration achieved. In 1972–73, 15 students took the preparatory year, five in physical education or dance and 10 in the education development and interdisciplinary studies components at Chelsea, and pursued the full-time year in 1973–74. For a time, numbers increased steadily but with diminishing financial resources, secondments for teachers were reduced and the part-time course became more popular.

From September 1975, students who had achieved two GCE 'A' level passes were eligible to take the three-year BEd degree course, validated by the School of Education, University of Sussex, instead of the Certificate in Education course. They studied all aspects of human movement and were prepared to teach physical education in schools.

Throughout the third era, the College provided many 'short' four or five week in-service courses for the Department of Education and Science. For example, movement in the middle schools; an advanced course in the science of movement; and physical education/movement education for teachers of mentally handicapped children. The College cooperated with the Chartered Society of Physiotherapists to provide a course in human movement studies for teachers of physiotherapy, and also linked up with other professional organizations to mount specific courses, as well as providing international workshops for American advanced students of physical education as a summer vacation course directed by Miss Hilary Corlett.

During the third era, the work of the College still focused, but not exclusively, on educating and training women teachers of physical education. There was, however, a distinct change in the academic content of the course with the emphasis on 'movement' as the core subject of study, and the opportunity for graduates to enter related professional careers.

Throughout the 1960s, the College continued to expand to meet the serious national shortage of teachers of physical education and in support of the development of the study of physical education. New buildings were erected or purchased and the processes of adaptation and alteration continued to meet the ever changing needs of accelerating growth. From 225 students in 1958–59, the College had grown to 550 by 1972–73 with corresponding staff increases from 21 full-time staff, including Principal and Deputy Principal, to 53 and a staff:student ratio from 1:10.7 to 1:10.3. Although residential accommodation had been increased for supplementary course students with a small hotel (The Lindens) (warden Miss A Elizabeth Cooper) by 1961–62, 50 second year students needed to be accommodated in approved lodgings. A temporary lodgings officer later to become permanent but part-time, Mrs Davies, was appointed to inspect and approve residences and then to allocate students to landladies.

By 1968, the Librarian was writing the '... transformation of Bishopsbourne into a day-time centre with crowded changing rooms and utility rooms where too many bodies chase too few feet (of space) and where garments and gear of all kinds are lost and found — and lost again. While this ceaseless activity does not make for the peace and quiet conducive to study, it does at least ensure that the library is now, for second year students at least, at the centre of College life, and the corresponding increase in its use over the last five years has been remarkable'.

In 1963, a further improvement project for the College was under discussion for the Gaudick Road site, followed by changes at the Welkin site and the purchase of new buildings along Gaudick Road between 1967 and 1970. The former involved pulling down the original chapel that had been converted into a laboratory in 1947–48, and building two gymnasia, a swimming pool, tutorial block, art rooms, music and practice rooms, the John Fulton Hall and cloakroom accommodation. This project was completed in 1967 when Lord and Lady Fulton officially opened the Hall on 6 December 1967. The project also included conversion work to the Welkin gymnasium and old dining room and kitchens, the former becoming the new dining room and kitchens, the latter the library.

As early as 1970, Miss Bambra had asked the governors to consider the building of a sports hall for the College to be erected in the gardens at the rear of Bishop Carey and Sunnymead in Gaudick Road. She justified the need for additional space and special needs in saying,

> Such a hall would serve not only present needs, but also would enable the College to extend its services to the community by providing a centre for:
> (i)   the training of talented sports men and women;
> (ii) sports events and tournaments;
> (iii) in-service courses in a wide variety of physical activities for school and club use; and
> (iv) physical recreation of all kinds for the public with leadership from the College staff and students.

The pressure was continued; papers were written; 11 reasons were given in 1972 as further justification for the provision of a sports hall and detailed plans were prepared. The project was approved in principle by the DES in March 1973, to be put forward as a bid for a major programme allocation, but the scheme was tied-up with the future development of the College and the changes brought about by the Local Government Act 1974. The project, however, was shelved. Miss Bambra's frustration at the lack of progress was expressed in 1975 when she wrote to the Chief Education Officer of East Sussex Education Authority, 'If we are to plan courses realistically, we need some clear reassurance that the Sports Hall project will be pursued with real concern by the Committees on whose judgment we now depend'.

The Government White Paper, *Sport and Recreation* (August 1975) from the Department of the Environment, stated in paragraph 62:

> The Sports Councils make substantial grants available to enable teams to travel abroad for international competition and for preparation training. Success in international competition has an important effect on national morale. Moreover, the standards set at international level, affect standards of performance at all levels and success stimulates the interest of young people to take part themselves. Accordingly, the Government are looking into means of diverting resources to those who are gifted in sport. A particular study is being made of the possibility of developing centres of sporting excellence at universities and other colleges, which would also provide for the general educational needs of selected young athletes. The Government do not interfere in matters affecting the admissions policies of universities and other educational establishments or their curricula and, any proposals arising out of the study, have to be discussed with the institutions or other bodies

concerned, but the response which has already been received is encouraging. The Government are also considering the possibilities of bursaries financed by commercial sponsors for established athletes to enable them to devote more time to sport, and other means of assisting outstanding sportsmen and sportswomen to train for and participate in, competition at the highest level.

It was clear to Miss Bambra, the staff and the governors, that Chelsea should be involved in this type of development and the provision of a sports hall therefore became a matter of vital importance. The College was, after all, already publicly acknowledged as a 'centre of excellence'. East Sussex County Council, however, continued to defer the matter pending negotiations related to the forthcoming merger with other colleges in the area.

As student and staff numbers increased and course content changed, a formalized departmental structure evolved within the College. The term 'department' was used to signify a major area of work for which a designated principal lecturer, later known as the Head of Department, held responsibility.

Figure 4.3: Staff structure: 1967

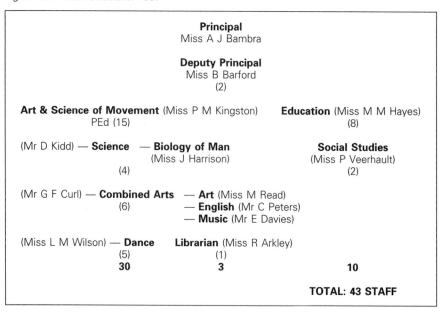

The *department* was conceived, by Miss Kingston, as having a 'free environment, in which ideas and opinions can be fully expressed, received with respect and are fairly evaluated'; conditions which, in her view, were vital for the proper functioning and development of the art and science of movement and physical education.

Miss Bambra had recognized by 1975, 'to hold a degree, is increasingly important in modern society'. This principle applied equally to staff and students. She went on to say to the Old Students, whom she was addressing, 'though we all know many excellent non-graduate teachers, yet it is clear that they will become less and less influential in shaping policy and development as seniority goes to those who hold better formal qualifications'. Old Students from home and overseas were writing for transcripts of their courses to enable them to be accepted onto a university degree course. As Miss Bambra responded in 1970 to one such request, 'Good luck for the degree. Its getting to be a must here, too, but I have decided to remain as part of the élite, those who have no degree!'. Her place and standing in the profession was already secure.

In 1958, of 21 full-time members of staff, six held Bachelors degrees in science, music, English or librarianship and one had also been awarded a Masters degree (education). By 1975–76, the 50 staff held 23 Advanced Diplomas, 16 Bachelors degrees or equivalents, 10 Masters degrees and one Doctoral award. Many went on to further study at postgraduate level in this and the next era. Correspondingly, there was an increase in attendance at conferences, presentation of papers, publications, research, appointment as external examiners/university assessors and sport/games honours, as well as academic awards.

Chelsea had always attracted students from overseas, either to the full three or four-year courses, to the one-year Junior Year Abroad course led from 1968 by Miss Joy Standeven or to the specially mounted courses of a more limited duration. The Commonwealth Bursary Scheme in 1964–65, provided a one-year course with a very flexible programme to cater for the needs of individuals from a wide variety of backgrounds. The Supplementary Course for Overseas Students accommodated individuals who had not gained Qualified Teacher Status in Great Britain, but were recognized in their own countries. Miss Lorna Turner took responsibility for overseas students and a tutor with overseas education experience, Miss Beryl Wardrop, was appointed to an additional lecturing post in September 1965 and tutored the bursars. The students received either the College Certificate for Overseas Students or the Commonwealth Bursary Certificate on successful completion of their courses. One of the highlights of the overseas one-year course was the annual visit to schools in the West Riding of Yorkshire. By 1972–73, the Commonwealth Education Study Fellowship Scheme had been established. On completion of their courses, the majority of students returned to their own countries; over 50 countries can be identified in the 1960s from all the continents of the world, where students returned to teach, coach, advise, lecture or inspect. As one Old Student commented, 'there is little opportunity to lead a sheltered existence at Chelsea College. The attendance of students and visitors from all over the world gives life at the College an international flavour'.

Minimum qualifications for the Teachers' Certificate and Certificate in Education courses were five GCE 'O' levels, suitability for the teaching profession, good health and physical ability. Each candidate was interviewed by the Principal and had to pass the College's practical tests. Selection for the fourth year of the BEd degree course was based on the College record, the Certificate in Education examination performance and initially, an interview. The choice of Chelsea College for potential students continued to be influenced by personal recommendations. Such comments as, 'Chelsea's reputation preceded me', or 'school staff suggestions influenced me' or 'I had contact with former Chelsea students, who encouraged me' were common. Reference, however, to an opportunity to take a degree, interest and ability in physical education, desire to teach, varied curricula available, were also reasons given for selecting Chelsea College.

In 1959, 12 college societies functioned, namely: sailing club, badminton club, athletics club, dramatic society, music society (including College choir and orchestra), art and craft society, photographic society, the Christian Union, camping and guide society, archery club, folksong and dance society, with the debating society restarted during the year. By 1973 there were 17 sports clubs connected to the evening activities programme, as well as Student Union clubs such as photographic and film club, production club, guide and outdoor activities club, sailing club linked to the Eastbourne Sailing Club and the Christian Union.

With the passage of time, there was a process of change in the affairs of the student body which formalized itself from informal students' meetings to the Students' Union in 1961, approved and constituted by the Governing Body. Under the new constitution, the Vice-President for Social Affairs took responsibility for *club evening* held every Wednesday. The Senior Student became the President and chaired all meetings. The former membership of two deputies, a second year student, secretary and staff treasurer was changed to seven officers, elected annually as the group of students responsible for the administration and organization of the Union and its activities. The Union, within its stated functions, should manage its own affairs, but the Principal retained the right of veto until 1968. Minutes of all meetings were now kept, standing orders were approved by the Governing Body and provision was made for financial arrangements with Student Union fees, as approved by the Minister of Education, as part of tuition costs. The proviso was, 'No part of the fee should be used to make payments to bodies not eligible for grant from public funds, such as political parties, National Union of Students and Students' Christian Movement, including College branches in each category. If students wished to support these bodies, they should do so as individuals'.

By 1973, the constitution had 17 main clauses and 17 sub-clauses. The Union was run by the Executive Committee, supported by the Student Council, with all registered students in membership of the Union. The students, since their course had been validated by the University of London, Institute of Education, had participated in its Students' Association events, particularly all the sports matches and tournaments. In 1959, the South Coast Colleges branch was formed and flourished until 1965.

Miss Bambra was fully aware of the contribution made by the Students' Union to the life of the College. When speaking to the Old Students at their Annual General Meeting in 1966, she said, 'The Student Executive has again proved its capacity to organize and guide the social life of the College and has shown increasing sense of responsibility also for standards of work'.

In 1958 students were not allowed to have scooters, motor cycles or cars on College premises. Men visitors were allowed on Saturdays only, but had to be out of hostels by 12.00 pm. Students requested, subject to signing in and out arrangements in hostels continuing, 'All students, after the first term, should have a leave until 11.00 pm on one evening per week'. By 1976, students were resident either in College or approved lodgings or had made their own domestic arrangements as non-resident students in Eastbourne. From 1958, each student had an assigned personal tutor who, throughout the course, was now concerned for academic progress and personal welfare. Students during this time were expected not to undertake an undue amount of paid vacation work and to return to College in good health, fully able to take part in a strenuous course. Paid work during term-time was not 'officially' countenanced; the course was very demanding.

The concept and practice of 'service' continued to be an integral part of the students extra-curricular activities. In 1961, Roger Catchpole from the University of Cambridge had, during his lecture to the students, when telling them of his experiences in taking refugee boys to camp in Austria, made a casual remark, 'So why not for girls?' Debra Turner, a first year student (who went to Israel to teach after completing her course at Chelsea), inspired and rallied her colleagues. With staff support and 'approval' of the United Nations Organization, they raised £1275 in three months to take two groups of 20 refugee 9–14-year-old girls to a chalet camp halfway up Hoekoenig Mountain, near Salzburg, each for two weeks holiday in the summer of 1962. Six students, Debra Turner (year II), Dairne Haggar (year II), Carol Burgess (year I), Sheila Pearson (year III), Marita Mottram (year III) and 'Frizz' (Pauline Gastall, a supplementary student), ran the camps, which were visited by Miss Bambra. The activities were recorded on film. Subsequently, children's camps have been organized annually in Burnham-on-Sea, Somerset; Cromer, Norfolk; and Eastbourne, the latter on the College playing fields at Hindsland for children from Birmingham, London, Manchester, Oldham, Bradford and Polish refugees resident in England. The London Borough of Hillingdon's Welfare Officer handpicked the 20 children, in 1973, who were 'in need of a holiday as they would not normally get this due to their unfortunate home backgrounds'. The programme the children enjoyed included visits to local attractions such as the Dolphinarium at Brighton, Drusillas Zoo at Alfriston or further afield to the castle at Arundel, Sir Alec Rose's 'Lively Lady' and HMS Victory at Portsmouth, or the observatory at Herstmonceux. Activities such as boat trips on the sea, walking on the Downs, playing on the beach, horse riding at a local stables have always been popular. College facilities were always available for use and many sports afternoons were held. Comments from students running the camps included, 'we were lucky in that we had no real problem children and could therefore devote all our time to giving them a really good holiday' or 'there was no shoplifting or stealing' or 'the children came from large families and needed individual attention to make them feel that someone was really interested in what they did'. Rachel Kingman was the first year II Chelsea student to participate in the residential Camp America programme as a swimming counsellor, during the summer vacation of 1974. Subsequently, groups of students have travelled annually to the United States of America for periods of up to eight weeks to contribute to this programme of sports activities for children.

A variety of charities, including World University Service, Children's Country Holiday Fund, International Social Service, Handicapped Children, National and

Local Charities, have been supported regularly. Students also contributed to days of gymnastics and dance for pupils from local secondary schools, the Saturday morning swimming club and the gymnastics club, assisted at local youth clubs, and with Brownies and Guides.

The College Games Association was very active during this era and, each week, the Principal and the Deputy Principal received written invitations from the team captains to attend matches. The fixture lists were expanded and matches were played against other physical education colleges, particularly Bedford, Dartford and Nonington, local clubs, local schools, two-year colleges, counties and the WRNS. The College also entered many tournaments, including those organized by the University of London Institute of Education Sports Association. Each weekend students continued to write games reports after each match and, for example, in 1968, the following account appeared on the Principal's desk, as well as being received by the Games Association and posted on the Games Association notice board.

> The weather was perfect for an afternoon's cricket. The fielding was good with each player concentrating hard and keeping the pressure on the batsmen the whole time. By taking quick singles and very good running between the wickets, B & J (Chelsea) soon had the fielders on the defensive. They took advantage of the few bad balls by hitting fours, but showed their ability to play 'respectfully' the good length, accurate balls, so strengthening Chelsea's position each minute. A marvellous win, and a most exciting and enjoyable game.

Other comments have included: 'The goalkeeper played well, and it was due to her we did not lose by more', 'A very competitive match evenly contested', 'Good team spirit', 'Good all round performance against an experienced side', 'Game won by visiting team in midfield (plus six goals)', and 'The team's performance was perhaps one of the best of the season'. Matches covering swimming, trampolining, athletics, badminton, table tennis, lacrosse, netball and hockey were also reported with comments on grounds, tactics, individual's play, as well as results. Specific comments have included: 'Fast and well fought game contested in a very sporting way', 'Chelsea replied late in the game with a well manufactured goal', 'A good match', 'Our starts and take-overs were noticeably faster than those of our opponents — despite the fact that there were no starting blocks' (away — swimming match), 'Passing high and inaccurate; attack uncoordinated' (lacrosse), 'Our shooters received good passes in the circle and made full use of them; court slippery' (netball) and 'Generally it was Chelsea's "body awareness" and quality that won the match' (trampoline). The first (men's) rugby game was played by Chelsea students and staff against Eastbourne College of Education in 1973; Chelsea won 32–0.

Students represented not only the College, but Great Britain, in the World Student Games. For example, in Tokyo in 1967, Maureen Barton (1965–68) competed in long jump (fifth 19' 2¹/₂"), Sheila Garnett (1965–68) in 100m hurdles, winning her semi-final and taking the silver medal in the final, and Linda Knowles (1964–67) in high jump, achieving the silver medal with a jump of 5' 5¹/₂". Linda had also represented Great Britain in the 1962 European Championships where she came third, and in the 1964 Olympic Games, both competitions prior to her entry to College.

Further examples of students' achievements include:

Judith Connors (1963–66)	Assistant Manager, Bulmershe Joint Sports and Youth Centre;
Judi Tarbutt (1966–69)	Started outdoor pursuits as a time-tabled activity, as well as an extra-curricular club;
Elizabeth Kelly (1967–70)	Was a member of the All England netball team that participated in the World Tournament in Jamaica in 1970;
Bridget Hathaway (1970–73)	Was a party leader to the Arctic Circle on the British Scout and Guide expedition;
Helen Rollason (née Grindley 1974–78)	BBC sports presenter.

Within the physical education profession Margaret Talbot (née Moir 1964–68) gained an MA Physical Education degree from the University of Leeds in 1971 and a PhD from the University of Birmingham (Social Science) in 1991. After teaching (1968 to 1970) lecturing (1971 to 1987) and Head of Department experience (1982 to 1987) she was appointed as Head of the Carnegie Department, Leeds Polytechnic in 1987. The first and, to date, only woman to lead a men's physical education department. She became a Fellow of the Physical Education Association in 1980 and was awarded a Personal Chair at Leeds Polytechnic in 1989. In 1990, she was designated the first Carnegie Professor, Leeds Polytechnic. Margaret was appointed Officer of the Order of the British Empire in the Queen's Birthday Honours List, 1993, for services to Physical Education and Sport. She has served on innumerable committees, travelled widely to give papers at conferences, contributed extensively to the published literature on physical education and women and sport and was elected President of the International Association of Physical Education and Sport for Girls and Women in 1997.

By the early 1960s, the Chelsea Old Students' Association was holding three meetings per year for social and educational purposes. The Association was saddened to learn in 1963 that Misses Fountain and Clark had been obliged to sell Domina's Cottage. Many Old Students had rented it but, alas, the fees received no longer covered the rates, maintenance and expenses.

By 1968, the meetings of the Association had been cut to two per year and the object was rewritten as:

(a) to unite the Old Students of the Chelsea College of Physical Education as an organised and independent body of Physical Educationists; and
(b) to keep in touch with educational developments.

By the 1970s, however, interest in joining the Association had waned and closure was discussed, but not implemented.

Old Students, from this era, continued to achieve honours in games at all levels and offered their services to local communities and governing bodies of sport. Examples of local groups include: Citizens Advice Bureau, Samaritans, Red Cross, play groups, meals on wheels, talking newspaper, day centres, prison fellowship and the Women's Institute. Some Old Students have become local councillors, mayors, District Commissioners for the Guides, school governors or been ordained. One has managed the England and Great Britain Under 20 and Under 23 athletic teams, another has captained the England Hockey Touring Team to Zimbabwe and a third became the Rhythmic Gymnastics National Coach. Naturally, Old Students were very successful within the physical education profession as teachers, advisers or inspectors. As one Old Student said, 'I was considered a teacher who was very concerned about teaching children'. Miss Bambra had 'followed up' the teaching experience of Old Students, with a five, 10 and 15 year enquiry. Results show that, on average:

50 per cent of students taught for five years
20 per cent of students taught for 10 years
10 per cent of students taught for 15 years

Well over 75 per cent of students were in posts of responsibility and at least 15 per cent of the students who were no longer teaching had held posts of responsibility earlier in their careers.

In 1996, one Old Student, who had been teaching for 31 years, wrote '. . . we are steeped in the preparation for a forthcoming OFSTED inspection; a far cry from the professional trust I experienced as a young teacher'. She continued, '. . . if it moves, you have to write a policy for it'.

All students remember well their uniforms, and this era was no exception; the long list cost £80 and included: Red 'dotty clotties' and yellow/red/black skirts for national dance; blue leotards for gymnastics and black for modern dance; Capri blue games skirts 3" above the knee, white poly cotton teaching shirts and black teaching trousers, cherry red 'Riding Hood' cloaks and woolly cardigans knitted by the blind; and a black and white Speedo slinky shaped swimming 'cozy'. Students received a £30 per annum allowance for equipment and clothing, in addition to the standard level of grant.

Students continued to give demonstrations of work for many organizations, both local and national and participated in international congresses. For example, in August 1969 at the International Association for Physical Education and Sport for Girls and Women VI Congress in Tokyo and, in 1973, at the VII Congress in Teheran, they formed part of the gymnastics and dance team from the women's colleges of physical education in the United Kingdom. Miss Kingston and Miss Wilson led the 1969 team and were responsible for the gymnastics and dance programmes, respectively. From Chelsea, Alison Smith and Penny Gale were in the 1969 team and Gill Aldis, Sue Harding and Linda Warwick were in the 1973 team.

The students' education continued to be extended in this era, through listening to and questioning eminent speakers on both general and specific topics and issues. Medicine, the arts, education, politics, charitable organizations and physical education are but a few of the areas covered in the external lecture programme. During the 1960s, these lectures were held in the evenings for the whole College but, during the 1970s, the lectures were often given to year groups during timetable time. Parties of schoolgirls continued to be welcomed and shown the work of the College. From these visits stemmed the course for fifth and sixth form pupils when they were introduced to the work of a physical education student in training. The course was primarily for enjoyment and advanced level play of a chosen game, but often resulted in a career decision.

The College had always welcomed visitors and the third era was no exception to this well established practice. On 28 October 1966, the College was honoured by a visit from Her Majesty The Queen and HRH the Duke of Edinburgh during their tour of towns associated with '1066 and the Battle of Hastings' and selected students 'stood like statues holding lacrosse sticks'. The Queen unveiled a plaque opposite the 'College Gymnasium'; photographs and the visitors book were signed. Miss Bambra and the Senior Student, Janet Sparkes, were presented and the visitors watched year III students demonstrating modern educational dance and gymnastics and coaching games on the College pitch. The one-year course students participated in a lecture/demonstration of observation and analysis of movement. The Duke, when leaving the College, delighted the students by saying 'The students are surprisingly unmuscular'.

The beginning of long-term changes for the College were foreshadowed in the 1966 letter from the Head of Teachers' Branch (Training), Mr P R Odgers. He wrote with specific reference to Chelsea:

1 That the short-term and long-term aspects of this College's future development could not properly be considered in isolation.
2 That the future of the Chelsea and Eastbourne Colleges of Education could not be considered in isolation either.
3 That the Department were thinking very much in terms of teacher training units of some size and broad scope, admitting both men and women students.
4 That, in the circumstances existing in Eastbourne it appeared that thinking was bound to move in the direction of a single institution of bilateral shape as the ultimate pattern, with a physical education side which would be a significant unit in its own right, both numerically and otherwise, and that, in this framework, the Chelsea College of Physical Education would provide a centre of excellence in the physical education field.
5 That immediate developments should be planned with the longer term in mind.

Mr Odgers and four officers at the Department of Education and Science met the Chairman and Deputy Chairman of the Governors and the Principal to discuss 'The future of the College'. By 1968 'The Secretary of State expressed the view that it would be appropriate to concentrate this expansion (planned for 1973–74) primarily on the extension of existing Colleges of Education, special attention being given to the possible enlargement and broadening of scope of some of the remaining specialist colleges for women'.

Within five years, circumstances, had changed and reductions in teacher training numbers were forecast because of the smaller school population. Chelsea's intake to initial teacher training was cut from 185 in 1972 to 160 in 1973 and 140 in 1974. In paragraph 17 of *Development of Higher Education in the Non-University Sector (Circular 7/73)*, further changes in the status and rôle of the College were foreshadowed:

> While it will be a major aim of planning to consider how places in colleges of education not required for teacher training can best be used for other higher education purposes, it would not be reasonable to suppose that all colleges of education should have a diversified role. In the Government's view there will continue to be a place for some institutions devoted solely to teacher education, and some of these may develop a national role in respect of particular aspects of professional training. But the number of such monotechnics cannot be large if proper provision is to be made for the uncommitted student and if institutions are not to be unduly at risk from future variations in teacher supply requirements.
>
> Some small colleges may need to be retained, perhaps on a reduced scale, as professional centres, while others not so needed or badly located for such a purpose may have to close. The potentialities of many may best be realised by incorporation in a polytechnic or by merger with other institutions. Finally, the policy outlined in paragraph 10 that advanced courses may co-exist in the same college with courses below that level should be regarded as applying to colleges of education also.

Towards the end of 1972, Miss Bambra enlisted the help of six senior members of staff to prepare brief statements under the following seven headings:

- the contribution of dance to education
- the contribution of dance in leisure and recreation
- physical education and leisure
- physical education and skill, including skill in everyday life
- physical activity as therapy
- physical education and health
- international importance of physical education

so that she could prepare a general document, for approval by the Academic Board, on the future of the College for the consideration of the governors.

With local government reorganization, the County Borough of Eastbourne ceased to exist from 1 April 1974 and the East Sussex County Council now embraced the County Boroughs of Brighton, Eastbourne and Hastings. East Sussex Education Authority was therefore now responsible for the administration and for the future of Chelsea, which had to be seen in relation to Brighton, Eastbourne and Seaford Colleges of Education and Brighton Polytechnic. In her report to the Old Students on 1 June 1974, Miss Bambra said, 'Here at Chelsea, we became alarmed that the decision that we should form part of a new College of Higher Education (with a new Principal and Governing Body) in Eastbourne was being made by people who know little of the work of this College, and before the *nature* of the new institution had been determined'.

The Further Education Sub-committee, by request of the college principals, established an Eastbourne Higher Education Working Party to consider the future of the colleges at Eastbourne and Seaford. In turn, the working party set up the Joint Academic Planning Committee to consider academic subjects, structure and related topics.

The processes of reorganization increasingly involved staff and students in lengthy meetings. The number of standing sub-committees of the Academic Board and its associated working parties, was accordingly expanded. The Principal, staff and students continued to prepare detailed papers for consideration by the Academic Board and the Governing Body or their sub-committees.

In her report to the Old Students' Association in 1973, Miss Bambra, expressed,

> ... appreciation of all that the County Borough of Eastbourne has done for the College in the 25 years since Chelsea came to the town and the Local Education Authority took responsibility for our administration. We have always had most generous treatment and have enjoyed the support of an excellent, liberal and thoroughly interested Governing Body and the kindness and understanding of the Chief Education Officer, Mr John Aspden ... Sir Sydney Caffyn, Eastbourne's last Mayor, (the Office of Mayor was continued under the new structure), is fittingly the Chairman of the Governors in this last year; we owe much to his well-informed and skilful leadership and his great interest in the College.

At the 'Farewell' evening to Eastbourne Borough Council, held 11 February 1974, among the guests were, May Fountain, Annie Rogers, John Aspden, Francis Busby and Ian Cowan. The students provided a programme of music and dance as entertainment.

At the last meeting of the 'old' Governing Body on 15 March 1974, the Chief Education Officer of East Sussex Education Authority, J Rendel Jones and the Senior Assistant Education Officer, Mrs S G Murton, were present. In closing the meeting and in his final remark, the Chairman, Sir Sydney Caffyn, encouraged the College to 'look forward with faith to the future'.

Chelsea governors had debated 'the future of the College' on many occasions, and were concerned (in 1974) that, if they supported a merger of the two Eastbourne Colleges and Seaford, as proposed by the East Sussex Education Authority, they would be reversing a decision made in 1973 (to retain independent existence) and that the tradition and international reputation of Chelsea built-up over the past 75 years would not be maintained. Anxiety was also expressed that the governors were being asked to 'agree a merger whose nature is not defined and which could lead to loss of prestige both nationally and internationally'. They, together with the Academic Board, wanted to preserve all aspects of Chelsea's work and tradition appropriate to new circumstances in higher education, to develop new courses to meet fresh needs in related fields of study and professions and to profit from new opportunities. In this they were supported by the Chelsea Old Students' Association, as a whole, and by individual Old Students. For example, Jennifer Wall

(Assistant Professor, McGill University, Chelsea 1952–55) and Mavis Berridge (Associate Professor, McGill University, Chelsea 1943–46) sent a cable/telegram on 5 May 1974, 'Are concerned re future of Chelsea, retain independent status and affiliation with the University. Support emerging discipline and specific research based on experience. Request input from Old Students throughout world'. The Chairman of the Association, Miss Maureen O'Sullivan, wrote to the Permanent Secretary expressing the concerns of Old Students about the uncertain future of the College.

The newly constituted Governing Body had first met on Monday 29 April 1974 when Councillor R G Edwardes-Jones (East Sussex County Council) acted as Chairman for the meeting. Subsequently on Wednesday 22 May 1974, Councillor T H B Mynors was appointed Chairman and Alderman Sir Sydney Caffyn, Deputy Chairman; staff members were Miss B Barford and Mr D Chapman and student members Miss J Grainger (President, Students' Union) and Miss G Washington.

The East Sussex County Council Plan was formulated by October 1974 and called *The Reorganisation of Higher Education in East Sussex.* In it the county proposed the expansion of Brighton Polytechnic by the inclusion of Brighton College of Education and the establishment of a new College of Higher Education, to be based mainly at Eastbourne, with the merger of the three colleges: Eastbourne and Seaford Colleges of Education and Chelsea College of Physical Education. The County Council had also proposed that, 'a new Principal and a new Governing Body be appointed as soon as possible after the proposal has been approved and that the national and international reputation of Chelsea College be safeguarded in any future organisation'.

The collective Chelsea position can best be summarized by the Principal's paper to the new Governing Body on 22 May 1974 which, in reality, demanded a series of requested guarantees:

1   The number of teacher places for Physical Education will be proportional to the present student intake.

2   Advanced level courses in the study of human movement will be retained and developed.

3   Plans for diversified courses for closely related vocations may be presented to the Regional Advisory Council without delay. These plans concern (i) youth, recreation and play leadership, (ii) health, therapy and work with the handicapped, (iii) sports coaching and management, and (iv) the performing arts.

4   The total intake of students to 1, 2 and 3 (above) should represent the present numbers at Chelsea College, unless it proves impossible to recruit candidates.

5   Present and proposed research projects be continued and extended as part of a continuing Chelsea contribution to the study of human movement, since this development is not adequately provided in Universities.

6   These initiatives be not interrupted while other sections of the institution come into balance.

7   There is, at least for an interim period, a component in the new institution, which is clearly identifiable by nature and title as the successor to Chelsea College.

Miss Bambra's personal position was best summarized in the statement, 'For an autonomous college to accept merger results in a much lower degree of self-determination and this in time inevitably slows progress in decision making'.

The College had prepared two proposals alternative to the six areas of study proposed by East Sussex Education Authority, namely: humanities, social and environmental studies, study of human movement, visual and performing arts, home, family and community studies and professional studies, for consideration at a specially convened meeting between the East Sussex County Council panel members and representatives of the Governing Body of Chelsea College of Physical Education on 20 June 1974. The College's proposals were based on either a bilateral college for human movement and visual and performing arts and community and social studies, or a National Centre offering not only teacher training, but preparation for many related careers, such as play leadership, youth leadership, therapy, work for the handicapped, sport and recreation and the performing arts — the solution preferred by Chelsea. The panel did not believe, however, that either of the alternative proposals put forward by Chelsea would meet the following three points raised by Miss Bambra:

1   the need for the new institution in Eastbourne to be viable and to have a distinctive character;
2   the need for the Authority to consider the provision of higher education in East Sussex overall; and
3   the need to ensure the effective contribution of the institutions concerned in any merger better than the Authority's proposal.

In the letter of 17 September 1974, from Hugh Harding (Department of Education and Science) to the Local Education Authority of East Sussex, the amalgamation of the three colleges was approved in principle. It would be necessary to reduce numbers further because of the slackening student demand for places and the economic situation. The letter continued:

3   In these circumstances, the Secretary of State attaches great importance to establishing an institutional structure in the Eastbourne area which will enable the three colleges to attract students to more general courses as their teacher training role contracts. He does not consider that any of the colleges is of a size which would enable it to do this independently and in competition with larger and more broadly based institutions elsewhere offering students a wide range of options and the opportunity to defer their career commitment. He is satisfied that a new institution formed by amalgamating the three present colleges would be very much better placed in this respect.

4   Accordingly, the Secretary of State sees great merit in the Authority's proposals as the one most likely to provide a sound structural basis on which to
found future developments. Subject to what is said below, he is pleased to
approve it in principle so far as his own requirements are concerned.

5   He has noted the reservations of the Governing Body of Chelsea College of
Physical Education about the academic issues raised by the proposed merger.

The Department of Education and Science formally agreed in a letter of
16 December 1974 to the proposal put forward by East Sussex County Council that
a new college should be established in Eastbourne.

To extend their perceptions of the current situation, Chelsea staff attended
various conferences, including the Brighton Conference, *Changing Patterns of
Teacher Education* held on 1 to 4 April 1975.

Figure 4.4:   Programme and speakers: Brighton Conference, 1975

The conference was addressed by:

Professor Norman McKenzie, University of Sussex
Introduction
David Hencke, *Times Higher Education Supplement*
An overview of re-organisation
James F Porter, Principal, Berkshire College of Education
Changing institutional patterns
Professor Alec Ross, University of Lancaster
Universities and colleges
Dr Edwin Kerr, Chief Officer, Council for National Academic Awards
Validation
Professor Anthony Becher, University of Sussex
Problems of curriculum design in Higher Education
Professor Roger Webster, University College of North Wales
Where is teacher education going now?
and a debate
FOR: Dr David Billings, Senior Assistant Registrar, Council for National
            Academic Awards
AGAINST: Kenneth Gardner, Senior Tutor, Brighton College of Education
That a modular curriculum is superior to its alternatives in Higher Education.

Miss Bambra continued to fight for Chelsea and visited Geoffrey Hall, Director of Brighton Polytechnic during 1974–75 to explain the steps being taken to
merge Eastbourne College of Education, Seaford College of Education and Chelsea
College of Physical Education to form the new East Sussex College of Higher
Education. She did not favour the proposed merger and would have preferred
Chelsea to merge with Brighton Polytechnic. During discussion, Miss Bambra
asked if there was anything Mr Hall could do to help her in her quest. His response
was that he had great sympathy for her concern about the future of Chelsea, but
there was little he could do as the East Sussex Local Education Authority had

already made its policy decision contained in its response *The Reorganization of Higher Education in East Sussex* to the Department of Education and Science. The College's concerns were strongly supported by the Chelsea Old Students' Association, teachers and physical education organizations, as well as by individuals.

Miss Bambra, together with Mrs P Bowen-West (Principal, Bedford College of Physical Education) and Miss M Jamieson (Principal, I M Marsh College of Physical Education) had also had meetings with Hugh Harding and Miss Pollard (Staff Inspector, Physical Education) during 1973 to 1975 to discuss, to reinforce her main concerns and to air her views on establishing 'a national college and place for physical education, physical recreation and sport'. Miss Bambra's overview of national needs was summarized in five points or objectives:

1   Preparation of teachers of physical education, provision of in-service courses; preparation of coaches, recreation and play leaders; education of sports coaches.
2   Development of the subject with supportive research into teaching methods and curriculum development.
3   Contribution of physical education to health and physical efficiency, orthopaedics, physiotherapy, nursing, health education and psychiatry.
4   Investigation into related fields of study; human and behavioural sciences, sociology, environmental and community studies.
5   Establish a centre of information, consultancy advice and provision for an international centre for comparative studies.

These objectives to be achieved through partnership of an associated group of colleges with a common Board of Governors.

Reorganization of colleges proceeded, however, when the Secretary of State, Mr Reginald Prentice, approved the inception of the East Sussex College of Higher Education with the amalgamation of Chelsea College of Physical Education, Eastbourne College of Education and Seaford College of Education, as from 1 September 1976. This College of Higher Education had been formed as a direct outcome of the James Report of 1972.

The Secretary of State's letter said '. . . while specific assurance, as requested by the Governing Body and Academic Board of Chelsea College of Physical Education, cannot be given in the form requested:

(a)   The Secretary of State recognises the important contribution made to physical education by Chelsea College in the past and will wish to ensure that, so far as possible, its specialist facilities and expertise are fully utilised and further developed in the future.
(b)   He believes that the prospect of this will be enhanced by the College's incorporation in a larger institution with greater resources; this will be in accordance with the Department's longstanding policy that, wherever possible, specialist teachers should receive their education and professional training in the same institutions as other intending teachers.
(c)   He expects that, in exercising control over teacher supply, successive governments will continue to look to Chelsea for an important contribution to the supply of specialist teachers of physical education.

(d) He hopes that the new institution will be successful in developing other courses of physical education outside the field of teacher training and believes that the national reputation of Chelsea College and the additional resources which the new institution will have at its disposal, offer substantial grounds for the belief that such developments will be successful. This will, however, depend on the institution's ability to attract students and obtain recognition from the Sports Council and other bodies of the qualifications it offers; these matters are not under the Department's control.

He concluded his letter, 'the Secretary of State believes that, on further consideration, the Governing Body and Academic Board of the College will recognise that their best interests lie in wholehearted support of the outline plans for the development of the new institution which your Authority has prepared and that it will be possible for detailed proposals for their implementation to be worked out between the Authority and the new institution to the mutual satisfaction of both parties'.

The County Council had also included a helpful statement in its submission to the Department of Education and Science, 'that the national and international reputation of Chelsea College be safeguarded in any future organisation'. There was, however, to be no post for Miss Bambra in the new institution; a source of regret expressed by Miss Barford, on behalf of her colleagues at the meeting of the Governing Body on 20 February 1976. At that same meeting, the Principal 'drew the attention of governors to what was considered to be the very limited influence which physical education would be able to exert in the new college, in view of the fact that the management structure of 10 persons established by the Formation Committee gave one post only to physical education, the Head of the School of Human Movement'.

Three days earlier, she had written to the governors,

There is no inbuilt requirement that any other member of the management team will have knowledge or interest in Physical Education; it is true that the newly-appointed Deputy Director is highly qualified in Physical Education, but there is nothing to ensure that any successor will be. In these circumstances, it is hard to believe that East Sussex County Council has fulfilled its undertaking to ensure that the national and international reputation of Chelsea College be safeguarded in any future organisation.

In her last report, as Principal, to the Old Students' Association in 1976, Miss Bambra said,

A community is fortunate if it can hold a balance of experienced staff and lively newcomers and this has been possible here. It is perhaps natural that I should think highly of the staff team, which is one of friends, as well as colleagues, but I can also make the professional judgment which, on this special occasion, enables me to say that they have been outstanding for their professional standards, in their selfless concern for the students' interests, and for their readiness, shown particularly in the Academic Board, to take time thoroughly to investigate issues, acting with academic detachment to get to the heart of a matter and to establish firm principles for action.

Whatever problems face the College will, I believe, be overcome by the goodwill and commonsense of a gifted staff and by students who hold the convictions which we all share that Physical Education is of crucial importance in the lives of children, and that teachers need a liberal education, both for their own development and to provide the resources on which they will draw in providing for the needs of their pupils.

My only regret is that, in the involved discussions which have preceded the formation of a new College here in Eastbourne, I have seemed unable to convince others that we have no wish to look backward (indeed we have sometimes thought ourselves to be daringly innovatory) nor to be exclusive. We are concerned solely to ensure that it is possible to sustain those features which have been good in our life and work and to maintain a supportive community appropriate to the needs of young people preparing for a profession of national importance.

The Chelsea College will be known as the Chelsea School of Human Movement within the East Sussex College of Higher Education under the leadership of Pat Kingston, a former student of the College, a highly respected and talented member of staff, who has skill, tact and good humour.

Miss Bambra found it very hard to give up the stewardship of the College.

During her time as Principal, Miss Bambra had also held many responsible positions, including Chairman (1968–71) and Secretary (1971–1976) of the Association of Principals of Women's Colleges of Physical Education; chairmanship of major conferences for the Keep Fit Association; Consultant and Trainer of Leaders for the Keep Fit Association; membership of the Academic Board of the Institute of Education, University of London; Governor of the London College of Dance and Drama; member of the Health Education Council by invitation of Sir Keith Joseph; and member of the Executive Board of the International Association of Physical Education and Sport for Girls and Women. In 1997, she was made an Honorary Member, for outstanding service to this Association as a committed member over many years and as the first editor of the Bulletin from 1981 to 1993. At the time of the first issue, January 1982, she wrote, 'it is hoped through this simple publication, to extend the influence of our Association in the years between Congresses, to keep alive professional friendships and ensure that members are kept informed of developments'.

Teaching and the range of professional experiences to which she was exposed, the varied views of colleagues worldwide, the numerous courses and conferences which she attended, ensured that her beliefs had not stagnated. Particularly influential were all the developments related to modern educational dance. Her experience pre-college had been in classical ballet. The talents of Miss Helen Wingrave had helped her to develop a wider range of dance styles. Laban's analysis of movement, however, opened up endless possibilities for her, not only in dance, but in gymnastics, where individual abilities could be developed far beyond the scope of formal gymnastic systems.

Days of National Dance, led by Miss Bambra, and normally held on Sundays, had been a feature of the College since she was appointed as Principal. Dances from the following countries had been included in the programme: Greece, Israel, Yugoslavia, Poland, Rumania, Turkey, USA, Estonia, Hungary, Czechoslovakia, France, New Zealand (Maori), Portugal, Bulgaria, Russia, Japan, Cyprus and England. Expert lecturers had included, Phrosso Phister, Anat Keren, Ken Ward, Judith and Jacob Borkan, Bert Price, Juditz Popiescie, Hamidi Ataoglu, Maida Riggs, Aily Eistrat, Alan Maclean, Hedda Klingrora, Simon Guest, Thora Watkins, Lucille Armstrong, Dan Lumley, Kristina Michael, Jill Gribbon, Geoargie Mikellidoue, and Joy McConachie-Smith.

Miss Bambra had given many outstanding lectures, particularly for the Physical Education Association and had contributed numerous articles in professional journals or sections in books, as well as being co-author of *The Teaching of European Folk Dance* with C Muriel Webster. Her study tours had included visits to the United States of America, Hungary and Russia. From each, she had absorbed 'the essence' of physical education or dance and utilized the newly-formed information in her adventurous thinking.

Under her guidance, courses at Chelsea had retained a balance between professional training, the acquisition of skill and academic study, but physical education and the study of human movement had been taken forward progressively. She had come to a realization that human movement is as fundamental an aspect of man's capacities, as are his intellect and his emotions, and as worthy of development through education. She felt, 'physical education should provide not only health-giving exercise and enjoyment, but an understanding of the importance of skilled and expressive action in every field of life'. The progression in her own thinking about physical education and the study of human movement was clearly demonstrated in her leadership of the College. Her vision for future development, that is both appropriate and possible, was enshrined in her contributions to discussions about the future of Chelsea and its incorporation within a larger institution years prior to her early retirement in 1976.

Miss Bambra was awarded the OBE in the Queen's Birthday Honours in June 1991, 'for services to sport and physical recreation' as a member of the Sports Council and the Central Council of Physical Recreation since her retirement as the Principal of Chelsea.

Her dominant personality, tireless energy, drive for perfection — second best was not acceptable — and enthusiasm, had permeated the whole College. During the period of Miss Bambra's leadership, the College had expanded, grown in stature and made a major contribution to physical education, both at home and overseas. Her years of distinguished service to the College were acknowledged by the Chairman of the Governors, in a letter, sent to her on behalf of the Governing Body.

Finally, and in her own words, she maintained, 'My career has been "made" by the impact of talented and unusual people. A philosophy of education is obtained by accretion. I was very fortunate in those that I met'. **She was 'A Principal with high principles . . .'.**

College badge depicting the coat of arms of the Earl of Cadogan – circa 1902–1908

The first Old Students' brooch – 1905

Face

Reverse

College blazer badge – I, II, III or OSA as appropriate – 1920–1956

College badge worn on track suit and scarf – 1957–1976

One logo used on sports clothing in 1997–98

Mabel Salisbury
in regulation
dress – student
1904–1906

Gymnastics –
skirt removed
for apparatus
work – 1902

Athletics – the start
of the 100 yards flat
race – 1910s

Cricket –
1st XI complete
with hats –
1920s

First college camp
– Minnis Bay,
Birchington, Kent –
27 June–9 July 1931

Netball on the
sands of Borth in
front of the Grand
Hotel – 1940s

Lacrosse at
Hindsland –
1950s

Advanced Dance
Group in the
Assembly Hall –
1960s

Hockey – Chelsea students
V Old Students,
Open day at Hillbrow
– 1970s

Rugby – mauling
practice at Hindsland
– 1980s

Swimming –
butterfly training
– 1990s

Students outside
Hillbrow main
entrance – 1998

5   Incorporation: 1976–1998

Patricia Kingston
Head of School (1976–79)
East Sussex College of Higher Education and Brighton Polytechnic

'. . . wise leadership maintained'.

Miss Patricia Kingston, born 29 July 1918, was a student at Chelsea College of Physical Education, from 1936 to 1939. After teaching for nine years in England, she joined the staff of Chelsea Polytechnic as Warden for Women Students, Physical Education Tutor, Secretary of the Social and Academic Council and Organiser of part-time release courses in physical education. Miss Kingston then taught in New Zealand and Canada, was on the staff of Lady Mabel College of Physical Education from 1954 to 1960 and, in 1960, was appointed Head of the Department of Physical Education at Chelsea College of Physical Education.

May Fountain wrote to her on 28 March 1960, to say 'I was delighted to know of it (your appointment to Chelsea) and rejoice to think of you at College — I do hope you will be happy there — I know you have so much to contribute and am glad to know Miss Bambra will have the support of someone like you, with stability and of complete integrity, as well as your professional assets'. On Miss Kingston's appointment, as Head of School on 1 September 1976 within East Sussex College of Higher Education, Miss Fountain wrote again, this time following her attendance at Old Students' Day in the summer of 1976, 'Especially I was glad to meet you and hear something of your new position, which I have every confidence that you will *fill* most ably. It is a great comfort to me that you have it'.

Miss Kingston's three-year period of office was unexpectedly, at least in 1976, to become a time of ever increasing pressures, unanticipated developments, great uncertainties for staff and unexpected changes in institutional allegiance arising from changes in government policy.

Following the work of the East Sussex Local Education Authority's Formation Committee, the East Sussex College of Higher Education was inaugurated on 1 September 1976. The new Director, Geoffrey R Tyler (designate from 1 January 1976), ensured that other members of the Directorate, Heads of Schools, teaching and the majority of non-teaching staff had been appointed to posts in the new structure by 1 April 1976. In the new structure, there were no former members of the Chelsea staff as members of the Directorate, neither were there any in the Schools of Home and Community Studies and Humanities. Twelve Chelsea staff were appointed to the Centre for Educational and Professional Studies, 38 to the School of Human Movement, two to the School of Visual and Performing Arts and one as Dean of Students of the College. The College Council, temporary Academic Board, its committees and three working parties, had been set up and the pre-launch programme of work completed. The problems of organization arising from bringing together three disparate colleges with very different academic philosophies, traditions and methods of operation had been successfully tackled by the working parties and acceptable compromises reached, in spite of the many difficulties and doubts encountered during discussions. The new College set out to grasp the new opportunities which were available and to create a distinctive role for itself in a spirit of cooperation and constructive collaboration.

A great deal had been achieved in a relatively short time, including the real-location of buildings, putting into place the academic and administrative structures of the College, agreement on an outline academic plan, the skeletal development of a common unitary course structure of 90 hours per unit, with 30 hours contact time and 60 hours non-contact or generated time, expansion of links with the University of Sussex and the Open University and a programme of extra-curricular activities involving the local community. The effective and economic utilization of staff expertise and College resources, both internally for the education of students and externally for the benefit of the local community, were clear priorities for the 'new college'.

The College's brief was to utilize existing resources, as the need for teacher training places contracted, and to devise new courses of higher education relating to staff expertise which was predominantly in the liberal arts. Many staff had to reorientate professional interests to meet the changing pattern of courses and to plan for developments, such as a field study centre and a centre for research. In the area of teacher training the opportunity arose to rationalize course content, to avoid expensive duplication and to bring together teams of lecturers in similar disciplines to service all courses, as appropriate. To the credit of all concerned, the new teams quickly cooperated to address the manifold problems arising from reorganization, not least the need to accept change, revise attitudes, abandon prejudices, cooperate with new colleagues and function as an academic community.

Two powerful influences affecting cooperation and collaboration were the regular (weekly) meetings of the Committee of Management, which was renamed the Director's Consultative Committee in January 1978, and the at least twice termly deliberations of the Academic Board to consider the best interests of students on a cross-college, cross-disciplinary basis. The Committee of Management consisted of Heads of the Centre for Educational and Professional Studies and the Schools of Home and Community Studies, Human Movement, Humanities and Visual and Performing Arts, the Academic Registrar and the College Directorate; it was serviced by the Chief Administrative Officer.

Within the new structure the Chelsea School had to adjust very quickly to the changed academic and administrative procedures. Decision making processes were inevitably elongated, within the larger community, leading to understandable frustrations when there were delays. Many members of the Chelsea School were nominated as representatives on College committees. They valued opportunity for discussion, but administration, organization and attendance at meetings created areas of potential conflict. When hurried decisions were made, without full consultation, these too were criticized; a balance had to be struck and items prioritized.

Distraction from the main purpose *the education of students* was a major cause of concern. Miss Kingston felt, 'true cooperation very often comes at a slower pace'. The collective enthusiasm for progress had to be tempered but 'time' was often of the essence in a fast changing educational climate where external political influences continually imposed new restrictions. This concern had also been expressed by the editor of the Chelsea Old Students' Association magazine, who had written in 1975, 'change should be exciting; it is fast becoming frightening because the rate of change is now so rapid that there is no time to evaluate the changes already made before more begin'.

The Chelsea School meetings, held under the chairmanship of Miss Kingston, with 40 members of staff and five students, were lively and long. The Standing Committee, with Miss Kingston as Chairman and 12 members of staff: two per area (aesthetic, practical, psychological, scientific and sociological) and two elected members from the teaching staff, was effectively the management team.

At the end of the first term Miss Kingston reported to the Academic Board in December 1976, 'In spite of the many problems involved in establishing a new College, designing diversified courses, planning the details of a unit structure, and attending meetings, the School of Human Movement has continued its work with enthusiasm'. With reference to courses and teaching practice, she said, 'the staff were pleased, once again, to be working with education tutors; the initial isolation from education had been a difficult situation to accept'. The School continued to offer four specialist physical education/dance teacher courses and three in-service courses, including the Teacher Award Scheme which carried awards of the University of Sussex, School of Education. On examining the Sussex validated three-year BEd (unclassified) course in 1978, the external examiners commented, 'It was noticeable that they (students) were encouraged to develop their own personalities and systems of recording, rather than all being forced into a particular mould'. Their report continued, 'There is no doubt that the opportunity for students to teach in well established schools within a tradition of regular physical education is invaluable to them at this stage of their teaching careers'.

The School offered two diversified degree courses in human movement which carried a BA University of Sussex Award. Seven women and three men completed the course. Four students qualified in human movement and human biology and six in human movement and sociology. They graduated in July 1978 and found employment in sports centres as recreational officers, research technicians in specialized ergonomic or pathological laboratories, work with the handicapped or they registered for postgraduate study in management and training or for MSc degree courses.

The School continued its overseas exchange programme for second year students and its one-year courses, particularly the Junior Year Abroad programme, for students mainly from the USA and Canada. For example, in 1976–77 two students went to the USA and two students to Canada for 15 weeks each; four students to Israel, two students to Spain, two students to Holland and two students to Germany for five weeks each.

Many activity days for school pupils and short courses for men and women teachers continued to be organized by the School. Within the national *Sport for All* campaign courses for potential and experienced coaches and officials in, for example, activities as diverse as association football and volleyball, badminton and trampolining, athletics and swimming were mounted.

In August 1975, the Department of the Environment had produced the White Paper *Sport and Recreation* in which it set out its plans for the development of centres of sporting excellence. In particular, the aim was the fulfilment of sporting talent at the highest level. 'Sport provides for many people a means of enriching their lives and developing their personality. In the sporting world, the pinnacle of achievement is to represent one's country. The government feel it is right to give special encouragement to sports women capable of performance at international level'. The Minister for Sport and Recreation, Denis Howell, set up a working party to consider 'centres of sporting excellence'. In the East Sussex County Structure Plan 1977 Review, reference was made to 'special emphasis on recreational and leisure facilities, including support for proposed fully equipped sport complexes'. Chelsea welcomed this statement and envisaged contributing to the design of facilities, provision of courses and an active role in study and research.

Chelsea was approved as the fourth 'Centre of Excellence' in England in September 1978 (the other three were Bedford, I M Marsh and Durham) to mount advanced courses for players and coaches, in collaboration with the All England Women's Hockey Association and the Sports Council, under the leadership of Miss Biddy Burgum. It was very successful and its work continued throughout the era. The Centre aimed to provide ongoing training and coaching opportunities of the highest possible level for gifted hockey players. The three objectives were:

(a) development of:
  (i) precision in personal skill;
  (ii) skill in the game, including vision and awareness;
  (iii) personal attainment and development in aspects related to hockey in fitness, strength, suppleness, speed and accuracy;
(b) testing and monitoring of personal fitness and skill; and
(c) to give advice concerning training schedules and playing commitments.

Initially, and for eight years, players were drawn from the 17 to 25 year age group and were of potential international standard. From 1987, Sussex juniors were the main participants and in 1990, the Centre became independent and catered for 50 local girls. From 1993 boys were able to participate and benefit from the programme. To date well over 400 young players have attended the Centre and benefitted from the programme of training offered by the advanced coaches with assistance from Chelsea students.

The School also contributed to the 'integrated coaching scheme' organized by the Greater London and South East Council for Sport and Recreation. This provision extended opportunities for children with potential physical ability within a 12 mile radius of the School for coaching from qualified coaches in tennis, table tennis and trampolining. Talented sportsmen and women made full use of the School's facilities and staff expertise.

National recognition was given to the School for its work, not only in hockey, but with individual Olympic athletes. For example, Steve Ovett benefitted from scientific testing for fitness and advice on subsequent training programmes. The development of excellence was in-built in the staff and students' expectations. A research programme set up by Dr Ray Watson, in collaboration with the Eastbourne District General Hospital, in the areas of cardiology and arthritis was operative.

On 9 November 1976, the Secretary of State for Education and Science, the Rt Hon Mrs Shirley Williams, announced in the House of Commons that the Advisory Committee on the Supply and Training of Teachers was considering proposals which her Department had submitted to them to reduce still further the number of teacher training places outside the universities from a target of 57,000 to about 45,000 by 1981. It was becoming clear from press reports at that time, that the government was actively reviewing and reassessing the need for teacher training places nationally to meet the requirements of primary and secondary schools in the foreseeable future. Account had been taken of the reduced birth rate, decreasing 'wastage' of personnel from the teaching profession, the return of married women to teaching and other relevant factors.

On 24 January 1977 the Rt Hon Mrs Shirley Williams announced proposals for the future reorganization of the education and training of teachers in England and Wales. She confirmed that the system should be reduced to 45,000 places including 10,000 for in-service education and training of serving teachers. In addition, and very important for Chelsea, her letter to East Sussex stated, 'Initial teacher training should also cease at the East Sussex College of Higher Education, except for the provision at the former Chelsea College of Physical Education, which should be continued as part of Brighton Polytechnic where total provision should be increased from 600 to 1000 places'. In practice, that was 400 places for physical education students equal to the number of students at Chelsea in January 1977.

On receipt of the letter, the Director immediately expressed his view to colleagues. He said, 'It was regrettable that the East Sussex College of Higher Education had not been given sufficient time in which to prove itself and gain the national and international reputation of which it was capable'. Despite deputations to the Department of Education and Science championing the College's continuation as a free-standing unit it was prudent, ultimately, to seek a solution within the terms of the Minister's proposals. Therefore, the Inauguration Ceremony for the new East Sussex College of Higher Education planned for Friday 18 February 1977, was cancelled and negotiations with Brighton Polytechnic began. East Sussex County Council established a Higher Education Advisory Committee to consider the future provision of teacher education in East Sussex, in the light of the Secretary of State's proposals, to advise the Education Committee on its response to these proposals and to consider the future of the East Sussex College of Higher Education.

The Further Education Sub-committee received the report on 24 March 1977, which concluded,

> ... the study of human movement and related studies in a wider context can best be secured in a single institution of higher education in the county which would develop a significant regional role in this and other areas, and recommended the County Council: to agree in principle that higher education in East Sussex should be developed in a single institution, the Polytechnic, based at Brighton, but with a substantial number of students at Eastbourne taking courses in human movement and related studies and such other courses as may be developed.

Nobody likes change, especially where there is an academic environment heavily steeped in tradition with a national reputation as a centre of excellence. Fears of losing identity in a merger were not unnatural and *integration* was the key word for all aspects of incorporation with the Polytechnic. It was not easy for staff and students to transfer their allegiance once again to a different institution while still retaining their loyalty to the Chelsea ideals and traditions with which they were familiar.

The students had been concerned to retain the name 'Chelsea' in the title of the School, in the original incorporation, and had based a paper to the temporary Academic Board of the new College 23 June 1976 related to the following three areas: foundation, tradition and reputation. The proposal was supported by the Board and the College Council and submitted to the Higher Education Advisory Committee on 18 July 1977. The Committee 'approved the retention of the name "Chelsea" for the duration of the life of the College'. This decision was formally reported on 14 November 1977. The students had achieved their objective; they were resolute and their resilience during change was evident in their determination to maintain standards and the name of the School.

'Standards' applied equally to levels of achievement, conduct and appearance. Guidance was issued and the following is but one example of the expectations of the School. In the School as formerly, 'A high standard of appearance was expected from students, in a professional capacity whilst on teaching practice, and every effort had to be made to wear the appropriate clothes, set out on the uniform list, for different activities'. (See Figure 5.1)

Any variations should be discussed with your physical education supervisor in advance. Jewellery should not be worn when teaching.

Teaching practice was organized so that year I students experienced serial and a two week block practice, year II students a five week block practice in Surrey,

Figure 5.1: Example of uniform to be worn on teaching practice in 1976

Gymnastics	— teaching blouse, teaching trousers or games skirt, teaching shoes or bare feet. NEVER GAMES OR TRACK SHOES.
Dance	— leotard and tights or skirt (DO NOT WALK ALONG SCHOOL CORRIDORS IN LEOTARD AND TIGHTS, PLEASE)
Games	— Teaching blouse, teaching trousers or games skirt, pullover, anorak. Track suit if very cold weather.
Swimming	— Teaching skirt or track suit trousers (PLEASE WEAR A SWIMMING SUIT UNDERNEATH IN CASE YOU NEED TO GO INTO THE WATER).

East Sussex, West Sussex, London (south east) or Kent, when a signed record was required for College certification, and year III students had a five week block practice both in and out county.

The Students' Union constitution of East Sussex College of Higher Education had as one of its four main aims, 'to encourage and develop the corporate life of the Union and its individual members in cultural, social, academic, education and athletic fields'. Accordingly, its nine officers had specific responsibilities, including external affairs, internal affairs, publicity, welfare, sport and social functions. The first President, a sabbatical officer, was Steve Hodgson (formerly Eastbourne College of Education); Jean Walker (Chelsea College of Physical Education) was the first Sports Officer. The Union was also concerned with all aspects of student welfare and cooperated with the Dean of Students, Mrs Lorna Jenner. It was fully represented at every level of the committee structure of the College, on both academic and non-academic committees. The Student Consultative Committee, with a majority of student members, was chaired by the Deputy Director and serviced by the Dean of Students. The Students' Union was well served by its staff members, Mrs Diane Lace and Mrs Maureen Taylor. Societies included, film, drama, choir, arts club, Christian Union and outdoor pursuits. The Community Action Group existed to coordinate student activities in social or charitable work outside the College, including the 'adopt a granny' scheme and weekly visits to homes for handicapped people. Games and sports clubs with matches for members were provided by the Students' Union through the Sports Federation in at least 13 sports and the evening activities programme covered a wide range of sports from archery to water polo, Olympic gymnastics to bar billiards.

It was inevitable that Chelsea students held the majority of places in the Students' Union Sports Federation representative College teams. 1978–79 was an exceptional year for the hockey squad. The first XI, under the captaincy of Ruth Hawes, won the first Women's English Hockey National Clubs Championship and, after raising the necessary funding of £5000, represented England in the preliminary and final stages of the European Club Winners Tournament in Prague and The Hague, respectively. Overall, they came seventh out of eight but under the circumstances of end of course final examinations, out of season competition and the youngest team playing continental sponsored, professional teams, this was a creditable result. In the same season the first XI had also won the Annual Women's Physical Education Colleges Tournament, the British Colleges South East Tournament and the British Colleges National Finals. Chelsea students continued to be very successful at county, territorial, national and international levels in a variety of games and sports, including hockey, netball, lacrosse, basketball, badminton, volleyball, table tennis, athletics and swimming.

The students' high success rate in appointment to first teaching posts was maintained, as was the level or standards of course work during the period of reorganization. As Miss Kingston said,

> The School naturally rejoices in the success of its students who achieve national and international sporting honours. Nevertheless, it is important to note that, while good performance in at least some aspects of practical work is important to all students for the maintenance of their self-esteem, the true emphasis of all courses lies in the study and understanding of the principles of human movement rather than on individual prowess.

She continued, the School '. . . now provides courses for men and women, whose career plans may take them outside the schools into new forms of service in sport, recreation and community health'.

Instead of being able to concentrate solely on establishing the Chelsea School of Human Movement within the East Sussex College of Higher Education, Miss Kingston had found herself, together with many members of staff and student representatives, very heavily involved in the next rounds of incorporation meetings with Brighton Polytechnic. It was predictable that following the latest government announcement (in the 1977 letter) on the future of the College, economies had to be faced. Administrative resources were reduced and Miss Kingston felt, taking the continuation of Chelsea within Brighton Polytechnic into account, 'It is important that the high level of work and teaching, which has given the College (Chelsea) its reputation, should be retained and developed, particularly in this time of reorganization; and that the necessary economies be looked for in other areas of College administration'. Miss Kingston found it hard after so many years to refer to Chelsea as the School.

As Geoffrey Tyler, Director of the East Sussex College of Higher Education, has written recently,

> Twenty-two years on from the creation of the East Sussex College of Higher Education, its brief existence might be regarded as having no more than minor significance in the evolution of Chelsea. At the very least, it provided a valuable experience in the transition from a traditional specific role of teacher training for women physical educationists to the cut and thrust of higher education in a wider context and prepared the way for incorporation into Brighton Polytechnic on 1 April 1979.

Under the changed circumstances, Miss Kingston set out to 'hold the School together' and expected detailed preparation and planning from herself and her staff; her essentially one-to-one style paid off and the School, under her leadership, remained united in its aims and work. In a letter to the Old Students' Association dated 22 January 1979, in both an optimistic and a reflective mood she wrote, 'May the link with Brighton be as helpful and creative as the link with Chelsea Polytechnic' and to the College Academic Board 8 February 1979 and 16 March 1979 respectively, she said, '. . . we look forward to a future, still full of change but with established goals and renewed enthusiasm;' and continued, '. . . perhaps our experience in one merger, and our increased understanding of the problems of large institutions will give us extra confidence in guiding the students to high standards in their work within the Brighton Polytechnic'.

The negotiations for the second incorporation involving members and officers of East Sussex County Council and members of the councils and staff and students of the Polytechnic and College were conducted between 1977 and 1979. On 1 April 1979, the Chelsea School of Human Movement was incorporated within the Faculty of Social and Cultural Studies of Brighton Polytechnic. The Director of the Polytechnic, Geoffrey Hall, had recognized the value of the name 'Chelsea'. As he commented, when tentatively asked if the name could survive, Chelsea is 'a College of national and international reputation with well-established traditions and high professional standards'. He readily accepted, much to the relief and appreciation of staff and students, that 'Chelsea' should be retained in the title of the School. It was his aim to achieve assimilation or full integration of all units into the Polytechnic structure. He was against any form of grafting on staff, departments or courses that were purely to save jobs. All new courses had to meet the Polytechnic's own standards before external validation for degree and higher degree courses and they had to contribute to the established ethos and future plans of the enlarged Polytechnic.

In this aim he was supported by the Chief Officer of the Council for National Academic Awards, Edwin Kerr, following the quinquennial review in March 1980 who, in his summing up said,

Integration — Firstly, may I say that we endorse the decision that the merging institutions should be fully integrated into the Polytechnic; we know that this is a difficult thing to achieve; we know that it will mean that more time is needed and more hard work is needed before it becomes fully achieved in all aspects; but we are convinced that in setting out to achieve an integrated institution, rather than a federation of a number of institutions on disparate sites, you were clearly doing the right thing.

In his Annual Report covering the year 1977–1978, the Director had written,

In this my ninth Annual Report, I must preface my remarks by emphasising that this Polytechnic has once again made considerable progress, indeed remarkable progress, in the face of continual change. At national level, there have been the DES papers on education in schools and on higher education into the 1990s and also the report of the Working Group on the Management of Higher Education in the maintained sector under the chairmanship of Mr Gordon Oakes. There have been the further pronouncements on teacher training which have given us the task of replanning in East Sussex to allow for the incorporation of the East Sussex College of Higher Education into the Polytechnic on 1 April 1979. This, in turn, has led to many of us being involved in almost daily meetings with our future colleagues in Eastbourne and with staff at County Hall in implementing this next merger. It is doubtful whether those outside our two institutions, especially those in Elizabeth House, can appreciate fully the enormous strains these reorganisations have on the Polytechnic or the almost unbearable pressures that fall on staff who suddenly find themselves uncertain of their future.

The organization of a relatively new field of knowledge — human movement studies — within Brighton Polytechnic, was to prove a complex exercise. It drew on the areas of the physical sciences, the arts, behavioural sciences, social sciences and philosophy in a multidisciplinary study of physical activity. It was applied in the contexts of physical education, social interaction, sport and recreation, the paramedical services, therapy, leisure pursuits, communication and ergonomics.

Miss Kingston had commented,

Initial discussions have indicated an appreciation by representatives of the Poly-technic of the significance of the specialist work in physical education and human movement studies and an interest in its place within the enlarged Polytechnic. Moreover, the teaching staff of the Chelsea School of Human Movement have regarded with considerable optimism the opportunities for their area of work which could spring from being an integral part of a Polytechnic with broad academic and technological preoccupations.

For the second time within three years with the change in institutional status and the development of changed or new courses, central job descriptions were rewritten and staff once again applied and were rigorously interviewed for posts within the Chelsea School.

In a letter to colleagues dated 7 July 1978 when they were applying for posts in Brighton Polytechnic, Miss Kingston wrote,

I would like to express my appreciation for the high standards that have been retained in the Chelsea School since the last merger, due entirely to the hard work, the determination and good teaching shown by the Chelsea Staff.

I am sure we can look forward to an exciting future with the support of a large and flourishing institution, with opportunities for the development of new ideas and courses in Physical Education that will continue to attract the very able stu-dents. Change is good, it will be a new and different organisation and an exciting challenge for everyone. (See Figure 5.2)

The fortitude and goodwill of staff throughout the reorganization process was commendable. It was, as the Director of the Polytechnic acknowledged later, also true to say, 'The extended work in leisure and sport, the developments in health related studies and the expansion of conferencing would not have taken place, in Brighton Polytechnic, without Chelsea's presence'. The contribution the School

The following staff structure was implemented:

Post number	Title
1	Head of the Chelsea School of Human Movement
2	Deputy Head of School and Coordinator of Initial Teacher Training
3	Course Leader BA(Hons) Human Movement
4	Course Leader BSc(Hons) Sports Science and Recreation
5–15	Physical education
16–22	Biological studies of human movement
23–30	Psycho social studies of human movement
31–37	Dance/aesthetic studies of human movement

also made to the recreational life of students in the Polytechnic, as a whole, was quickly appreciated and welcomed.

Miss Kingston retired on 31 August 1979, secure in the knowledge that, in her imperturbable and determined way, she had successfully led the Chelsea School of Human Movement through the first phase of the fourth era.

Gillian Burke
Head of School (1979–84)
Brighton Polytechnic

Mrs Gillian Burke, born 18 February 1942, was educated at Felixstowe High School from 1953 to 1958, Leiston Grammar School from 1958 to 1961 and I M Marsh College of Physical Education from 1961 to 1964. She had qualified with a Certificate in Education of the University of Liverpool, Institute of Education achieving a Distinction in Movement Studies and Education and, later, in 1971 and 1974 respectively, she was awarded the Diploma in Advanced Study of Education and Master of Education from the University of Manchester. Her teaching experience as Head of the Physical Education Department at Christ's Hospital School was followed by lecturing experience at Endsleigh College, Hull and I M Marsh College of Physical Education.

Prior to her appointment to Chelsea, Mrs Burke, as the BEd Course Leader, had lived through protracted discussions for one merger with a polytechnic: that of the I M Marsh College of Physical Education and Liverpool Polytechnic. Therefore, she had a considerable grasp of the standard practices on monitoring, evaluation, staff appraisal and course validation to which Chelsea was rapidly having to adjust. Understandably, the *systems approach* used by large institutions was viewed by many Chelsea staff as unnecessarily bureaucratic. Mrs Burke's experience in the design of new courses and the preparation of course documents was to prove invaluable for Chelsea. Equally, her participation in tough negotiations stood her in good stead.

The Head of Chelsea was responsible for the academic leadership of the School, its internal organization, ex-officio representation on major committees of the Faculty and appropriate committees of the Polytechnic (22 in total), the maintenance of high academic standards in the work of the School in teacher education and in the developing BA and BSc courses in human movement and sports science, respectively, and the further academic, professional and research development of the School. Specific duties included coordination of School activities, liaison between course leaders, cooperation with other faculties, especially Art and Design and Education Studies with whom the School needed to develop particularly close ties, and contribution to the teaching and research programme of the School.

The incorporation with Brighton Polytechnic produced some further changes to the well-established practices within the School. The School had to adjust to, for example, new roles, costing time, space and materials; staff were understandably puzzled by Mrs Burke's first attempts to 'cost' their time. They did not appreciate or understand that the excellent work they did with children and students on Saturdays, Sundays, and in the evenings could not 'count' because no money was being received by the Polytechnic for these services. This well established practice of voluntary service to the local community, benefitted both pupils and students. The schools, to some extent, were repaid for their goodwill in hosting students on teaching practice, while the students had opportunities to teach in an informal atmosphere and often with small groups of pupils whom they soon came to know well.

The School was also puzzled by the 'seat occupancy factor' and its resulting anomalies, which were employed by the Polytechnic to assess use of accommodation. Gymnasia, dance studios, playing fields and the swimming pool were left out of the equation because there were no seats! Groups of 45 students in the nearly fully timetabled lecture theatre led to a result of only 50 per cent occupancy because half the seats were empty.

The Polytechnic, for its part, had to adjust to accommodate the specific professional needs of Chelsea and recognize and accept that teaching groups of

90 students was not appropriate, especially in practical subjects in the gymnasia, dance studios or swimming pool.

The School included a Division of Physical Education and Recreation based at Falmer, with H J (Frank) Dain as Coordinator, which contributed to courses on that site. The Division was also responsible for organizing a scheme of physical recreation for all members of the Polytechnic at Brighton and maintaining also association with the Sports Federation of the Students' Union.

Departments in the Polytechnic's central administration included: Academic Affairs, Administrative Services, Bursary, Communal Services, Personnel, Physical Resources, Learning Resources, Registry and the Computer Centre. These units were based at Brighton with small representative 'local' offices at Eastbourne. From being under 'one roof' or just 'down the road' the perceived 'power house' was now 25 miles away. An *Administrative Handbook* (255 pages) was produced, to assist staff in finding their way around the system. For some members of staff, it only served to increase the 'feeling of detachment', for others it reinforced the 'sense of bureaucracy' as the all-important method of operation.

There were other difficulties and concerns that arose from the general principles of responsibility applied throughout the Polytechnic. For example, with the Faculty of Education Studies taking responsibility for all teacher training courses, including those of the physical education students and with Ralph Homer (now in the Faculty of Education Studies, but formerly in the Chelsea School) appointed Course Leader for the BEd(Hons) Physical Education degree course, the 'principle of servicing' had been taken further than in the previous incorporation. The staff of the Chelsea School were now concerned that 'The School's national reputation, which is at the moment high, will be lowered if it appears that the School is no longer capable of planning its own physical education degree course'. The School's policy was based on the belief that,

> The relationship between physical education and education has, in the past, been one of close cooperation, but the main emphasis in preparing teachers of physical education has been, and will continue to be on the content and study of the advanced level work in physical education.

The Standing Committee of the School wanted an 'internal' appointee, 'by virtue of professional qualifications, experience and personal qualities' as Course Leader. At the time of incorporation the Director of the Polytechnic had written to the Head of the Chelsea School, 'This (application of the principle of responsibility) sounds rather formal; I am confident you will find that, in practice, there will be fewer difficulties than you envisage at the moment'. The increase in internal administrative structures, whilst appearing heavily bureaucratic, was the inevitable result of the need to have clear structures from which to make appropriate links between faculties in the delivery of courses.

To assist staff with the clarification of their new roles in June 1981, Mrs Burke summarized the:

(a) responsibilities of Course Leaders as administration of approved courses, monitoring, evaluation, course development, together with 17 specific responsibilities;

(b) responsibilities of Area Coordinators as subject interests, chairman of area meetings, advise Head of Department, together with 10 specific responsibilities; and

(c) responsibilities of Subject Coordinators as link between Course Boards and areas; share work with Course Leaders, together with nine specific responsibilities.

The implications of being part of a changed higher education environment meant many adjustments for staff and students. In particular, in Mrs Burke's view, the staff required to meet, for Honours Degree programmes, the following criteria:

1 academic expertise in terms of qualifications;
2 academic expertise in terms of higher education attitudes, appropriate teaching/learning strategies, commitment to research, knowledge of the real world; and
3 practical expertise over and above initial training.

Ideally, the BEd staff should meet all three criteria.

The School needed staff not only to teach, but also to take a more systematic academic approach to the day-to-day administration and monitoring of courses. Expertise was needed in evaluation, curriculum design, assessment of performance, modular systems of timetabling and record systems. Above all, the School required people with clearly developed ideas about the future of physical education, human movement, sport and recreation, who were prepared to articulate these views in open meetings.

The Polytechnic's policy on validation had been recommended by its Academic Development Committee and supported by the Academic Boards and Councils of the East Sussex College of Higher Education and the Polytechnic in April 1978, as follows, 'The Polytechnic works towards having its degrees validated by one body and that should be the Council for National Academic Awards'. This decision to have one major validating body resulted from widespread debate. It meant that the University of Sussex courses had to be redesigned and converted to validation by the Council for National Academic Awards. Thus, the whole period of Mrs Burke's tenancy was characterized by massive course development. The plan to diversify using staff strengths and the range of disciplines which underpinned physical education, embraced science to develop the BSc(Hons) Sports Science degree; social sciences to develop a BA(Hons) Human Movement Studies degree; and arts to develop a BA(Hons) degree course in Dance and Related Arts. The BSc Sports Science course was an early success under the leadership of Trevor Wood. It was one of the first in the United Kingdom to be validated in 1979 and mounted in 1980 when it recruited 26 students. There were 16 men and 10 women, on the first course, with the consequent requests for sports specialisms in cycling, body building, soccer and rugby, together with competition level pitches, first class weight training facilities, access to minibuses for matches and a definite need for upgraded provision for changing and showering facilities in the School. The students all qualified in July 1983 with one student awarded a first class honours degree, nine upper seconds, 12 lower seconds and four achieved degree standard. The main aims of this innovative course were: to establish an understanding of sport through the synthesis of biological, psychological, social and practical perspectives; to produce an honours graduate able to play a prominent and constructive role in the development of sport in our society. The course linked results of research from sports medicine and the natural sciences with expertise from the world of coaching. It was 'based on the premise that sports science is an academic study of the scientific basis of preparation and performance in sport', and that 'practical experience is an important aspect of the course, providing a focusing point for the academic study'. It was a coherent course with a clear focus; it was also quite different from the teacher training courses for which Chelsea was renowned and brought into the institution a very different kind of student and staff with different areas of expertise. One intrinsic feature was a field trip to a mainland European Institute of Higher Education; on the first in 1981–82, second year students visited Amsterdam University.

The new BEd(Hons) course achieved the Council for National Academic Awards validation for a September 1981 start and, in turn, attracted more male students with at least one surprising outcome. A group of first year BEd men asked to see Mrs Burke about dance and, contrary to expectations, requested *more*, not less. Their argument, if they were going to be adequately prepared for teaching the subject, they needed more dance in their programme than the women students; at the time they were receiving slightly less. This excellent, professional attitude was a mark of the calibre of student attracted to the School.

Success was, however, diluted, in that the School and the Faculty failed to persuade the Polytechnic's Validation Committee of the viability or rigour of a BA in Human Movement, even although it had been operating, with some success, with University of Sussex validation. It was surprising that an institution which could allow its largest department to be called the Chelsea School of Human Movement, could also deny the existence of human movement as an academic discipline. In many other institutions, such courses were developed and have progressed from strength to strength, to provide a particularly strong foundation for students entering teaching via the Postgraduate Certificate in Education route. The development of the BA(Hons) Expressive Arts degree was undertaken in the Department of Combined Arts within the Faculty of Art and Design, to which four members of the Chelsea dance staff had been appointed at the time of incorporation.

Other developments were, however, successful. For example: a one-term Polytechnic Diploma course in Sports Management and Administration for overseas students was successfully developed by Miss Joy Standeven, in cooperation with the Management Centre in the Faculty of Management and Informatics, and recruited its first students in 1981–82. It attracted students from Malaysia, Nepal, Nigeria and Israel, namely, Sagir Garba, Mahmood Binkaking, Omar Masa Khalil, Pias Kasimawo Laloko and Mamal Buhadur Thapo. One Khalil (Director of Physical Recreation, Bethlehem University) joined the Working Group that developed the short course into a one-year Polytechnic Diploma course. This full-time Diploma course was run on a full cost basis and recruited 13 students in 1982. It was based on an incremental process and incorporated distance learning modules as an alternative for students to being full-time at Chelsea. The course aimed to develop an understanding of sport and physical recreation within the wider context of leisure and society. It also developed skills and understanding of modern management and administration of sports facilities.

The development of higher degrees was a natural outcome of successful undergraduate programmes. The MA Physical Education course, in both full-time and part-time modes with a Postgraduate Diploma option, was developed between 1981 and 1984. Specific aims covered the development of analytical and critical powers; breadth of vision; analysis of theories of teaching and learning relationships between physical education, sport and dance; increase of subject knowledge; development of research skills; and continuing professional commitment. It was validated by the Council for National Academic Awards in 1985, and recruited its first students in September 1987 on the part-time mode. 'The focus throughout was on physical education as an activity *one practices*, on practical issues of teaching, but necessarily informed by theory'. Originally, the course was planned as a joint degree with the MA Art Education course with Ralph Homer as the Programme Coordinator. The two courses were separated in 1988, when it was agreed to run them independently, one within each Faculty.

At the outset, and during the planning process, Miss J C McConachie-Smith was the Course Leader of the MA Physical Education course. In 1988, when the course was operative, Dr Graham McFee was appointed to this role. The course was based on two summer schools of 10 days each and 12 weekend schools. The catchment area for recruitment of men and women teachers or lecturers was both national and international. The majority of home students took the part-time mode because financial secondment for full-time students was very limited. Of the initial intake of 11 students, six held Honours degrees in physical education, one an Honours degree in social science and a Postgraduate Certificate in Education, and three were exceptional entries; one was eventually unable to attend. This course proved, until its closure in 1993, to be a very strong source of critical and reflective study of the teaching of physical education within an expanding academic field of study.

From 1 April 1979, physical recreation within the enlarged Polytechnic became the responsibility of the Chelsea School of Human Movement with the Recreation Committee contributing new ideas, advising on and approving the annual programme. The staff of the Recreation Service had as:

General Aims
1.1 Provide a service that complements:
    1.1.1 the Students' Union Sports Federation, Clubs and Societies, and staff programme; and
    1.1.2 educational aims of the institution — personal development of students outside the parameters of the academic counsellor.

1.2 Cooperate with local and regional services; extend recreational opportunities for the local community; contribute to the adult education programme.

1.3 Offer comprehensive recreation programmes.

Specific Objectives

2.1 Liaise and work with officers of the Students' Union Sports Federation, clubs and societies.

2.2 Provide 'closed' and 'open' courses and make provision for instructor, coach, trainer, official in a wide variety of recreation activities.

2.3 Organize intramural competition.

2.4 Encourage 'casual' recreation.

2.5 Implement programme agreed annually by the Recreation Committee.

2.6 Advise the Recreation Committee on all matters pertaining to the Recreation Service.

In January 1980, a new post of Recreation Tutor was created for the Eastbourne campus. Edward Twaddell was appointed, with responsibility for: the organization and development of sport and recreation for all students on the Eastbourne site; participation in the planning, administration and implementation of coaching; the provision of coaching courses in physical recreation activities; and the development of Polytechnic/local community links with sportsmen, sportswomen, sports organizations and clubs in Eastbourne and the surrounding district. Except for a break of three years, he served on the Eastbourne Council for Sport and Recreation from 1980 to 1998. During that time, he held various offices, including the post of Secretary.

The School and the Recreation Service cooperated with the Sports Council in the national *Sport for All* campaigns. 1981 was designated International Year of the Disabled, when the Chelsea School of Human Movement organized an open day of *Come and Try* events for the handicapped. In 1983, under the title *50+ All to Play For* 'taster' courses in swimming, canoeing, badminton, tennis, rambling, jogging, archery, folk/old tyme dancing and tennis were arranged at Eastbourne. At Falmer, the Recreation Service designed and mounted the *Give it Five Fitness Scheme*. These taster days led directly to the formation at Eastbourne, on Friday evenings, of a club for the disabled, organized by Mrs Sally Murphy, where members participated in swimming, archery, short mat bowls or wheelchair dancing and the 50+ tennis and swimming clubs. The students raised £1068 during 'Rag Week' in 1981–82 so that a 'hoist' could be purchased for the swimming pool. In cooperation with the Eastbourne Sports Development Officer, the School organized and hosted a 'Sports Day for the Disabled' in 1990 and in 1991. The members of the Friday evening club who played bowls also joined the local league (for able and disabled bowlers). They were successful in winning the league on at least one occasion and competed in other specific and joint local and national events, including those at Stoke Mandeville. The above three clubs continued to function throughout the fourth era and were very popular amongst members of the local community.

The School had always cooperated with the local sports clubs and, for example, in 1980 Hindsland was used by seven outside organizations:

> Seven Sisters Football Club
> Willingdon Evening Centre for Yoga
> Polegate Community Centre for Football
> Hailsham Hockey Club
> Polegate Football Club
> Prince Albert Stoolball Team and
> Debenhams Stoolball Team.

Territorial lacrosse selections, courses for the cricket teachers' award scheme, Sussex under 14 hockey tournament, a day of athletics and a day of cricket for school pupils continued to be part of the ongoing wider community programme.

Between 1980 and 1985, eight dance residences were organized by Mrs Ann Cole with financial support from South East Arts and other agencies: in 1980, 1981 and 1982 with the Mantis Dance Company, 1982–83 with the London Contemporary Experience, 1983–84 with the Phoenix Dance Company, and 1985 with the ACGB Extemporary Dance Theatre. Staff and students of the Polytechnic, together with teachers and pupils from local schools participated in workshops and members of the local community were able to see the final dance productions.

Increasingly, over the period 1980 to 1985, Mrs Burke had been invited to give keynote papers at national conferences, including the Physical Education Association of Great Britain and Northern Ireland; the British Association of Advisers and Lecturers in Physical Education; the Public Schools Physical Education Association; the National Association of Teachers in Further and Higher Education — Physical Education and Dance Sections; and the Standing Conference on Physical Education and to contribute to many Department of Education and Science courses as either a member of the staff team or as the course leader.

Of particular interest was her paper, prepared following formal and informal discussions on the place of gymnastics in the new BEd degree course and entitled, 'Development in gymnastics: The educational viewpoint'. She explained her understanding of gymnastics in the context of education and the nature of gymnastics construed as an educational activity. There was a historical précis with philosophical connotations, context and rationale and she developed ideas concerning ways of structuring the activity for individual development within educational gymnastics, which represented the teacher's perspective. In her lecture given in October 1981, *What is Physical Education For?* at Reading, she had outlined the major difference between physical education and sport as *not* in *what* is done but in *how* and *why*. Physical education and sport was to become a topical issue at national level with ever increasing emphasis on the role of physical education and sport in the National Curriculum, in the remainder of the fourth Chelsea era. It was also a key topic for the Sports Council that led to the production and publication of *Young People and Sport: Policy and Framework for Action* in 1993 and subsequent national, regional and local strategies, documents and schemes for talent development.

Mrs Burke was the first Head of Chelsea to resign when, on 1 September 1984, she became an HMI (PEd) and moved to the North West. On her arrival at Chelsea, Mrs Burke had been met with some suspicion, for she was an appointee from a 'rival' institution, the I M Marsh College of Physical Education. Soon, however, she had 'won over' the staff through her intellectual powers, open mindedness, honesty, well-considered opinions, managerial expertise and capacity to work. Following discussion, many documents were produced 'overnight' and succinctly expressed agreed decisions. At other times, she wrote thought provoking papers, which led to important changes. The staff and Mrs Burke quickly learnt to work together. She was acutely observant of other people's reactions and her calm exterior often hid her deep inner concerns for staff, students and the School. Her advice was sound and led to pragmatic solutions and innovative projects. She believed in straight talking to achieve ambitious objectives, was articulate and skilfully guided the School through its first Council for National Academic Awards quinquennial review in 1980; a traumatic experience for the uninitiated. A persuasive manner combined with stamina enabled her to steer, nudge, cajole or push staff and students, as the situation demanded. These characteristics, combined with a sense of humour, which was very evident at times of crisis, created a dynamic and positive outlook and the right environment to surmount the challenges facing the School in the second phase of the fourth era. There was also a 'lighter' side to Mrs Burke's nature. For example: in the staff pantomime *Snow White and the Seven Dwarfs* she abseiled, sporting a wicked grin and hissing loudly into the arena of the John Fulton Hall from the balcony. On appointment as Head of the Chelsea School in 1979, Mrs Burke had had a clear vision of achievable objectives. Her lucid, critical and analytical approach to the study of physical education, human movement and sports science and her incisive leadership had been effective. Her influence was apparent in the progress made by the School, in the development of both new and existing courses and in the recruitment of a wider range of students of both sexes. Under her leadership, the Brighton Polytechnic system was mastered and successfully implemented within the Chelsea School of Human Movement.

Joy McConachie-Smith
Acting Head of School (September 1984 to February 1985)
Brighton Polytechnic

From the time the School was incorporated with Brighton Polytechnic on 1 April 1979, Miss Kingston, followed by Mrs Burke and later, their successor,

Miss Elizabeth Murdoch, were very ably supported by the Deputy Head of School, Miss Joy C McConachie-Smith until her untimely death on 4 December 1994. She had been appointed to Chelsea College of Physical Education in 1969. As the Deputy Head of the School, she had been responsible for academic development and coordination of teacher training. She had general responsibility for academic standards and staffing and convened and chaired many committees and working parties. She was also in membership of many School, Faculty and Polytechnic (later University) committees and her input was always valued. Miss McConachie-Smith was 'special' to everyone who met her, not just within the School, but also throughout the institution and outside it. She had a great sense of humour and was able to share many laughs with colleagues and students. The Director of the Polytechnic said, 'I always enjoyed meeting her and talking with her'.

Miss McConachie-Smith, in spite of her vast experience as a teacher and lecturer in physical education in New Zealand, the United States of America and England, and her wide range of knowledge, particularly in the psychological aspects of physical education and human movement studies, was modest, meticulous, loyal, gentle, calm and, above all, especially in the last year of her life very courageous. She was a natural scholar with the ability to explain knotty problems simply and to share ideas in a way that made you think they were your own. Miss McConachie-Smith was a versatile teacher; one who was able to establish an easy rapport with children, students and staff alike. Her breadth and depth of understanding and her vision about education came from the unique blend of academic and professional experience, coupled with intensive thought and extensive reading.

Through her involvement in psychology, she became a recognized leader in the field of child development within physical education. Miss McConachie-Smith also made a positive contribution to the development of the National Curriculum, particularly in two different areas namely: progression in learning and assessment in physical education. Her research, publications and presentations were innumerable and earned her worldwide respect from professional colleagues. Amongst the many professional associations and councils that welcomed her contributions, were the Physical Education Association, of which she was a Fellow; the Standing Conference of Physical Education; the British Council of Physical Education; Southern Sports Federation; British Society of Sports Psychology; the South East Council for Sport and Recreation; the School Sport Forum; the International Association for Physical Education in Higher Education; and the Department of Education and Science. In 1992 she was awarded a Churchill Fellowship, which led to the report, *Sport in Schools and the Community in Australia and New Zealand*.

Her effective leadership of the School during the autumn term of 1984 and January 1985 meant that the transition from one Head of School to the next was smooth, efficient and well organized. She had spared no effort in carrying out her duties; her attention to detail was prodigious and every file was in order and tabulated when handed on to Miss Murdoch.

Following this experience as Acting Head, Miss McConachie-Smith continued her loyal service as Deputy Head of the School and combined this with her contributions to the Faculty, to the Polytechnic (later University) and to external organizations.

For example, first, her paper entitled, 'Physical education and the National Curriculum: The current issues' was developed around the following three questions to make her teacher audience 'think'.

1 What do we expect children to *learn* in physical education?
2 What range and categories of activities/experiences would we expect children to show their capabilities in?
3 What cross-curricular themes and general and personal abilities can be included in the physical education programme of study?

This paper as her contribution to an inset-course 'Physical Education: Preparing for the National Curriculum' brought forth the following letter from Mrs Margaret Coleman, the East Sussex Education Authority Physical Education and County Curricular Adviser dated 2 March 1990, 'Thank you for your typically generous response and thoroughly professional approach to my request for support in mounting the in-service experience yesterday'. The letter concluded with the words, 'It was good to observe a professional of calibre, working in harmony with the "team"; tackling issues that could have been "threatening" to the individual, in a manner which was totally supportive and will facilitate growth amongst the members of the group'.

Secondly, following her paper 'School and sport — the way forward' detailing the education perspective for the Southern Sports Federation Conference at Bisham Abbey on 7 October 1990, she received a letter from the Honorary Secretary, Jeff Stimpson in which he said, 'thank you for your outstanding contribution, sensitively delivered'.

Elizabeth Murdoch
Head of School (1985–98)
Brighton Polytechnic 1985–92 and University of Brighton 1992–98

Elizabeth Murdoch, born 26 May 1937 and educated at Marr College, Troon, Scotland from 1949 to 1954 and Dunfermline College of Physical Education from

1954 to 1957, was appointed as Head of the Chelsea School of Human Movement on 1 February 1985. Her teaching and lecturing experience included Kilmarnock Academy, Dalmellington High School and Dunfermline College of Physical Education. At Dunfermline, as well as lecturing and researching, she held the posts of Head of Department of Physical Activities and Movement; Head of Department of Rehabilitation, Movement and Physical Education; and Head of Department of Movement Studies. Personal further study, all successfully concluded, included the special one-year course at the Art of Movement Centre, the BEd(Hons) degree of the University of Leeds and the MSc(Bioengineering) by research at the University of Strathclyde.

Before her appointment, Miss Murdoch had been a member of the visiting party to Brighton Polytechnic and, in particular, to the Chelsea School when the BEd(Hons) degree course, including the physical education secondary route, was validated by the Council for National Academic Awards in 1981. Subsequently, she had been the external examiner for that course, had met Chelsea staff at conferences and therefore, had an insight into the ethos and work of the Chelsea School.

On appointment, her track record for the development of courses, in-service work, research, publications and presentations was very impressive. During her tenure at Chelsea, she added to that outstanding profile at both national and international levels and contributed greatly, with the support of her staff, to the standing and reputation of the School and to the academic development of physical education and movement studies and to producing further diversified courses.

It is interesting and important to consider, in particular, the development of her thinking and her personal beliefs about physical education within the context of the progress of the Chelsea School during the past 13 years. In *The nature of Physical Education* she wrote, 'Physical Education is essentially the study of the area of experience afforded by physical activity in an educational context. This, traditionally, has been identified by a range of physical activities that have been used as vehicles for learning. To encourage learning at all ages, the Physical Education programme needs also to be even more varied and flexible'.

Learning embraced four aspects:

- knowledge of and about physical activity and the individual activities themselves, and the ability to participate and perform;
- the development of desirable social attributes;
- the development of positive/appropriate attitudes to physical activity; and
- the enhancement of fitness for participation and performance.

The distinction between participation and performance was characterized by two distinct approaches to involvement in physical activity:

- that of the individual who engages for the experience at a level appropriate to needs; and
- that of the individual who engages with the intention of reaching a high level of achievement.

Miss Murdoch felt that both approaches must be catered for in the width of the experience offered within the programme and the manner of presentation of these experiences. Such width encompasses the needs of a population ranging from pre-school to adulthood and old age. The purpose of physical education is to offer to each individual a breadth and variety of experience and to ensure that each has the capacity to allow full benefit from this involvement. Physical education and the teaching of it, is a practical and a theoretical area of study that is approached both in theoretical and practical mode. The resulting matrix identifies the main approaches to the study in teacher education:

Figure 5.3:   Four interrelated approaches to study in teacher education

	Theory	**Practice**
Theoretical	The theory studied in theoretical mode.	The theory of practice of both teaching and physical activity.
Practical	Laboratories/workshops where theory concepts are examined practically	Practical participation per se. Teaching practice.

Balance amongst these four aspects characterizes a course in terms of content and the methodological approaches. Study in all four areas is essential to a rounded and full understanding of the area. The above summary sets out the context of Miss Murdoch's beliefs and her aspirations in the teacher training field for the Chelsea School during her term of office.

In 1986, Miss Murdoch was also concerned that, 'Some Physical Education teachers are not willing to question the evolution of the subject'. She continued,

> This stems from a strongly held conviction that Physical Education is a practical subject and it is through the doing that most is achieved. This tends to beg the question of the role of the teacher, firstly, as an educator responding to changing needs and demands of young people in society and reinforces a traditional approach since, if changes are made in tune with changes in the individual's activities over time, then the programme is seen as updated and relevant.

Miss Murdoch set out, with the support of colleagues, to question and find answers to the many problems facing the profession in the late 1980s and early 1990s, to widen horizons and to increase the diversified programme of courses offered by the School.

Her breadth and depth of knowledge was reflected in the innumerable well-researched papers, chapters or books she has subsequently written. All her contributions have been logically structured, analytical in style, clear in presentation and progressive in thought, ideas and subject development. Central, however, in her thinking was the *learning theme* which can be traced throughout her writings. It appeared, for example, in approaches that ranged from 'What is the process of learning?', through 'Learning to learn', 'How children learn', 'Learning in the real world' to 'Independent student learning'. The latter was a strategy that many students in the Chelsea School found difficult and a few even unacceptable. They had experienced direct teaching as their primary mode of learning at secondary school, and expected the same approach in higher education. Nevertheless, they had to come to terms quickly with this 'new' method of study which had fast become an integral feature of degree courses, particularly in the 1990s. Miss Murdoch's views were supported by an Office for Standards in Education/Department for Education and Employment report which stated, 'Setting targets makes you focus on what children are actually learning not what you think you are teaching'.

It was made very clear to Miss Murdoch at the time of her appointment as Head of the Chelsea School, in February 1985, by the Director of the Polytechnic, Geoffrey R Hall, that the School's research profile should indeed be raised. Since becoming a department of the Polytechnic, the School had been working to develop its research function. By 1983, a project, 'Motor Control in Downs Syndrome Children', under the direction of Dr John Allen and Miss Joy McConachie-Smith, had been approved. The first Polytechnic supported research assistant, Shelagh Lawton, to be based in the School was appointed in 1984 to undertake the above research at Master's level, and the first Honorary Research Fellow, appointed to the School in 1985, was Professor Stanley Parker, BSc MSc PhD (London). Under Miss Murdoch's leadership, the School, after lengthy discussions, decided to concentrate on three areas of rigorous academic scholarship for research, namely: leisure and recreation, health and fitness (later retitled sport and exercise) and curriculum research in teacher education. The first area was established, in cooperation with the Department of Service Sector Management, as the Leisure Research Unit in 1986 with its focus on 'people'. Its aims were:

> to strengthen leisure research in the two departments, to provide research data, case studies and improve expertise for courses in leisure and leisure management across the Polytechnic, to liaise with agencies in the statutory, voluntary and private sectors, to provide applied research into leisure and to provide forums for critical discussion on the nature and significance of leisure.

Lesley Lawrence was the first student appointed to this unit in October 1986, to research 'Education for Leisure' with Dr Joy Standeven as her tutor. She gained her PhD in 1990–91; her thesis was entitled 'Understanding teachers' leisure aims and practices in secondary school physical education'.

The work of the staff and researchers in this Unit centred at that time on leisure pools, public sector markets in sport and leisure, comparative sport and leisure studies and sports consumption. The members utilized sociology, social history and cultural analysis of leisure and physical recreation as their academic tools. Between 1987 and 1992, 27 projects had been completed successfully and seven were ongoing in the Leisure Research Unit. In 1993, the Unit was recognized by the Economic and Social Research Council as a 'research centre of excellence in the study of leisure'. As a direct outcome of the early research work of this Unit, the Chelsea School cooperated with the Department of Service Sector Management, based at Eastbourne, to develop the BA(Hons) degree course, entitled Leisure Policy and Administration. Dr Joy Standeven was the first Course Leader and, from 1995, Udo Merkel took over the course leadership. Twenty-four students were recruited as the first cohort in September 1993. The general aim of the course was to produce graduates who had an understanding of leisure policy and competencies appropriate to a wide range of professional tasks of leisure administration. The seven specific aims led to seven learning outcomes. Twenty-two students graduated in July 1996; one gained a first class degree, seven upper seconds, 13 lower seconds, one a third class award and two students qualified for the Certificate in Higher Education: Leisure Policy and Administration.

On the basis of experience in running this course, in September 1997 the field of leisure was developed into two distinct routes with a total intake of 59 students. The first route; BA(Hons) Leisure and Sport Management, had as its focus: physically active forms of leisure and the management of people's free time; historical, sociological and political aspects of sport and leisure; entrepreneurial skills; technical knowledge; and business acumen. The second route, BA(Hons) Leisure and Sport Studies had as its focus: theory related to practice; in depth academic study of selected aspects of leisure and sport; and appropriate vocational emphases.

By this time, the Unit had been renamed the Sport, Leisure and Cultures Group and was entirely within the Chelsea School. It comprised Professor Alan Tomlinson, Professor Graham McFee, Dr John Sugden, Mr Udo Merkel, Miss Gill Lines (academic staff), Dr Stanley Parker, Mr Andrew Jennings (Faculty Fellows) and Professor John Hargreaves (Visiting Professor). The Group now focused upon critical sociological research into contemporary and modern historical sports and associated leisure cultures and forms. Between 1992 and 1996 members had supervised to successful conclusion seven PhDs and two MPhils and aimed to have six to eight doctoral students at any one time. Typical examples of its projected work included, comparative sports systems in Europe; sport in divided cities/societies; the philosophy of free will; the sociology and social history of consumption; and Olympic ideology and sports/media consumption.

The second area, the Human Performance Research Unit, under the leadership of Paul McNaught-Davis was set up in 1986–87. It focused on four areas, namely: developmental field tests for measuring performance and anaerobic threshold; sports injuries and rehabilitation; training and performance; and mental rehearsal programmes. The staff and research students utilized the academic perspectives of physiology and psychology of sport performance and exercise. Sarah Rowell (Chelsea, BSc(Hons) Sports Science 1st Class 1981–84) was the first student based in this Unit to successfully complete her PhD Studies. Her thesis was entitled 'The aetiology of running injuries'. Her work was funded between 1985 and 1989 by the Health Promotion Research Trust. Sadly, Sarah Rowell had herself been a victim of a sports injury, and so the research topic was of especial interest and relevance to her. Subsequently, she was appointed Sports Science Programme Manager, National Coaching Foundation, Governing Body Service Section and from 1997 became a self-employed consultant. Examples of projects successfully carried out by the Unit included: *The Trip to Death Valley* shown as a BBC QED programme

Attempt to Run the Valley, in 1987, and the joint project with the Women's Cricket Association when the aim was 'Winning the World Cup in 1993', which was successfully accomplished. Both were staffed by Dr Jonathan Doust and Steve Bull, and the latter project had Mrs Ruth Prideaux, Coach to the England Women's Team, as Adviser/Consultant. Individual athletes of national and international standing, including Evonne McGregor, Chris Boardman, Paula Radcliffe, Sally Gunnell and Kelly Holmes, as well as various governing bodies of sport, have continued throughout the fourth era to utilize the services of the Unit. In 1995, Dr Jonathan Doust was responsible for the Sports Science Cluster and, by 1996, the Unit had defined three specific areas for further research: sports and exercise psychology, children in sport, and physiology/related sciences. Staff had successfully supervised three PhDs and one MPhil award. The Unit had raised £85,157 externally between 1992 and April 1996 to support its work. In 1996 it was staffed by: sports and exercise psychology — Dr Stephen J Bull, Dr Chris Shambrook and Dr Adrian Taylor; institute for the study of children in sport — Dr Martin Lee and Dr Jean Whitehead; and physiology/related sciences — Dr Peter Bale, Mr Adrian Burden, Dr Jonathan Doust, Mr Peter Keen and Dr Craig Williams. In June 1997 the Chelsea School shared £2.7m from the capital English Sports Council's Lottery Fund awarded to the National Sports Medicine Institute to the extent of £100,000 to purchase new scientific equipment (isokinetic dynamometer, an on-line mass spectrometry gas analysis system, a range of ergometers, additional computers and refurbishment of patient reception room) for the School.

These two units, the Sport, Leisure and Cultures Group and the Sports Science Cluster formed the Chelsea School Research Centre in 1988, as the administrative focus for research activity under the management, directorship and coordination of Dr, later Professor, Alan Tomlinson. He chaired the Faculty's Research Committee, sat on the two University research committees; was Course Leader for the University's Certificate in Research Methodology; and led the Leisure Research Unit (later the Sport and Leisure Cultures Group). In 1992 he had been appointed reader in the sociology of sport. Since its inception, the Centre organized the graduate seminar research training workshop programmes for the School's research students, research meetings and joint writing programmes. The postgraduate students contributed to undergraduate teaching.

The third area, Curriculum Research and Teacher Education later renamed Curriculum and Youth Sport Research, was developed within the MA programme where strong professional links had been established. Later it cooperated with the School's Research Centre. Students' dissertations focused on critical work in the physical education curriculum, evaluation and assessment procedures in physical education and young people's informal school cultures in relation to sport. Following the 1992 Research Assessment Exercise, in 1993–94 the area was divided with psychological work included in the sport and exercise section of the Human Performance Unit and pedagogically driven output returned to education. The Physical Education in School and Teacher Education Group was led by Professor Murdoch; its work was directed to meet challenges posed by the National Curriculum and new patterns of partnership as they affected physical education. Under the theme

Curriculum and Pedagogy such topics as: how children learn; implications for school practice; modes of assessment; learning processes in specific subjects, for example, athletics and gymnastics were researched. Under *Partnership for Physical Education*, such topics as: dance artistes in education; cooperation between physical education and sport; and university/school partnerships were pursued. This Unit, in 1996, was staffed by Professor Murdoch, Miss Ann-Marie Latham, Mrs Margaret Carroll, Dr Jean O'Neill and Dr Ann Cole.

In pursuance of its research programmes, the School created partnerships with, for example: sports councils, local authorities, private companies, the Tourist Board, Regional Arts Council, local health authorities, Harwell, Royal Sun Alliance Insurance, FIFA, Sussex Cricket and the National Governing Body of Sport for Basketball. It has had joint projects with other institutions of higher education including, Bedford, West Sussex, Crewe and Alsager, Birmingham, Exeter, I M Marsh Centre (Liverpool John Moores), Queen's (Canada), Newcastle, Glasgow, North East Missouri State, Goldsmiths, Montpellier, New Brunswick and Queen Mary Westfield.

In the 1980s Chelsea had gone out into the open market and won contracts against prestigious competition. The profile had been raised and this paved the way for the *structured* submission of research output with the Higher Education Funding Council for England: Research Assessment Exercise in 1992, 1996 and the anticipated exercise in 2001. The School entered the exercise with submissions in all three areas of its work and, in 1996, gained '3' ratings in all three areas. This resulted in the award of £84,000 per annum to the School to support the next four years research production.

The University of Brighton's own academic review report in the summer of 1994, concluded, the

> . . . success in the 1992 Research Assessment Exercise provided further resources to strengthen this (model of research organization and administration) through developments in staffing and administrative support, . . . the School had developed an effective research infrastructure and programme which was likely to provide a strong underpinning for the School's continuing academic excellence.

During the period from 1992 to 1995, staff had been involved in 82 publications. The School's decision to focus its development in the field of higher degrees by research, rather than in taught higher degrees, had been successful. The reputation and academic excellence of the School had been enhanced. (See Figure 5.4)

In 1990 Miss Murdoch was made a Fellow of the Physical Education Association and gave her lecture, entitled 'Physical Education and the National Curriculum' on 5 December 1990 in a room at the House of Commons. She took this opportunity to revisit her 1986 paper, 'Future trends in physical education, sport, recreation and leisure' and summarized the major changes in the intervening four years as:

- the great media debate;
- the Education Reform Act 1988; and
- the National Curriculum with physical education as a foundation subject from 1989.

Figure 5.4:   Staff publications, 1992–95

Unit	Authored books	Co-authored books	Monographs	Edited volumes	Peer reviewed articles	TOTALS
Leisure Research Unit	3	9	7	4	3	26
Human Performance Research Unit	1	7	23	6	0	37
Curriculum Research and Teacher Education	1	3	11	4	0	19
TOTALS	5	19	41	14	3	82

The stability of the profession, the clarity on the nature of physical education, the 'running out of time' for the profession and the need for proven research were all questioned. She said there was progress towards: first, consensus on a progressive and developmentally based programme of physical education for 5–16-year-olds; second, preparation for leisure; and third, a positive approach to health and fitness. With its focus on learning, physical education was an educational force. Assessment and achievement could be measured with examinations at GCSE 'O' and 'A' levels requiring learning by employing imaginative teaching strategies.

In Miss Murdoch's view, further progress would be achieved through *Partnership in Action* and clarification of the role of the physical education teacher.

In 1991 Miss Murdoch became a Professor of the Polytechnic and gave her inaugural lecture, entitled 'Choreutics — An alternative perspective on Plato's Choric Art', on Thursday 13 February 1992. This illustrated lecture was structured with three main themes or areas of interest: first, the study of choreutics based on the original works of Rudolf Laban; second, the significance of this analysis of movement to the learning child, an area in which she used her own knowledge and experience and Mark Johnson's work, to develop the theme; and third, Plato's writings. In a scholastic and compelling way, Professor Murdoch also developed the thesis of the importance of a good well planned movement programme for children where the experience of moving was central to learning. As she concluded, children should, '... become so harmoniously adjusted to their movement, that they will move with ease, efficiency and flow and stand in stillness with confidence'. Or as Johnson said, they should be viewed as, 'Putting the body back into the mind'. Or, as Plato remarked, 'the just man will always be seen adjusting the body's harmony for the sake of the accord of the soul'.

In 1986 the Polytechnic's internal restructuring had led to the demise of the Faculty of Social and Cultural Studies. Chelsea was transferred to the newly-formed Faculty of Health, under the deanship of Malcolm Parker. The opportunity was also taken to develop a five-year plan and within the Chelsea School to restructure the organization, leading to seven divisions which reflected the focus of professional development, and were operative under leaders as follows:

Teacher Education (Physical Education)	Joy C McConachie-Smith (Academic Health and Staff)
Sports Science	Trevor Wood
Leisure and Recreation Studies	Joy Standeven (External Affairs)
Health, Fitness and Coaching	Paul McNaught-Davis (Finance)
Special Needs in Physical Education and Sport	Ruth Prideaux
Dance and the Arts	Varina Verdin (Students)
Research	Dr Alan Tomlinson (Academic Health).

Even with the redistribution of duties and responsibilities, Miss Murdoch commented, 'surprisingly, one of the most difficult things to achieve is to allow staff time and resources for personal academic reflection and growth'. She was very aware of the need for staff to keep abreast of developments within their own specialist fields and to achieve continuing scholastic success.

Following Corporate Status for the Polytechnic on 1 April 1989 when it became:

- responsible for its estates
- the employer of all its staff
- responsible for its own budget
- free to encourage entrepreneurial activities and create increased income

the institution's strategic plan, *Towards 2000* was prepared. In it the Polytechnic's Mission Statement read, 'The corporate goal of the Polytechnic is to develop an institution, accessible to all who can benefit, which encourages excellence in teaching and learning, research, scholarship and creativity'. In September 1991, the reformed Faculty of Education, Sport and Leisure, with Mrs Ann Markham as Dean and Professor Murdoch as Assistant Dean, set out to bring together the Chelsea School of Human Movement and the Faculty of Education to form a Faculty that 'reflects the strengths of both'. A corporate unit was envisaged that strengthened its academic profile; made more effective use of resources; extended its professional partnership in training; focused on outreach activities; responded to demands for consultancy; and developed research. Its philosophy was based on the following three principles, a holistic view, a client centred approach and development of a joint philosophy. The common goals were set out as: flexible structures leading to dynamic response to change; partnership approaches to client bodies and other areas of the Polytechnic; outreach activities from the decentralization of the balance of Faculty activities; and a harmonious balance between increase of provision, maintenance of quality and consultancy delivery. The School was renamed the Chelsea School of Physical Education, Sports Science, Dance and Leisure and members of the former Education Department moved back into the School.

The School's (departmental) goals had been defined in February 1991 during the discussion process as:

1   To provide courses for full/part-time students of the United Kingdom and other countries in physical education, dance, sports science, coaching, exercise and health and leisure studies.
2   To contribute to a programme of in-service and professional development.
3   To promote and conduct research in areas of academic and professional study related to expertise and specialisms.
4   To initiate and respond to requests for consultancy related to areas of expertise and specialism both individual and collective.
5   To promote professional and, where appropriate, personal development for members of the Department.
6   To be ready to respond to perceived need, as appropriate, in the initiation and development of new areas of academic and professional work.

In carrying out its remit, the Head of the School said, 'The Department seeks to operate an equal opportunities policy in the pursuit of its goals'.

The attainment of Corporate Status led to further changes in management style with, in particular, the devolving of financial control and decision making. Pressure was two-fold: first on the School to generate income and secondly, as a cost centre with a devolved budget. The Polytechnic, Faculty and School, were active constituent parts of the market economy culture. The School's Management Group evolved as Head of School (Chair), Deputy Head of School, Manager of the Research Centre, Field Coordinators, and Head of the Recreation Service; all other Principal Lecturers advised the Head and assisted with policy making and implementation. The Management Group met on a weekly basis which integrated with termly meetings of the School Board of Study. Members acted as a channel of communication with other members of staff. Decision making was, if possible, shared through solution seeking and corporate responsibility but, if necessary, the Head took hard management decisions. Professor Murdoch had incorporated an ideas-based approach to development with significant delegation that was, at the same time, both stimulated and supported by the Head of School.

Professor Murdoch summarized the *tensions* that would arise under the new structure in the following way:

Figure 5.5: Tensions

Partnerships	↔	Need to Survive
Central Policies	↔	Professional Credibility
Quality Assurance	↔	Declining Resources
Academic Standards	↔	Delivery Demands
Market Economy	↔	Service to Community
Management	↔	Teaching/Research
Education	↔	Sport, Leisure, Health

The management responsibilities were complex and were set out as a figure. The agenda items ranged from Academic Board reports to timetable details and from the dangers arising from using old buildings with asbestos in their structures to securing large research grants.

Figure 5.6: Management responsibilities

STAFFING

To MONITOR staff conditions and workloads
To MONITOR the implementation of the timetable
    as it effects staff, conditions and workload
To PROPOSE and set up staff conferences
To PROMOTE staff development and appraisal
To OVERSEE appointment of new staff

FINANCE

To REVIEW finance management
    strategies and align with
    Polytechnic procedures
To CHECK the accuracy and security
    of the internal system
To PROPOSE financial policy in
    relation to internal needs and
    the implications of external
    developments
To DESIGN the format and set
    timetable for annual budgeting
To ENSURE free exchange of
    information re-finance within the
    Department

ACADEMIC

To OVERVIEW academic standards
To CLARIFY the distinctiveness of
    courses
To INCULCATE in staff a sense of
    career development and balance
    this within the Department
To ENCOURAGE professional debate
    among students and staff
To PROMOTE academic development
    of the Department
To ENCOURAGE a full understanding
    of the detail of courses throughout
    the Department

M A N A G E M E N T

EXTERNAL AFFAIRS

To LIAISE within the Department, the
    Polytechnic and external groups/
    committees
To PROMOTE the Department, and the
    Institution
To BRING to the Department relevant
    influences from the market place
To INITIATE from outside influences
To CONSIDER the relationship of
    various 'arms' of the Department to
    central policies
To MONITOR student recruitment and
    relevant publicity
To DESIGN a strategy for short courses

STUDENTS

To FACILITATE dialogue and
    information flow to students
To COORDINATE the work of
    the academic tutors
To MONITOR the resource
    support for students
To MONITOR the quality of
    the learning environment
To ENCOURAGE student
    representation on committees

The Faculty redesigned its courses on a two semester modular basis, with a new committee structure and with the Chelsea School taking a lead role in the implementation of the scheme from September 1994.

Figure 5.7: Modular scheme

Basic characteristics	• student responsibility and choice for learning • credit accumulation and transfer • progressive assessment • coherence of student experience • tutorial support
Semester	• two per year • 17 weeks each: one week induction, two weeks administration, 14 weeks study
Levels	• one • two • three
Tracks	• fast: seven modules • normal: six modules • slow: five modules • exemption for mature students
Modules	• two hours direct contact per week • eight–four hours per module • permitted: constructed choice, count towards minimum requirements • discretionary: not necessarily part of field, free choice
Structure	• field: coherent academic area, expertise, experience, scholarship • route: educationally associated or groups of modules • pathway: individual leading to outcome • outcome: end product
Study hours	• 1008 per year • 3024 leading to honours degree • 4032 leading to honours degree and qualified teacher status

As the institution grew from 1976 to 1998, it seemed to many that 'decision making' was further and further removed from the 'grass roots'. In an effort to overcome the feeling of 'isolation', the Directorate met once per term and the Council/Board of Governors once per year on the Eastbourne campus. Staff and students had opportunities to share concerns with the Directorate and Council/ Board of Governors and the Directorate and Council/Board of Governors to see ongoing work. The Polytechnic Director's concern was that the Academic Board should discuss in some detail and then formulate academic policy for the formal approval of the Council/Board of Governors. Below this layer, the Faculty Board had an important role which was underpinned by departmental input. This practice was to be continued by the Director of the University of Brighton.

The School's development plan for 1990 to 1995 included the development of new courses, the extension of research and consultancy, continuation of staff development and an international and a European commitment. The latter point was endorsed by the International Committee under the chairmanship of Dr Joy Standeven, 'Chelsea needs to become more European in its thinking, in view of the Polytechnic's geographical location and its commitment within its strategic plan to increase collaboration with European partners'. First Erasmus projects were successfully pursued and, later, Socrates projects were negotiated.

The 1991 White Paper, *Higher Education — A New Framework*, envisaged a graduate force equipped to deal 'with the demands of a rapidly changing working environment'. These expectations of transferable skills were considered and incorporated into the redesigned courses to include the ability to communicate readily and the development of the powers of critical thinking in a range of contexts.

Professor Murdoch felt, '. . . the School needs people with clearly developed ideas about the future of physical education and human movement who are prepared and able to articulate these views in open meetings. People who can lead, initiate, innovate within the framework of the many constraints within which we will have to operate'. Between 1986 and 1992, Professor Murdoch made a major contribution to debate and recommendations at national level. Her experience and knowledge was of direct relevance to the Sports Council and to developments within the School. In 1986 the 'great media debate' had been initiated by the press. It launched an attack on physical education for letting down the nation and failing to provide, through the schools' programmes, an adequate base for the emergence of international sportsmen and sportswomen. The Sports Council, in its strategy *Sport in the Community — The Next Ten Years*, published in 1982, recognized the role of education in the development of sport and recreation. The London and South East Councils for Sport and Recreation established a joint working party, with Miss Murdoch as a member, and issued a report, *Physical Education*, in September 1986. 'The Working Party concluded that identifying the problems and offering solutions on paper was relatively easy. However, if the time spent discussing the issues is to be of any value, then the deliberations must be translated into practical action'. The report contained 35 targeted recommendations for implementation.

Within the same year (November 1986) and arising from the joint Department of Education and Science and Department of the Environment seminar *Sport in Schools*, Miss Murdoch was recruited and commissioned by the two Departments (a first) to write a *desk study*. Her remit was to consider and report on the place and state of physical education and sport in schools in England and Wales. That was translated as 'the place of sport in the physical education curriculum' and the inquiry ranged more widely than the original remit to encompass extra-curricular activities, out of school and post-school activities. Her report, *Sport in Schools*, published in May 1987, identified seven major issues to be addressed, and was accepted as the working document to guide the School Sport Forum. This was established at the request of the two Departments, under the chairmanship of Miss Bambra in April 1987 and of which Miss Murdoch, appointed by the British Council of Physical Education, was a lead member.

The School Sport Forum report, *Sport and Young People: Partnership and Action*, published in July 1988, contained 69 recommendations, targeted at specified agencies. The report was sent to the Ministers of both Departments, and led to a government response which outlined the extent of national support and also the setting up of a select (all party) Committee of the House of Commons. For the first time, there was acknowledgment by the government of the day that the physical education profession could not carry alone the responsibility for the total sport experience to be offered to young people.

Parallel to the sport debate, the government issued, in 1986, the White Paper *Working Together — Education and Training*. The government was committed to expanding participation rates in higher education.

The 1988 Education Reform Act provided for the implementation of the National Curriculum. The aims of education had been set out in the White Paper *Better Schools* in 1985, and preparations had been ongoing leading to the consultation document, *The National Curriculum 5–16*, published in July 1987. The physical education profession welcomed the inclusion of the subject as one of 10 foundation subjects in the National Curriculum, although it was the last area to be developed. Its inclusion reinforced, within the world of physical education and sport, the principle of the teacher of physical education as the key provider and facilitator.

Miss Murdoch and Miss McConachie-Smith had responded to this document on behalf of Chelsea, and both contributed to the interim 'Working Group on Physical Education in the National Curriculum' established by the British Council of Physical Education. Its report contained nine principles and was used by the Physical Education Working Group of the National Curriculum Council, set up on 10 July 1990 under the chairmanship of Ian Beer and with Miss Murdoch as a member, as its working document. As Margaret Talbot, also a member of the National Physical Education Working Group said,

> Physical education, when it is introduced in September 1992 as a foundation subject in the National Curriculum, should provide the opportunity for all school-aged children, whatever their talents and interests, to experience a wide range of sport and dance activities.

With Miss Murdoch and Miss McConachie-Smith making major contributions to the work of the National Curriculum Physical Education Working Group, or its sub-groups and while this input took place off campus, the School, nevertheless, had the benefit of up-to-date and advanced thinking and some early knowledge of possible forthcoming policies useful in the reconstruction of both its initial teacher training programme and its in-service education and training work for the 1990s. The philosophy for the development of the physical education programme and the individual subjects can be encapsulated in the following figure:

Figure 5.8: Related areas in the development of a physical education programme

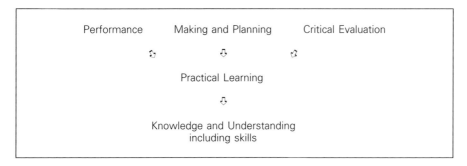

During 1979–80, the four-year BEd(Hons) degree course with a compulsory two 'A' level entry qualification, a step towards raising standards in the teaching profession, had been reconstructed. The specialist physical education route was led, within the School, by Miss McConachie-Smith. She commented,

> The physical education component has been designed to reflect the major aims of the whole course, that is, a concurrent professional honours degree. Subject and teaching studies are integrated within the component so that the students' personal education progresses in combination with the development of professional competence.

The course provided experience in a wide variety of physical activities, appropriate theoretical perspectives, study in depth, synthesis and evaluation, together with teaching practice in both primary and secondary schools and in serial and block modes. Initially validated by the Council for National Academic Awards for the September 1981 intake, the BEd(Hons) degree was reviewed during 1985–86. In February 1987 it was the first Polytechnic course to be revalidated under delegated authority, granted to the institution by the Council for National Academic Awards in April 1986. The first group of men to complete the BEd(Hons) degree course graduated in July 1986, with Glen Pierce the first male student to hear of his successful appointment to a teaching post at Eton College and in 1997 he was still working there. The external examiners reported, 'It is clear from the examination of this cohort of students (1982–86) that thorough and competent preparation for the teaching profession is considered a major concern of the School'. By 1989–90 external examiners commented, 'we were left with the impression of a strong developing, well-managed professional degree, which is certainly up-to-date and, in many important ways, anticipates and prepares for change'. In 1990, Miss McConachie-Smith prepared a paper for the Teacher Education Division of the School, entitled 'Model of a physical education teacher'.

The essential points can be summarized as:

Model = teacher with a subject specialism;
Teacher = empathy with, and understanding of, children;
wide variety of teaching strategies and skills;

an understanding of their own and children's learning processes;

a capacity to be self-critical;

a capacity to think and make professional decisions independently; and

a broad view of their role as an educator.

Subject = understanding physical education and physical activity,
Specialism involvement across the full age range from toddlers to the
(PE) elderly;

concept of physical education which links the school subject with community involvement and the world of sport and the arts;

an appreciation of different roles they may have in dealing with different client groups of participants and performers in the school and the community;

through studying their own and a second teaching subject/ area an awareness of the cross curricular potential of their subject.

At the same time, the Muska Mosston Spectrum of Teaching Styles developed in the United States of America from research conducted in the 1960s, was used to '... alert students to the necessary bond between teaching, learning and desired outcomes'. The 10 styles, integrated into one structure as the 'Spectrum', were progressive in nature. They ranged from command or directed; through practice; reciprocal or peer; self-check or self-evaluation; inclusion; guided discovery or convergent thinking; divergent thinking; individual programme or learners design; learner initiated; to self-teaching and were applicable irrespective of subject or discipline.

In 1991 Barry Copley was appointed Course Leader of the BEd(Hons) Physical Education degree course and Senior Internal Examiner. He continued to coordinate a very professional degree course on which students also achieved a high standard of practical work and were well versed in issues concerning the National Curriculum — physical education component.

The Council for the Accreditation of Teacher Education was established under *Circular 3/84* and published its criteria for the approval of courses, which included,

> For the continued accreditation of teacher education courses, the Council for the Accreditation of Teacher Education, requires that staff concerned with such courses in higher education, should have recent, relevant school experience and that this experience should be the equivalent of one term in every five years.

This policy led to changes in the staff development programme with identified staff spending 20 days teaching in primary or secondary schools, during the course of an academic year.

Staff development was a continuous process and the main areas for training, experience or study can be grouped under seven general headings as follows:

(i)   teaching/lecturing/supervision, coaching and managerial experience;
(ii) membership of committees, working groups and panels, both internal and external to the Institution;
(iii) study for further academic and/or professional qualifications;
(iv) presentation of keynote papers to professional organizations by invitation;
(v)   research and consultancy;
(vi) publications; and
(vii) attendance at conferences/conventions of professional organizations, of which they are members.

Under the staff development policy, each member had evaluation and appraisal sessions annually with the Head of School when a programme for the following year, based on analysis of the previous year's development, was agreed. A willingness and determination to meet challenges was continually displayed and was essential if staff were to keep abreast of changes in education and subject development.

The Council was reconstituted in 1989 with accreditation granted under *Circular 24/89* arrangements plus *Circular 18/89*. The Education (Teachers) Regulations 1989, made provision for and led to the establishment of BA(Hons) degree courses with Qualified Teacher Status. In September 1993, the BEd course was therefore replaced by the BA(Hons) Qualified Teacher Status course and met the criteria set out in *Circular 9/92*. Initially, five routes were offered; one with the single subject physical education and four with physical education and a second subject. Professor Murdoch noted,

> There is evidence that some students would prefer to concentrate more specifically on chosen aspects of physical education, dance, sport and recreation to enhance their depth of knowledge in subject studies. In the light of the increased interest in GCSE '0', 'A' level and National Vocational Qualifications in physical education, dance and sport studies, and the emerging scenario of professional developments in coach education and community recreation, this would seem to be an appealing and viable alternative.

The role of the physical education teacher was seen in the future to,

> . . . encompass primary work, secondary work and community links, especially with sports clubs, enabling children to have greater opportunities for participating in sport and dance and to improve continuity in progression from 5 years to school leaving to adulthood.

To fulfil this brief, the opportunity was taken from September 1996 to offer only the single subject route, physical education and, from September 1997, approval was given by the Teacher Training Agency for Chelsea to offer specialist physical education courses for potential teachers, for the National Curriculum Key Stages II and III. The Teacher Training Agency, from 1995, had taken responsibility for student number allocations and the funding of teacher training places in institutes of higher education.

Within the BA(Hons) PEd QTS course from September 1996, students were offered more subject specific modules such as a complete module covering examination work together with modules in community issues, sports management and leisure. More time was devoted to practical activities and there were whole modules covering the content of gymnastics, dance, games, athletics, swimming and outdoor activities, mainly for year I students followed by modules on pedagogy for each of the six areas. There had also been dramatic changes in the supervision of students on school practice from 1992/93 under the Department for Education *Circular 9/92* for initial teacher training secondary and the Department for Education *Circular 14/93* for initial teacher training primary with schools undertaking the major responsibility for training students.

The partnership school-based model in initial teacher education can be set out as follows:

Figure 5.9: Essential features of a partnership model

SCHOOL PERSONNEL	UNIVERSITY PERSONNEL
CO-ORDINATING/PROFESSIONAL TUTOR	**LIAISON/LINK TUTOR**
Introduction to school based issues beyond subject knowledge and teaching. Induction into teaching as a profession. Liaison with Link Tutor. Monitoring of student assessment.	Liaison between schools and higher education institution. Monitoring quality and coherence of school based aspects of the course. (10 to 12 schools per tutor, per practice)
MENTOR	**SUBJECT TUTOR**
School based subject specialist. Student support, guidance, assessment and instruction.	Focus on craft knowledge at higher education institution. Subject specialist support when needed during school based aspects of the course.

Through the Partnership Resource Scheme, schools were remunerated financially for their services. There was now a shift in the balance of the course from theory to practice, less reliance on educational disciplines and a focus on classroom competence.

The setting up of a joint research project *School based Teacher Education Partnerships* in 1994 previously piloted by Liverpool John Moores University (I M Marsh Centre) with the University of Brighton (Chelsea School of Physical Education, Sports Science, Dance and Leisure) enabled the collection of valuable data from the first two years of operation of the enhanced school involvement in initial teacher training. A number of publications have resulted from this cooperation.

A team from the Office for Standards in Education had visited Chelsea from 29 November to 3 December 1993, 15 to 18 March and 18 to 29 April 1994 to inspect teaching, management and partnership with teaching practice schools. The members of the visiting party had used the following six areas for assessment:

• Quality of admissions policy and the selection procedures
• Quality of the training process in developing the teaching competencies
• Quality and consistency of assessment of students' competencies
• Students' subject knowledge for teaching the relevant age range
• Students' planning, teaching and classroom management
• Students' assessment, recording and reporting of pupils' progress.

The summary of the OFSTED report stated: 'The quality of the undergraduate training is very good in physical education . . .'. 'In the PGCE, the training is very good in dance . . . and satisfactory in physical education'. Other comments made reference to the National Curriculum orders, attainment targets, planning and evaluation.

The OFSTED report also made reference to facilities available to the Chelsea School in the following way,

> In physical education, because of the number of different courses that has to be sustained, accommodation at Eastbourne is under serious pressure. The lack of a sports hall and the shortage of rehearsal spaces at some times during the year are major weaknesses for an intensive practical course. Students have to be transported to off-site spaces for some of their course work, and this is a further drain on resources. It is also becoming increasingly difficult to carry out routine maintenance.

From February 1994, the University of Brighton established a Partnership in Education Committee, which provided an additional tier of management and was seen as part of the chain of consultation between schools and the institution to reinforce the place of partnership within the overall management structure of the institution. Chelsea had always made a major input to in-service education and training at local, regional and national levels. In this fourth era provision ranged from: practical courses in a variety of activities; school based consultancies related to the development of the National Curriculum in physical education; the East Sussex INSET programme; mentorship training days; the Essex Partnership, the induction of newly qualified teachers, led by Miss Joyce Allen and Dr Laurie Bolwell; out county courses on teaching styles; pupil profiling and records of achievement; to postgraduate work at Certificate, Master and Doctorate levels.

Another important partnership developed when, in 1987, the National Coaching Foundation was designated the coaching arm of the Sports Council with responsibility for the coordination of coaching and coach education. Within the space of a few months' discussion, the National Coaching Foundation, South East base, was opened in September 1988, with Chelsea as the designated resource centre housing the unit in Hillbrow Cottage. Suzanne Law, a BSc(Hons) Sports Science graduate from Chelsea (July 1988) was appointed as the Regional Development Officer (later Senior Coaching Development Officer) and Roger Neuss, a member of the Chelsea staff, acted as the Regional Coordinator. The centre's brief was to develop a coach education programme in the Sports Council's South East Region covering Kent, Surrey, East and West Sussex. Over its 10 year existence, it has worked with the Sports Council, the National Governing Bodies of Sport, staff of the Chelsea School and other institutions of higher and further education, the local authorities and clubs, to provide quality initial and in-service education for coaches at all levels and to raise the profile and status of coaches and coaching in the South East.

In 1991, the National Champion Coaching Scheme for 11–16-year-olds was established locally under the title ACCESS (Active Champion Coaching for Eastbourne Schools Sport) with the Chelsea School as headquarters. Seven sports were offered: badminton, basketball, cricket, hockey, netball, soccer and tennis, 152 children were enrolled and 27 coaches participated in the scheme. The long-term intention was for ACCESS to become Active Champion Coaching for East Sussex Schools but, from 1995, the National Champion Coaching Scheme became one of the major programmes within the new National Junior Sports Programme.

The Council for National Academic Awards had granted associated institution status to the National Coaching Foundation and the Coaching Diploma for Senior Coaches was developed and validated. Fifteen members participated in the deliberations with Paul McNaught-Davis as the Brighton Polytechnic representative on the Working Party and Mrs Gillian Burke, the HMI member; Sue Campbell, Director, National Coaching Foundation, took the chair. The first students graduated in 1996. With the demise of the Council for National Academic Awards, the National Coaching Foundation Consortium Council took responsibility for the review process and future development of the course. Further direct links with the community and the Sports Council were established when the following very representative group of the East Sussex School Sport Development Officer, the East Sussex Adviser/Inspector of Physical Education, two East Sussex Curriculum Development Officers, the Regional Officer for the British Sports Association for the Disabled, and the Education and Training Officer for the Sports Council (South East) were also based in Hillbrow Cottage, Chelsea School. The latter post was jointly funded by the Sports Council and the Chelsea School, with a remit to develop programmes for Sports Development Officers. The close cooperation that resulted from easy access between the above group members and Chelsea staff and students led to joint projects which benefitted both the local schools and the regional sports community.

From the time the incorporation with Brighton Polytechnic was formalized, the students had taken part in the discussions leading to the amendment of the constitution of the now enlarged Students' Union. Paul Finnerty, Chelsea School, was elected by the students as Vice-President (Eastbourne) for 1979–80. His role was to coordinate Brighton Polytechnic Students' Union activities across all Eastbourne sites. Bishopsbourne, where the permanent secretariat was based, was retained as the Students' Union office, together with the union bar, laundry and other facilities, and provided amongst its many services, the ticket outlet for events, the Union shop, bulletin board, minibus terminus and lost property office. Chelsea students continued to have membership rights on Brighton Polytechnic, and later, from September 1992, the University of Brighton committees following formal elections, but as members of the student body as a whole and not necessarily as 'Chelsea' students, except for the School's boards and committees. With an enlarged institution, changes in relationships were seen with, for example, from 1993–94, the University of Brighton producing a 194 page Student Handbook, containing advice and information on the following 12 sections: becoming a student; your rights; your obligation; money matters; a guide to learning resources; computer services and facilities; students services; Students' Union; where to eat at the University; leisure and cultural activities; shops, travel and general; student regulations and disciplinary procedures. It was compiled by the Academic Registry in cooperation with Student Services and the Students' Union. Students also received Chelsea supplements with information about each course and module outlines. The Eastbourne package included information about entry to local nightclubs, discount facilities on University of Brighton Students' Union run entertainments and cheaper membership of the Sports Federation. The year started with Societies Fairs when contact could be made with officers and clubs.

Chelsea students representing the larger institution have always acquitted themselves well in the British Colleges' Championships, the British Polytechnics' Championships and the British Universities' Championships. In addition and, in order that all Chelsea students fulfilled the mandatory requirements for experience in playing and officiating in a number of games and sports under competitive conditions, the Professional Studies Association was established and a sum of money was specifically allocated for this purpose. The double dilemma of allegiance to Chelsea and/or representing Brighton Polytechnic had been resolved. Chelsea students have represented Great Britain in the World Student Games and Olympic Games and their own countries in the Commonwealth Games. For example, Chelsea had 11 students at the World Student Games in Edmonton in 1983, where Sarah Rowell won the Gold Medal in the Marathon; she competed in the London Marathon and the Olympic Marathon in 1984 when she came third and 14th respectively and, in 1985, she achieved the British Record of 2 hours 28 minutes 6 seconds in coming second in the London Marathon. Her success continued in 1986 when she was the outright first in the Seven Sisters Mixed Marathon. She entered the World Mountain Running Trophy five times from 1989 to 1995 winning the Silver position in 1992, and was the British and English Fellrunning Champion in 1995 and in 1996. Ricky Burrell had been a member of the Bronze Medal 4×100 metres freestyle team when a British record of 3 minutes 30.10 seconds was set in the 1978 Commonwealth Games in Edmonton. He won a silver medal in the 4×100 metres freestyle team event with a new British record of 3 minutes 26.98 seconds (Ricky swam his leg in 50.97 seconds) at the British Commonwealth Games held in Brisbane in 1982.

Ricky was captain of the Brighton Polytechnic men's swimming team, when 17 teams participated in the British Polytechnic National Swimming Championships held in the Chelsea School's swimming pool on Saturday 13 March 1982. He will be remembered for his enthusiasm and encouragement of other Chelsea competitors. His delight bubbled over at the end of the evening when, even though he was soaking wet, he enthusiastically embraced and kissed the Director's wife, Mrs Elizabeth Hall, as she presented him with the men's swim team pennant.

The women's team were equally successful under the captaincy of Karen Harper and won the women's swim team pennant. The mixed medley relay team won the Speedo Cup and the combined men's and women's results led to the retention of the Wilkinson Sword Trophy for another year. Early in 1998, the University of Brighton men's basketball team won the Halifax BUSA National Championships beating Loughborough University on their home court by 77 goals to 64 goals. In so doing, the team claimed the coveted number one position in the United Kingdom. As an integral part of their training, Chelsea students learnt to organize, administer and officiate at sports events. This expertise was put into practice when the World Student Games were held at Sheffield in 1991. Volunteer Chelsea students, trained by Roger Neuss, '. . . assisted in day-to-day management of the Games'. Students assisted at the Special Olympics held at Brighton in 1986. From 8 to 15 May 1987, 17 students from the adapted physical education course acted as officials at the Special Olympic Games held on the Isle of Wight, under the leadership of Mrs Ruth Prideaux.

Starting in 1977 with the Federation Cup, year II students ball-girled or acted as line judges for the next 10 years at the annual International Ladies Tennis Championships at Eastbourne, sponsored by firms such as Pilkington Glass, Volkswagen and BMW. The students valued the experience of working and mixing with international tennis players like Martina Navratilova, Chris Evert, Billie Jean King, Betty Stove, Wendy Turnbull, Helena Sukova and Jo Durie.

Chelsea children's camps continued to be organized each summer by students at Hindsland for pupils from London schools, following the raising of funds to support this venture and service. Opportunities to assist in educational cruises, with the physical programme during voyages and, at Camp America, teaching sports activities to children in residential camps, continued to be readily grasped by year II and year III students.

Each year, courses within the School were reviewed and evaluated and changes made to improve their quality or appropriateness. Part of this evaluation process depended on student feedback, either through the completion of questionnaires or through discussions with tutors or through presentations and reporting of views at Subject/Course Board meetings.

When the polytechnics were granted university status, the Mayor of Eastbourne, Councillor Maurice Skilton, hosted a reception on behalf of the Borough, in the Gold Room at the Winter Garden on Thursday 10 September 1992, to launch the University of Brighton in Eastbourne. On Sunday 20 September 1992, *A Festival of Sport and Fun* was hosted by the University at The Saffrons ground, Eastbourne, in aid of Chailey Heritage (Challenge). The Director, Professor David Watson, captained the University of Brighton XI in a cricket match versus an England Ladies XI, which was umpired by Mrs Ruth Prideaux and honourably drawn. Councillor Skilton, with the agreement of David Watson and the ladies' captain, Karen Smithies, presented the cup to the women's team at the end of the afternoon to be retained until a re-match could be arranged. £1330 had been raised for the charity. Will a return match be played during the Chelsea Centenary celebrations in the summer of 1999?

The institution has always encouraged 'excellence' in sport and, from 1989–1990 to 1996, the Polytechnic (continued by the University) awarded five sports scholarships to talented students each year, worth up to £500 to the individual student over his/her course.

Initially, to inaugurate the scheme, larger sums of money had been allocated, for example:

1989–90   £3000
1990–91   £12,000   (year leading to the World Student Games in Sheffield)
1991–92   £8500
1992–93   £5000

The intention of the scheme was to attract good quality sports people to the Polytechnic/University. By 1996 there were no applications for a scholarship from prospective students. The scheme was, therefore, revamped and a fund of £2000 per year identified and allocated to assist high quality performers with competition expenses. Normally, the sum awarded was between £250 and £300 but students were able to reapply for further support.

Chelsea had always kept detailed student records which were often used to make course transcriptions, and, in this era, as well as this formal information, students' personal profiles were also kept. These were a record of development: practically, professionally, academically and other related information compiled by the students, in consultation with tutorial staff. The detail included: an initial self-assessment of strengths and weaknesses; goals/objectives; summary of progress; and general comments/observations on physical education expertise or practical ability in each area of work. The move towards more independent learning and self-responsibility was therefore continued in this way.

Recruitment to the School and particularly to the undergraduate degree courses had been consistently buoyant with, for example in 1993, 17 applicants for every BA (QTS) PE place; 18 for a BSc Sports Science place; three for a BA Leisure Policy and Administration place and five for a Postgraduate Certificate in Education place, giving a total of 3282 applicants for 206 places on the undergraduate courses. There were 160 applicants for 32 places on the postgraduate course. (See Figure 5.10)

While the School tried to implement an equal opportunities policy in student recruitment, applications from ethnic groups remained at the 2 per cent level, but applications from mature candidates have risen from 7 to 22 per cent.

Employment rates were equally impressive with, in 1989:

BEd(Hons) Physical Education	96 per cent employed with 87 per cent into teaching posts
	2 per cent into further study
PGCE Physical Education/Dance	95 per cent employed with 89 per cent into teaching posts

The Challenge of Change in Physical Education

BSc(Hons) Sports Science

61 per cent employed
23 per cent into further study.

By 1992 the figures were:

BEd

91.8 per cent employed
84 per cent into teaching

PGCE

83 per cent into teaching

BSc

66.5 per cent employed
22 per cent further study.

By 1996 the figures were:

BA QTS PEd

88.7 per cent employed
82.5 per cent into teaching

PGCE PEd/Da

98.3 per cent employed
80.7 per cent into teaching

BSc

62.7 per cent into employment
16.2 per cent further study

BA

78.2 per cent into employment
21.7 per cent further study.

Figure 5.10: Student numbers — September 1997

Course	Year I	Year II	Year III	Year IV	TOTALS
BA(H) QTS Physical Education	92	94	79	85	350
BA(H) QTS Upper Primary/Lower Secondary	21				21
BSc(H) SE Sport Science/Sport Exercise	112	104	93		309
BA(H) Leisure Policy and Administration		32	28		60
BA(H) Leisure and Sport Management	25				25
BA(H) Leisure and Sport Studies	34				34
PGCE	33				33
TOTALS	317	230	200	85	832

Figure 5.11: Staff in the School — September 1997

Head of School	1	Visiting Research Fellows	4
Teaching and Research	24	Research Students	18
Administrative	9		
Technical	5		
TOTAL	39		22

162

While Chelsea Old Students continued to be successful in teaching, advising, lecturing, inspecting, counselling, coaching, further study, and community service in physical education, sport and recreation, their Association had ceased from the 1970s to attract new members and it folded in 1982. The Association was reactivated by Miss Wendy Burrows, a member of staff, in 1985 because of 'genuine interest and desire', by that set of students to, 'keep in touch' but, to date, no male student has joined the Association, although some of the BSc men graduates met the same weekend as Open Day in 1989. With Miss Murdoch as Chairman, Miss Burrows as Secretary and Newsletter Editor, Vanessa Hall, Treasurer, Jeanette Pollitt, Assistant Secretary, and a Committee of seven (Linda Jeffery, Venetia Cosia, Lee Burlinson, Nicola Cherry, Miss McConachie-Smith, Miss Verdin and Mrs Tatlock) the Association issued its first Newsletter in 1986 with 640 Old Students on the mailing list. Since 1985, there has been an annual meeting and newsletter and the Chelsea Centenary Committee, under the chairmanship of Ann-Marie Latham, was formed in 1994. With the establishment of the University of Brighton Graduates' Association, in 1994, and the Chelsea Old Students' Association not a driving force within the University, it was agreed at the AGM in 1996 to review the future of the Association during the Chelsea Centenary Conference to be held from 28 to 31 May 1999. The current dilemma for the Association was summarized in the following two questions: *to retain a sense of permanence through continuation* or *to become a part of the alumni of the larger institution?*

At the second University of Brighton degree ceremonies held on 15 and 16 July 1993, the first Honorary Degree (Doctor of Science) nominated by the Faculty of Education, Sport and Leisure was awarded to Susan Campbell who, at that time, was the Chief Executive of the National Coaching Foundation, for her services to coach education, youth sport and a continuing commitment to physical education. In her acceptance speech, she questioned how we could be optimists in a world that seemed hell-bent on destruction, and responded by suggesting that the adoption of the five Hs — 'Hope, Humility, Have-a-go, Honour and Humour could make dreams come true for ordinary people'. At the February 1997 Ceremony, Chris Boardman, the Olympic Gold Medallist in cycling, was similarly honoured.

In the approved development plan for 1996 to 2001, prepared in October 1996, Professor Murdoch and her staff envisaged that the work of the School, over the next five years, will concentrate on:

(i)   creating as good a learning and working environment as possible against a diminishing resource base;

(ii) providing appropriate new accommodation for the academic work of the School through completion of the sport development plan, which includes a bid for a contribution towards a regional academy/institute of sport;

(iii) developing and implementing a strategic and focused research policy;

(iv) pursuing a modest development in the academic profile of the School to allow for current national developments to be encompassed;

(v)   maintaining a leading role in professional and academic development at regional, national and international level;

(vi) developing and implementing a realistic income policy.

These aims were not necessarily in priority order. The planned expansion was from 757 students in 1996–97 to 1140 in 2000–01.

Throughout the fourth era, as the 'incorporation' proceeded, the desire on the part of staff for personal participation in the running of Chelsea did not wane. This attitude was understandable, although it was also very time consuming. The practice of delegation appeared to exclude some and to give power to others. A balance had to be achieved if the rapidly expanding School within an evergrowing institution was to function efficiently, but with everyone feeling involved and able to contribute to the policy making process. Chelsea aimed through its committee structure of School Board, sub-committees, subject boards, working groups and School meetings to retain the democratic involvement of all staff. Presentation of papers was followed by open discussion with awareness of current developments, support for the implementation of appropriate innovations and universal recognition of the need for accountability evident before policy decisions were made.

Resilience, stamina, adaptability, capacity to work and courage of convictions have all been required by the Head and staff of Chelsea during the fourth quarter of the century. During this era, there had been two separate proposals and feasibility exercises to move Chelsea to the Falmer campus. The first proposal and exercise followed an Audit Commission investigation of the financial affairs of the Polytechnic in 1986 and was detailed in the consultation document published by the East Sussex County Education Officer in July 1987, *Brighton Polytechnic: Consolidation at Brighton*. The second proposal within the Polytechnic's accommodation strategy suggested that, '. . . the Chelsea School . . . should be established at Falmer . . .'. The Board of Governors received a progress report on 9 July 1990 and reaffirmed the intention to withdraw from Eastbourne. In the *Strategic Plan for 1992 to 1996* the following commitment was made:

> the rate and pattern of growth in the Polytechnic's student population will require the maintenance of a significant presence in Eastbourne for the current planning period and beyond. Work in education, human movement and sports sciences and the paramedical areas will be based there until at least 2002, and accommodation for it will be maintained and improved accordingly.

The resolution, by the Directorate and Board of Governors in March 1992 led by its Chairman, Michael Aldrich, for the institution to retain a flourishing campus in Eastbourne was welcomed, not only by staff and students but also by the local community with whom good relationships had been fostered and cemented, personal contacts established, partnerships forged, service given and mutual respect attained. In the *Strategic Plan for 1998–2003*, agreed by the Board of Governors in

January 1998, one of the University's priorities was, '. . . to improve further facilities across the University with a particular focus on the Falmer and Eastbourne campuses'. By April 1998, an institutional *Strategy for Sport and Leisure to 2006* had been produced and approved. It included the following statement,

> Major new provision on the Eastbourne campus will include a sports hall and artificial turf pitch on the Hillbrow site. A later project will provide refurbishment of gymnasia and the swimming pool, a science park of eight laboratories and analysis areas for biomechanics, motor skills and physiology, and a centre for research staff and students. If possible, the development will include a community leisure provision and links with other local providers will increase potential through shared use.

Throughout her period of leadership of the School, Professor Murdoch's willingness to pursue 'scholastic/academic' subject development, was reflected in the progress made by the Chelsea School in achieving the research objective set by the Director of the Polytechnic, in new course development, in growth in student numbers and student and staff academic, personal and professional development. By 1997, the curriculum was presented to students through a simplified modular scheme with more independent learning structures and fewer team teaching modules. The success of the students' independent learning was based on their ability to set and achieve self-motivation targets and rigorous self-monitoring and evaluation. Flexibility in provision of course content and opportunities to learn had been progressed and modernized.

The School, however, and particularly with the implementation of the recommendations contained in the Dearing Report, *Higher Education in the Learning Society*, published in July 1997, can never stand still and rest on its laurels. The Report produced by the National Committee of Inquiry in Higher Education and quickly dubbed by students 'pay as you learn', will provide a political opportunity for renewal of the social and economic mission of higher education. There was a government response to this Report entitled, *Higher Education for the 21st Century*. 1999, therefore, brings the dawn of a new era, the dawn of a new millennium and further changes for the Chelsea School.

Professor Murdoch retired on 31 July 1998 and was honoured by the University of Brighton; she was made Professor Emeritus from 1 August 1998. Six key elements and characteristics or hallmarks of her leadership and success as the Head of the Chelsea School during the third phase of the fourth era can be summarized as:

- *learning* at all stages of education;
- *academic and professional development* in physical education, dance, sport and leisure;
- expansion of *research* within the School's programme;

- implementing a *delegated management style*;
- building and maintaining a visible School and personal *profile* at national and international levels;
- original *ideas*.

Even if, because of the pace of change, Professor Murdoch did not always have the time to fully develop an idea before moving on to the next she, nevertheless, had the capacity to take Chelsea forward from 1985 to 1998 and '...**to progress the best ideas**'.

6   Conclusions

Hillbrow   Location, 1998

... 'to know and understand tradition'.

To know 'Chelsea' is to appreciate that there has always been a 'pioneering' spirit of optimism manifest in the outcomes of the wide range of work and achievements of staff and students from 1898 to 1998. This characteristic attitude and philosophy stemmed from the vision of its founder, Dorette Wilke, through the initiatives of its various leaders and staff to the progressive contribution of its students and Old Students as committed professional members of communities, whether general, specialist, local, regional, national or international. It is true that 'Chelsea' has had many troughs, as well as peaks, in its history, but it has always been recognized as 'a centre of excellence' in academic, practical and professional terms of which it and its various parent bodies can be proud. Such recognition, however, has only been attained through consistency of purpose and dedicated work.

The colourful personality of Dorette Wilke enabled her to influence persons in authority, to enthuse staff and students to work hard to attain both personal satisfaction and public recognition and to instil in staff and students an attitude of professionalism and service to the community through teaching and voluntary work. Her indomitable spirit and farsightedness led to the establishment of an institution that, despite its numerous traumatic experiences, has grown in stature and status and flourished for 100 years. As one Old Student wrote in 1939,

> In Domina, we had put in front of us an example of gaiety and tremendous vitality in work — of great courage in personal and professional difficulties — of great generosity, again both personal and professional — an eager investigating spirit in work — and a great love of children and of humanity. It is a great picture to keep in front of us.

167

Has that picture been to the front throughout the College's first century? The early and continuing strong external reputation, achieved through persistent effort, creativeness and, above all, a capacity to identify, analyse and then rise to meet new crises, always placed the Chelsea College/School in as favourable position as possible to face the challenges of the future. That premise holds true today and should encourage the School to go forward with renewed confidence. 'Her beginning was small, but sincere and built on a basis of sound principles'.

In contrast to the flamboyant Domina, May Fountain was unassuming, almost to the point of being a retiring personality. She was, however, knowledgeable, persistent, thorough and an efficient organizer. Staff, students, governors, parents and official visitors were impressed and influenced by her genuine concern for the College in the service of education and for physical education in the service of humanity. She had both a professional integrity and a humane approach to problems. At times, especially ones of intense pressure and stress, her energy and enthusiasm seemed inexhaustible. The pioneering role of creating training opportunities for women as physical educationists that paralleled the emancipation of women, was extended during May Fountain's term of office, albeit in a quiet but, nevertheless, effective way. The very turbulent and disturbing times of her era seemed to act as an additional challenge and challenges were there to be faced and conquered. Perhaps it was her strict self-discipline, incorporating the full acceptance of personal and professional responsibilities towards the individuals of the community as a whole, of which she was part, that enabled her to achieve so much. As one Old Student commented, 'Miss Fountain was severe, but absolutely fair' and 'dedicated to physical education at Chelsea'.

In contrast again, Audrey Bambra had a dominant personality. She was a fiercely independent perfectionist to whom second best was not acceptable. Her thinking was often way ahead of her time but, again, her tireless energy and neverending enthusiasm enabled her to drive herself, her staff and Chelsea forward to be in the vanguard of changes in physical education and human movement studies. The role and status of both College and subject was prized and jealously guarded. In contending with numerous changes in government policy, the next change being proposed almost before the last one had been implemented, she made various determined attempts for the retention of Chelsea either as an independent institution or as the focal and key member of any new organization. When it was clear to her that, continuing as an independent institution was not possible, she first suggested and discussed with senior members of HMI a 'national college'. This idea had previously been suggested by Miss Fountain, but this time Miss Bambra envisaged each of the existing specialist women's colleges of physical education developing a specific focus. Her second alternative proposition envisaged Chelsea, as the core of the new Eastbourne College, with other fields of study in supportive roles. While the 'new' governors, officers of the local education authority and committees of East Sussex County Council, from 1974, appreciated the strengths of Chelsea they had, nevertheless, to operate within the wider perspective of higher education within the county of East Sussex and they had areas of greater responsibility than one college. Both proposals were rejected and, therefore, it seemed inevitable to Miss

Bambra that, through merger, Chelsea College would lose the position of leadership in physical education that it had earned during the past 75 years. In practice, her fears did not materialize but she remained and will be remembered, as 'a powerful leader with an individual style'.

Patricia Kingston and Gillian Burke within the East Sussex College of Higher Education and Brighton Polytechnic, respectively, identified a forward looking role for the Chelsea School. At the same time, they were cognizant of previous professional and academic standards as well established traditions, which they upheld.

Elizabeth Murdoch, with typical Scottish durability and resourcefulness, in post as Head of Chelsea School for 13 of the last 22 years, maintained the high profile for Chelsea, physical education and sport internally first, within Brighton Polytechnic and secondly, within the University of Brighton and externally at home and overseas. Her influence through both the written and spoken word extended from talking with local teachers and taking part in radio and television programmes, to addressing delegates at international conferences and through being a member of innumerable groups to holding key offices in many professional associations. Keen to develop partnerships and networks to assist new developments for the Chelsea School, for the professional progress of teachers, coaches, sports development officers and sports managers, she conducted two-way dialogues, rather than use the 'aggression of survival'. Her philosophy assumed that little would be achieved by threat, insecurity or undermining confidence. As far as possible, she retained the personal approach of meeting individuals, discussing and resolving issues. A solution, however, of 'seeking by approach' achieved through 'shared decision-making', also carried with it 'corporate responsibility'. During all the vicissitudes of the last era, she always remembered the importance of 'children's learning through moving' as the first and most important foundation block from which to achieve 'excellence' in physical education, dance, sport or recreational leisure.

Under her leadership, have the staff, students, and old students worked through the insecurities that arose as each specialist group developed and now attained the confidence to accept that there is no longer the need to identify each component area of work in the title of the department? Clearly, *The Chelsea School* is universally recognized and accepted for its integrity, its academic standards, its expertise and for its professional contribution to physical education, sport, dance, health, recreation and leisure.

Many tensions and dilemmas arising from the rapid pace of change have been evident in the fourth era. In leading discussion of topical issues, Professor Murdoch has sought to clarify and resolve the present complicated position. In facing up to the stark choices that had to be made, the foundations are now in place for the next period of academic, curriculum, professional and research development in the Chelsea School. In this next phase, *flexibility* could be seen to be the key quality required for progress to be achieved.

The College/School has moved from being free to train as many students as possible, through expansion and contraction, to meeting target numbers set by a central agency. The influence of education acts, official reports, political policies, government departments circulars and the Dearing Report, *Higher Education in the*

Learning Society, which challenges the next century, have been crucial in determining the size of the student body, the direction of courses, the scope of curriculum development and the basic funding to support the School's work. In the future, it would appear that *quality* will be examined through regular assessment and inspection, measured by the attainment of academic, professional and research standards and judged in scrutinizing the consequent ranking or allocated position in various league tables.

As far as possible, within financial constraints, students with appropriate qualifications, qualities and potential aptitudes have been drawn from every social class and every type of school in the United Kingdom and from many 'overseas' countries. The rich experience of meeting people with different life assumptions, may be viewed as an important by-product or as an essential element of the Chelsea-style courses and the Chelsea educational process and experience.

Was there ever a Chelsea hall mark? Was it 'loyalty'? The following quotations serve to express the students' perspective.

> Chelsea students feel a strong sense of connection with the School, and this extends to links which are maintained long after graduation.
>
> Our physical education staff came from Chelsea and I was determined to follow them and to train there.

Was it 'identification'?

> ... my abilities seemed to fit into the Chelsea requirements best.
>
> The School has a very strong identity as a centre of learning and excellence in sport and physical education, to the point that some students perceive it as a self-contained sports college and, to some extent, almost as a university in its own right. There is an interaction of factors involved in this identification with Chelsea: a strong identification with the School itself — its traditions and history — but also an identification with Eastbourne as an academic community in its own right, of which Chelsea is one part. This identity is also closely allied to a 'sports' culture. The panel was informed during the review that Chelsea School students were known by other students outside the School as 'sporties' and that there is considerable student pride in the distinctiveness of the School and its work. The student community is closeknit and relationships with the staff are good.
>
> My physical education teacher was from Chelsea and she encouraged me to apply there for my 'first choice'.

Was it 'professionalism'?

> We were particularly impressed by the good relationship within students' groups and between staff and students, and by the development of trust, consideration and cooperation. From year one to year four, students showed levels of commitment and articulateness that will make them valued members of the profession.
>
> I came away with a very strong sense of duty and responsibility and conscious that it was necessary to be a good example.

Was it enthusiasm for the subject, whether as academic study, a practical experience or a vocational outcome?

I loved the training and hated leaving College.

I loved it all, theory and practical, and shall always be glad that I had such an interesting training.

Because I was best at this at school.

Because I had good natural physical ability and was successful in all physical education at school.

The thrill of teaching and knowing that one *could* teach.

One seems to learn most in one's first years of teaching, but Chelsea gave us all that was necessary to be able to continue learning through teaching.

Or was it a combination of qualities, the accumulated outcome of their experiences as students of 'Chelsea'?

Students have always been 'heard' and 'heeded'. The high level of participation in decision making processes from informal 'drop in' to formal student/staff consultative groups and membership of the institution's committees, has had positive outcomes. The student body has been lively, loyal, vocal, influential and successful. Naturally, their *sporting* successes have been recognized and contributed not only to the standing of Chelsea, but also to that of Brighton Polytechnic and the University of Brighton within the wider and less differentiated system of national higher education.

Has the major aim of Chelsea, to educate and train 'professionals', whether they be teachers, sports scientists, sports psychologists, sports coaches, sports development officers, managers or voluntary workers, changed over the century?

The prospectus has changed its wording from 'a sound education in Physical Training' in 1898 via physical education as an academic discipline studied through aesthetic, scientific and social aspects and the study and understanding of the principles of human movement, to 'prospective secondary teachers, not only as subject specialists in physical education, but professionals with a wide understanding of their role in the school and the local community' in 1998. However, the aim of Chelsea College for the first students to qualify was to make the basis of the curriculum as broad as possible, so that they were acquainted, not only with the details of each branch, but also understood the fundamental physiological principles on which the systems of gymnastics were founded. As Sidney Skinner, the Principal of the South Western Polytechnic, said in 1906, 'The aim of the course is to give a course of physical training on a broad basis (ie not confined to teacher training). We should always have a higher aim than leading to the teaching profession only'.

By 1998, the wide range of physical activities studied was supported by relevant academic and professional studies, including physiological, psychological and social aspects of physical education. Core aspects were requisite for all students on the BA(Hons) Physical Education with Qualified Teacher Status degree course with opportunities to select areas, such as exercise and health, leisure and recreation, competitive sport, dance appreciation, special needs, gender or multicultural issues. In the 'diversified' courses: sport science focused on the sports performer and on traditional competitive sport, maximizing an individual's or team's performance; exercise science focused on exercise as a means of recreation for fitness and health promotion; leisure and sport management focused on physically active forms of recreation and dealt with many different management aspects of sport and leisure, ranging from top level competition to recreational sport; and leisure and sport studies focused on the social-scientific study of sport and leisure. These courses prepared students for careers in public, private and voluntary sectors, as professional sportsmen and women, sports centre managers, recreation officers, countryside rangers, sport/leisure development officers, community sports leaders, events promotion officers or in the fields of health promotion and consultancy. The courses offered at Chelsea have always been developed using, as appropriate, the arts and the sciences. First, however, the curriculum included theoretical studies based on the scientific principles of the day as a key feature of the course. Such an approach enabled students to understand the content of the practical elements of their training and the effects of physical exercise on the human body. Secondly, the change in emphasis, from the sciences to the arts occurred when a more aesthetic approach to the work was adopted. Finally, with the development of diversified courses, in particular the BSc(Hons) Sports Science degree, and the advancement of knowledge and methods of coaching and training, the scientific approach returned as the main focus of the undergraduate courses.

With changes in ratios of women to men staff and women to men students, has there been a cultural change in the ethos of the School?

The College had always employed both full-time and part-time women and men members of staff with each member an expert in her or his own field. The ratio, however, of women to men has changed during the century from 46:54 in 1898, to 80:20 in 1929, to 90:10 in 1958, to 68:32 in 1976 and to 31:69 in 1998. The first teacher training course was for women only with a one-year course for men only running from 1908 to 1912. The pattern of recruiting only women to courses then continued until the early 1970s although men had attended some of Domina's classes in the early 1900s. Men students were recruited first to the PGCE course, secondly to the Supplementary course and in the 1980s to the BEd courses, although they were eligible to attend specific short courses offered as in-service work. The diversified courses have always been open to women and men candidates. By April 1998, the ratio of women students to men students, in the School, was 50:50 with a ratio of 59:41 on teacher training courses and 41:59 on diversified courses. The transition, as compared with the pioneering role in higher education for women in the early days, to today's 'mixed' environment is in line with the University's aim of gender balance among the student body. The School has achieved that objective.

At no time has the College or the School had totally ideal buildings, facilities or resources, but it has always been regarded, both nationally and internationally, as a 'centre of excellence and progress', for its contribution to the education and training of students, initial and mature, undergraduate and postgraduate.

At the beginning of its second century, will the much needed sports hall, new laboratories and refurbished facilities materialize? So many times in the first century plans have been made, and feasibility exercises carried out, and so often Chelsea has had to wait for new facilities to be built or seen its 'dreams' remain unfulfilled. The latest ambitious University *Strategy for Sport*, published March 1998, indicates that the answer to that question is '*yes*'. The School will, however, have entered its next century before these plans materialize and can be fully implemented.

Throughout its history and irrespective of changes in its collegiate position and physical location, the Chelsea College and the Chelsea School have created and cemented good relationships with the local population through community service.

Professor Sir David Watson, the Director of the University of Brighton (appointed 1 September 1990), has written:

Any major change of institutional status can be a painful and worrying time for staff, students and their external supporters. I am deeply impressed by the way in which Chelsea has handled its institutional 'transformation' over the years, the manner in which its members have maintained a sense of positive contribution and the constructive effect they have had on others. I also think that this has been helped by the role of Brighton Polytechnic (now the University) as a congenial 'host' because of its strong commitment to professional practice, its more specific mission in teacher education (maintained while a lot of similar institutions 'wobbled' in this respect), and its understanding of the strengths brought by Chelsea. The University looks directly to Chelsea for leadership, not only in the field of teacher education, but also in science, social science and some of their key applications.

The University is a rich, diverse and complex organization. I believe that it is also, against a lot of the odds, a remarkably cohesive and purposeful one. The sum of its parts is a greater whole and, within it, there is a healthy sense of mutual respect across these parts. Chelsea is a vital component of this important collective enterprise, and will remain so as it forges into its new century.

The community of the University of which the Chelsea School is but a part, has developed through positive team work, supported by the ever present power of relentless goodwill and courtesy. Individuals have been encouraged to work hard, to think constructively, to utilize opportunities, to contribute to the growth of knowledge, to participate in the communication revolution and to share experiences with partners. Chelsea staff and students have played their role in the achievement of this ideal.

Chelsea has always been led by *Heads* who were *ahead of their time*. Each leader was able to rise to new challenges and to motivate staff and students to do likewise.

In 1938, at the time of the 40th birthday celebrations of Chelsea College of Physical Education, an Old Student wrote,

This College has grown up in a Polytechnic, a place where men and women work together, each with special work, but part of a larger whole. We, and all students of the College feel that this circumstance should help us to realise that all our work is part of a greater whole and it must be our pride to see that our contribution is the best we can make it.

A second Old Student said,

Rightly, we honoured Domina for her work as Founder and the first Head Mistress of the College, but brilliant and inspired though a founder's work may be, it could not succeed, or continue to flourish, without loyal support in its beginning, and vision and courage in its continuing.

The Chelsea 'spirit' has survived and, in the current search for equality of opportunity in the 'living institution', the stable central core of 'professionalism' with 'vocational relevance', accompanied by 'academic excellence' and 'research skill', has created a secure platform from which the Chelsea School can boldly enter its second century.

'. . . the challenge continues'.

Appendix I Sources of Information

Archives

Chelsea School, University of Brighton

Correspondence; magazines — COSA; minute books — COSA; minutes — Academic Board, CCPE; minute books — Chelsea School Board; memorabilia; memoranda; newsletters; newspaper cuttings; miscellaneous; papers from office of the late Miss J C McConachie-Smith; photographs; prospectuses; record books 1898–1920; regulations; reports; syllabuses.

Chelsea Library, Chelsea Old Town Hall

Annual reports and prospectuses 1895–1955 SW Polytechnic — Chelsea Polytechnic; maps; newspaper cuttings.

East Sussex County Record Office

Minute books — CCPE, governors meetings; minute books — ESCC, Education Committee.

King's College, London

Documentation — S W Polytechnic and Chelsea Polytechnic.

Physical Education Association

Archival material held at Liverpool University Library; books held at Sheffield City Library; journals from 1950 held at PEA, West Malling; minute books from 1990 held at PEA, West Malling.

Contributions from senior staff CCPE; ESCHE; Brighton Polytechnic; University of Brighton.

Personal

Correspondence; interviews; notes; papers; questionnaires; minute books of the Association of Principals of Women's Colleges of Physical Education.

Theses

Unpublished — see Select Bibliography/Further Reading p. 193.

Appendix IIa   Chelsea College of Physical Education — Staff 1929–30

Position	Name	Qualifications	Subject
Head Mistress	Miss M Fountain	Dip CCPE	
Senior Mistress	Miss R Clark	Dip CCPE	Dancing, gymnastics
College Medical Officer	Dr M L Dobbie	MD	
	Miss C Partridge	Dip CCPE	Games
	Miss O Legg	Dip DCPE	Games
	Miss H Grafton	Dip CCPE	Dancing, gymnastics
	Miss S Kreuger	Southport	Gymnastics
	Dr V Coghill	MB ChB	Anatomy
	Miss R E Procter	MA MB ChB	Hygiene
	Dr G W Halsey	Dip CCPE	Psychology
	Miss L J M Holtzmann	BSc	Physiology
	Miss D Wood	MRCS LRCP	Medical gymnastics
	Mr A E Ludlam	MSc	Mechanics
	Mr W H Kerridge	MA Mus Bach (Cantab) FRCO ARCM	Singing
	Miss H M Bruce	BSc	Physics and chemistry
Secretary of the Polytechnic	Mr H B Harper		

Appendix IIb   Chelsea College of Physical Education — Staff 1958–59

Position	Name	Qualifications	Subject
Principal	Miss A J Bambra	Dip ACPE LDTPPE	
Deputy Principal	Miss B Gough	BA	Drama
	Miss J E Baggallay	Dip DCPE LDTPPE	PE and games
	Miss C H Baker	Dip DCPE	PE and athletics
	Miss M Cadel	Dip CCPE	PE and games
Head of Science	Mr R A Collier	BSc TcLDip	Physiology
	Miss F S Cook	BSc MA	Education
	Miss G M Coombes	Dip BCPE MISTD CSP	PE and games
	Mr E T E Davies	BA BMus LRAM	Music
	Miss B M G Edwards	BA	Education
	Miss J M Harrison	BSc Teachers' Dip	Anatomy
	Mrs J M James	Dip ACPE CSP LDTPPE	PE and gymnastics
	Miss G J Jasper	Dip DCPE CSP	PE and health education
	Miss J Langridge	Dip CCPE CSP LDTPPE	PE and dance
	Miss E W Lewis	Dip BCPE CSP	PE
	Miss B Pont	Bishop Otter Dip Sup CCPE	PE and games
	Miss C Powell	Dip CCPE	PE
	Miss P W Tanner	Dip DCPE	PE
	Miss L E Turner	Dip CCPE CSP LDTPPE	PE
	Miss B W West	Froebel Teachers' Cert	PE and games
	Miss L M Wilson	Dip BCPE AISTD LDTPPE CSP	PE and dance

Appendix IIc   Chelsea School of Human Movement — Staff 1976–77

Position	Name	Qualifications	Subject
Head of School	Miss P M Kingston	DipCCPE DipPE(Lond)	
Head of Division	Mr J R Homer	MA MA(Educ)	
	Miss J E Allen	DipDCPE DipEd	Human movement
	Dr P Bale	PhD DipEd MIBiol	Human movement, science
	Mrs M Britton	BA	Human movement, sociology
	Miss B F Burgum	DipBCPE DipPE(Lond)	Human movement
	Miss W Burrows	DipBCPE CertEd	Human movement
	Mr D E Chapman	ATC NDD	Human movement, art
	Mrs L W Collin	Teachers' Cert	Human movement
	Miss A E Cooper	DipDCPE MSc DipPE(Lond) MCSP	Human movement
	Miss H Corlett	DipBCPE DipPE(Lond) MCSP	Human movement
	Miss M Cutland	DipACPE DipPE(Lond) MCSP	Human movement, science
	Miss G Denton	DipACPE CertEd	Human movement
	Miss W Ellis	DipIMMCPE Teachers' Cert ACDipEd	Human movement
	Miss M E Fogo	DipDCPE	Human movement
	Mrs M E Fox	DipIMMCPE DipPE(Lond) MCSP	Human movement, science
	Miss M C Kent	LMCPE Teachers' Cert	Human movement
	Miss J Langridge	DipCCPE DipPE(Lond) MCSP	Human movement
	Mr D L K Leggett	BA DipREd MI Biol	Human movement, science
	Mrs R Limb	Teachers' Cert AL (CS)	Human movement, drama
	Mr E C Loader	St Mark & St John Teachers' Cert ACDipEd CarnDipPE Leeds AdvDipPE	Human movement
	Miss K Lynn	DipDCPE Teachers' Cert AdvDipEd	Human movement, dance

Position	Name	Qualifications	Subject
	Mr R P Malley	CertEd ABSM	Human movement, music
	Mrs S M Murphy	DipIMMCPE As GSM & D	Human movement, dance
	Mr G J McFee	MA	Human movement, philosophy
	Mr E J McKenna	Teachers' Cert Carn	Human movement
	Mr J P McNaught-Davis	BEd MSc	Human movement, science
	Miss O C Napper	CCPE Teachers' Cert	Human movement, dance
	Mr R Neuss	Teachers' Cert, DipEd	Human movement
	Miss S O'Hanlon	Teachers' Cert, CCPE SupCert, AGSM & D	Human movement
	Miss M M Preece	DipTL Des PGWO Des LSIA	Human movement, art
	Mrs R E Prideaux	DipACPE DipPE(Lond)	Human movement
	Mrs S Shaylor	CCPE Teachers' Cert	Human movement
	Miss JC McConachie-Smith	(Otago) MEd DipTch(NZ) Dip PE	Human movement
	Miss J Standeven	NCPE BEd CertEd	Human movement
	Mr A Tomlinson	BA MA PGCE	Human movement, sociology
	Miss V Verdin	BCPE Teachers' Cert LRAM ALCM FISTD	Human movement, dance
	Dr R Watson	MSc Phd DipPE Carn AdDip, PE(Leeds) ResFSpC	Human movement, science
	Miss J Wilkinson	Teachers' Cert	Human movement
	Miss L Wilson	Dip BCPE DipPE(Lond) MCSP AISTD	Human movement, dance
	Mr TC Wood	Westminster and Carnegie Teachers' Cert DipPE(Carn) AdvDipPE(Leeds)	Human movement

Temporary appointments — replacements for seconded staff 1976–77

Position	Name	Qualifications	Subject
	Miss E Aggiss	CertEd	Human movement, dance
	Mr L Quilty	CertEd, DipEd, BEd	Human movement

Appendix IId   Chelsea School Staff — 1997–98

Position	Name	Qualifications	Subject
Head of School	Professor E B Murdoch	Dip Dunf CPE Cert MSc (Strathclyde) LAMS BEd (Leeds)	Pedagogy/curriculum PE and dance
Deputy Head of School and Course Leader for the BSc (Hons) Sport Science, Exercise Science	Dr J Doust	PhD (Nottingham) BSc (Loughborough)	Exercise physiology
Year 1 Tutor BSc (Hons) Exercise Science	A Burden	BSc MSc	Biomechanics
	B Carrington	BSc PG ResMeth (Leeds Met)	Sociology and cultural studies
Coordinator for the PGCE Dance	Dr A Cole	CertEd DipEd Adv DipEd (Dance) MA Dance (Ed) (London) PhD (Surrey)	Dance
Course Leader for the BA(Hons) PE with QTS	B Copley	BA (Manchester) DipPE (Carn) AdvDipPEd (Leeds) PGCE (Leeds) MSc (Sussex)	Psychological and social aspects
Coordinator Area 1	Miss M Dorobantu	BEd (Bucharest) MSc (Exeter)	Sport psychology
Route Leader for the BA(Hons) Leisure and Sport Management and University Recreation Service Coordinator	J Fairclough	CertEd (St Lukes) BEd (Exeter) MSc (Washington State) DMS (PNL)	Leisure service delivery

Position	Name	Qualifications	Subject
Coordinator games modules; Special Needs Link Tutor	S Hayes	BEd (St Paul's & St Mary's) MSc (Leics)	Games, professional and special needs
Admissions Tutor for the BA(Hons) PE with QTS, Coordinator Initial Teaching Practice, Year 1 Tutor for the BA(Hons) PE with QTS, Coordinator of the Chelsea School tutorial system	Miss A-M Latham	CertEd BEd (Sussex) MA PEd (Brighton Poly)	Games; professional studies
Principal Research Fellow	M Lee	CertEd (Exeter) BEd (Leeds) MSc (Washington State) MA PhD (Oregon)	Dissertation Supervisor
Admissions Tutor for the BA(Hons) Leisure degree courses	Miss G Lines	CertEd BEd (Sussex) MA PEd (Brighton Poly)	Social perspectives and professional studies
	P Lopes	Nurse (Toulouse) BA (Ulster) DEUST (Pau)	Physiology
	Professor G McFee	BA MA (Keele) PhD (London)	Philosophy
Coordinator for the PGCE Secondary PE, Coordinator of athletics and gymnastics, Year 11 Tutor for the BA (Hons) PE with QTS	S McKenzie	BEd (Jordanhill) MSc (Loughborough)	Professional studies
Coordinator for the Undergraduate Modular Scheme	P McNaught-Davis	CertEd BEd (Birmingham) MSc (Loughborough)	Anatomy, environmental physiology
Coordinator for School Admissions	N Maxwell	BA MSc	Exercise physiology

Position	Name	Qualifications	Subject
Course Leader for BA (Hons) Leisure Policy and Administration and the BA(Hons) Leisure and Sport Studies and the BA (Hons) Leisure and Sport Management degree courses contact for the SOCRATES bid	U Merkel	BA BSc (Cologne FRG) MA (Leicester)	Social history, sociology, politics
Coordinator for Professional Studies and Joint Coordinator for Chelsea School/ Community partnerships	Dr J O'Neill	CertEd (BCPE) (Cambs) BA (OU) MA (Ed) PhD (Sussex)	Professional studies
Coordinator for the BA(Hons) PE with QTS Coordinator for the dissertation and Admissions Tutor for the PGCE Secondary PE	Dr R Royce	BA PGCE MA(Ed) MEd PhD	Philosophical aspects
Year 3 Tutor Coordinator for Dance	Miss F Smith	BEd (Sussex) MA (London)	Dance, gymnastics
	Dr C Spray	BA (North Staffs Poly) PGCE (Loughborough) PhD (Exeter)	Sport psychology, child development learning
Reader in the Sociology of Sport	Dr J Sugden	BA (Essex) PGCE (Liverpool) MA PhD (Connecticut)	Comparative studies
Coordinator for the Junior Year Abroad	Dr A Taylor	BSc PGCE (PE) (Liverpool) MSc (Ithaca, NY) PhD (Toronto)	Sport, exercise and health psychology
Reader in Sport and Leisure Studies and Course Leader for the Certificate in Research Methodology	Professor A Tomlinson	BA (Kent) PGCE (London) MA PhD	Social and cultural studies, sociology

Position	Name	Qualifications	Subject
Recreation and non-curricular use of facilities	E H Twaddell	DipPE (Borough Road) Teachers' Cert(London) DipMS (PNC)	Practical studies
Principal Research Fellow	Dr J Whitehead	Teachers' Cert (DCPE) (London) DipAdvStEd MEd (Manchester) PhD (Oregon)	Sport psychology, motor learning
Admissions Tutor and Year 3 Tutor for the BSc(Hons) Sport Science	Dr C Williams	BEd (Exeter) MSc (Alberta) PhD (Exeter)	Exercise physiology
Coordinator for Key Stages II and III of the BA (Hons) PE with QTS	Miss J Williams	BEd (Sussex) MA PE (Leeds) USPTR	Professional studies, games

Appendix IIIa Chelsea Old Student's Association Officers

President

1904–29	Dorette Wilke
1931–82	May Fountain

Chairman

1904	E M Cartwright		1923–24	E Parkinson
1904–05	G M Polgreen		1924–25	W Warren
1905–06	H Ironside		1925–26	F Morgan
1906–07	R Skelton		1926–27	R Clark
1907–08	V Charter		1927–28	Mrs V Charter-Dibdin
1908–09	R Clark		1928–29	W M Saunders
1909–10	M Appleton		1929–31	G M Cater
1910–11	M Blomfield		1931–32	Mrs S B Thomson (née Rennet)
1911–12	R Skelton		1932–35	J G Stephen
1912–13	M Fountain		1935–38	E Sutch
1913–14	H Ironside		1938–39	B Holmes
1914–15	M Appleton		1940–43	R Clark
1915–16	D Nevill		1943–47	G M Cater
1916–17	R Clark		1947–50	K McConnell
1917–18	E Willmer		1950–53	Mrs S B Thomson (née Rennet)
1918–19	L S Crowdy		1953–60	R Clark
1919–20	L S Crowdy		1960–65	Mrs Catchpole (née Lacey)
1920–21	M Fountain		1965–73	Mrs M Housden (née Buckle)
1921–22	M Fountain		1973–82	Miss M O'Sullivan
1922–23	R Clark			

Secretary

1904–05	R Skelton		1918–19	T Edgel
1905–06	M Hughes		1919–20	W M Saunders
1907–09	R Skelton		1920–21	Mrs V Charter-Dibdin
1909–10	G Martyn		1921–22	Mrs V Charter-Dibdin
1910–12	S C Sparger		1922–25	H Campbell
1912–14	L E Crowdy		1925–27	G Cater
1914–15	K W Trayler		1927–29	Mrs S B Thomson
1915–16	Mrs V Charter-Dibdin		1929–31	A Engel
1916–17	K W Trayler		1931–35	D M Soley
1917–18	T Edgel		1935–46	Mrs S B Thomson (née Rennet)

1946–47	J Sharpe		1955–62	Mrs M Housden (née Buckle)
1947–51	D Foster		1962–81	Mrs B G Smith (née Bennett)
1951–55	D Clark			

Treasurer

1904–05	R Skelton		1919–20	WM Saunders
1905–06	M Hughes		1920–21	Mrs V Charter-Dibdin
1906–07	I Bramham		1921–28	Mrs V Charter-Dibdin
1907–09	R Skelton		1928–29	Mrs S B Thomson (née Rennet)
1909–11	L E Crowdy		1929–31	A Engel
1911–13	S C Sparger		1931–35	D M Soley
1913–14	L E Crowdy		1935–45	Mrs S B Thomson (née Rennet)
1914–15	K W Trayler		1945–47	J Sharpe
1915–16	L E Crowdy		1947–51	D E Foster
1916–17	K W Trayler		1951–52	Mrs D Clark (née Mundy)
1917–18	T Edgel		1952–54	Mrs M Housden (née Buckle)
1918–19	T Edgel		1955–81	Mrs F Coppen (née French)

Appendix IIIb   Chelsea Old Students' Association — Officers

Chairman

Professor Elizabeth B Murdoch	1985–91
Ann-Marie Latham	1991–

Secretary

Wendy Burrows	1985–91
Claire Brown	1991–96
Helen Cassady	1996–

Treasurer

Vanessa Hall	1985–90
Margaret MacFarlane	1990–

Appendix IIIc   One Year Course

1935	formed OYSA	K M Richardson	Chairman
		P Hoyland	Secretary
1936		M Fountain	President
		K M Melhuish	Secretary
		N Bland	Treasurer
1938		G M Battley	Vice President
		I M Hooking	Treasurer
1947	Appears to have ceased as a separate Association.		

Appendix IV Countries outside the United Kingdom from which students have been recruited to study at Chelsea

Students recruited from, and appointed to, schools in all parts of the United Kingdom (England, Northern Ireland, Scotland, and Wales)

Students recruited from, and appointed to, schools in various countries in the world including:

Antigua
Australia (Queensland, Western)
Bahamas
Barbados
Bermuda
Canada (British Columbia, Vancouver, Ontario, Halifax, Quebec, Toronto, Montreal, Dalhousie)
Ceylon
Channel Islands
Cyprus
Denmark
Dominica
Egypt (Alexandria, Cairo)
Germany (East, West)
Ghana
Gibraltar
Greece
Grenada
Holland
Hong Kong
Hungary
Iceland
Indonesia
Iran
Ireland (Eire)
Israel
Jamaica
Japan
Kenya
Leeward Islands
Malawi
Malaya (Malaysia)
Malta
Mauritius

Montserrat
Nepal
New Zealand
Nigeria (East, West)
Norway
Pakistan (East,West)
Phillipines
Poland
Portugal
Rhodesia (Southern)
St Lucia
St Vincent
Saudi Arabia
Seychelles
Sierra Leone
Singapore
South Africa (Cape Town, Cape Province, Johannesburg, Natal, Pretoria, Transvaal, Transkei)
South America (Venezuela)
South Korea
Spain
Sri Lanka
Sweden
Trinidad
Tobago
Uganda
United States of America (Massachusetts, Ohio, Connecticut, New Jersey, Michigan, Pennsylvania, New Hampshire, Illinois, Kansas, Missouri, New York, Idaho, Georgia)
West Indies
Zambia

Appendix V Examples of the associations/organizations with whom Chelsea staff and/or students have worked

AELLA   All England Ladies Lacrosse Association
AENA   All England Netball Association
AEWHA   All England Women's Hockey Association
AEWLA   All England Women's Lacrosse Association
AAA   Amateur Athletic Association
ASA   Amateur Swimming Association
AAHPER   American Alliance for Health, Physical Education and Recreation
APPEL   Association of Polytechnic Physical Education Lecturers
APWCPE   Association of Principals of Women's Colleges of Physical Education
APPTC   Association of Principals of Physical Training Colleges
ACHPER   Australian Conference of Health, Physical Education and Recreation

BAE   Badminton Association of England
BAAB   British Amateur Athletic Board
BAGA   British Amateur Gymnastic Association
BAALPE   British Association of Advisers and Lecturers in Physical Education
BANC   British Association of National Coaches
BASES   British Association of Sport and Exercise Science
BASM   British Association of Sports Medicine
BATD   British Association of Teachers of Dancing
BASS   British Association of Sports Scientists
BAF   British Athletic Federation
BCU   British Canoe Union
BCSA   British Colleges Sports Association
BC   British Council
BCPE   British Council of Physical Education
BMC   British Mountaineering Council
BOA   British Olympic Association
BPSA   British Polytechnics Sports Association
BPS   British Psychological Society
BSA   British Sociological Association
BSAD   British Sports Association for the Disabled
BUCPEA   British Universities and Colleges Physical Education Association
BUPEA   British Universities Physical Education Association
BUSA   British Universities Sports Association

CAHPER   Canadian Association of Health, Physical Education and Recreation
CCPR   Central Council of Physical Recreation

CCPRT	Central Council of Recreative Physical Training
CSMMG	Chartered Society of Massage and Medical Gymnastics
CSP	Chartered Society of Physiotherapy
CNAA	Council for National Academic Awards
CPFA	County Playing Fields Association (Sussex)
DS	Dalcroze Society
DCNA	Durham Netball Association
ECSR	Eastbourne Council of Sport and Recreation
EBBA	English Basket Ball Association
EFDSS	English Folk Dance and Song Society
ESC	English Sports Council
EFSP	European Federation of Sport Psychology
FIFA	Fédération Internationale d' Football Association
FIEP	Fédération Internationale d' Education Physique
FIMS	Fédération Internationale Médecine Sportive
FOSRSE	Federation of Sport and Recreation — South East
FA	Football Association
GLC	Greater London Council
GDA	Greek Dance Association
HEC	Health Education Council
ISTD	Imperial Society of Teachers of Dancing
ISTM	Incorporated Society of Trained Masseuses
ILAM	Institute of Leisure and Amenity Management
IAAF	International Amateur Athletics Federation
IAPESGW	International Association of Physical Education and Sport for Girls and Women
ICSP	International Committee of Sports Pedagogy
ICAP	International Congress of Applied Psychology
ICHPER	International Council of Health, Physical Education and Recreation
ICSPE	International Council of Sport and Physical Education
ICSSPE	International Council of Sport Science and Physical Education
ICSS	International Council for Sport Sociology
IDTA	International Dance Teachers Association
ISSP	International Society of Sports Psychology
JAPEW	Japanese Association of Physical Education for Women
KFA	Keep Fit Association
KNA	Kenya Netball Association
LAMG	Laban Art of Movement Guild
LTA	Lawn Tennis Association
LSA	Leisure Studies Association
LSEVA	London and South East Volleyball Association

MS	Medau Society
NAOPE	National Association of Organisers of Physical Education
NATFHE	National Association of Teachers in Further and Higher Education
NCF	National Coaching Foundation
NCSS	National Council for Schools Sports
NDTA	National Dance Teachers' Association
NFBPWC	National Federation of Business and Professional Women's Clubs
NGBS	National Governing Bodies of Sport
NOGC	National Organisation of Girls' Clubs
NPFA	National Playing Fields Association
NASSPA	North American Society of Sport and Physical Activity
PEA	Physical Education Association of Great Britain and Northern Ireland
PEAUK	Physical Education Association of the United Kingdom
PSPEA	Public Schools Physical Education Association
RFU	Rugby Football Union
RLSS	Royal Life Saving Society
SSRC	Social Science Research Council
STM	Society of Trained Masseuses
SECSR	South East Council for Sport and Recreation
SES	South East Sport
SPRITO	Sport and Recreation Industry Training Organisation
SAF	Sports Aid Foundation
SRA	Squash Rackets Association
SCOPE	Standing Conference of Lecturers of Physical Education
	— Dance Section
	— Physical Education Section
SCFA	Sussex County Football Association
UKSCLRS	United Kingdom Standing Conference of Leisure, Recreation and Sport
USPTR	United States Professional Tennis Registry
ULIESA	University of London, Institute of Education Sports Association
WCT	Winston Churchill Trust
WAAA	Women's Amateur Athletic Association
WCSP	World Congress of Sports Psychology
WCA	Women's Cricket Association
WI	Women's Institute
WSF	Women's Sports Foundation
WSFSG	Women's Sports Foundation — Sussex Group
YMCA	Young Men's Christian Association
YWCA	Young Women's Christian Association

Select Bibliography/Further Reading

Books of Particular Interest

BARCLAY, J. (1944) *In Good Hands*, Oxford: Butterworth Heinemann.

BEAR, B.E. (1920) *The British System of Physical Education*, London: G. Bell & Sons Ltd.

CHAPMAN, M.J. (1856) (2nd Edition) *Ling's Educational and Curative Exercises*, Oxford: Balliere.

COGHLAN, J.F. and WEBB, I.M. (1990) *Sport and British Politics Since 1960*, London: Falmer Press.

CRUNDEN, C. (1974) *A History of Anstey College of Physical Education 1897–1972*, Sutton Coldfield: Anstey College of Physical Education.

EVANS, H.J. (1974) *Service to Sport — The Story of the CCPR 1935–75*, London: Pelham.

FLETCHER, S. (1984) *Women First: The Female Tradition in English Physical Education 1880–1980*, London and Dover, NH: The Athlone Press.

FOX STRANGWAYS, A.H. (MCMXXIII) *Cecil Sharp*, Oxford: OUP.

FRANCIS, A. (1975) *I M Marsh Anniversary 1975*, Liverpool: I M Marsh College of Physical Education.

HODGSON, J. and PRESTON-DUNLOP, V. (1990) *Rudolf Laban — An Introduction to his Work and Influence*, Plymouth: Northcote House.

KARPELES, M. (1967) *Cecil Sharp — His Life and Work*, London: Routledge and Kegan Paul.

KIRK, G. (ed) (1995) *Moray House and Change in Higher Education*, Edinburgh: Scottish Academic Press.

MACLEAN, I.C. Dr (1976) *The History of Dunfermline College of Physical Education*, Dunfermline: Dunfermline College of Physical Education.

MAWER, E. (ed) (1996) *Mentoring in PE: Issues and Insights*, London: Falmer Press.

MAY, J. (1969) *Madame Bergman-Österberg*, London: Harrap.

MCINTOSH, P.C. (1952) *Physical Education in England since 1800*, London: G. Bell & Sons.

MCINTOSH, P.C., DIXON, J.G., MUNROW, A.D. and WILLETTS, R.F. (Revised Edition) (1981) *Landmarks in the History of Physical Education*, London: Routledge and Kegan Paul.

PHYSICAL EDUCATION ASSOCIATION (1964) *Nine Pioneers in Physical Education*, London: Physical Education Association.

POMFRET, A. (1985) *Dartford College 1885–1985*, London: Thames Polytechnic.

PRESTON-DUNLOP, V. (1998) *Rudolf Laban — An Extraordinary Life*, London: Dance Books.

Books of General Interest

ASPDEN, J.C. (1978) *A Municipal History of Eastbourne 1938–1971*, Eastbourne: Eastbourne Borough Council.

BEALE, D. *History of the Cheltenham Ladies College 1853–1904*, Cheltenham: Cheltenham Ladies College.

BRUNER, J.S. (1960) *The Process of Education*, Vintage Books.

BRUNER, J.S. (1966) *Toward a Theory of Instruction*, Cambridge, MA: Harvard University.

BUTLER, D. and B. (1994) *British Political Facts 1900–94*, London: Macmillan.

DES (THE MCNAIR REPORT) (1944) *Teachers and Youth Leaders*, London: HMSO.

DES (THE ROBBINS REPORT) (1963) *Report of the Committee on Higher Education* (Cmnd 2154), London: HMSO.

DES (THE WEAVER REPORT) (1966) *Report of the Study Group on the Government of Colleges of Education*, London: HMSO.

DES (1972a) *Education: a Framework for Expansion* (Cmnd 5174), London: HMSO.

DES (1972b) *Teacher Education and Training* (The James Report), London: HMSO.

DES (1987) *Higher Education — Meeting the Challenge* (Cmnd 114), London: HMSO.

FLOUD, R. (1997) *The People and the British Economy 1830–1914*, Milton Keynes: OUP.

GRIGGS, C. (1983) *The Trades Union Congress and the Struggle for Education 1868–1925*, London: Falmer Press.

HENKE, D. (1978) *The Re-organisation of Teacher Training 1971–7*, London: Penguin Books.

KAMN, J. (1958) *How Different From Us. Miss Beale and Miss Buss*, Oxford: Bodley Head.

LAWSON, J. and SILVER, H. (1973) *A Social History of Education in England*, London: Methuen.

MACLURE, J.S. (1986) *Educational Documents. England and Wales 1816 to the Present Day*, London: Methuen.

MARWICK, A. (1970) *The Nature of History*, London: The Macmillan Press.

MOSSTON, M. (1981) *From Command to Discovery*, Spectrum.

MURDOCH, E.B. (1987) *Sport in Schools — Desk Study*, London: DES/DOE.

NATIONAL COACHING FOUNDATION *Annual Reports*.

NATIONAL COACHING FOUNDATION (1992) *After School Sport — 24 Recipes for Action — The Story of Champion Coaching*, London: National Coaching Foundation.

NEVINS, A. (1962) (Revised Edition) *The Gateway to History*, New York: Doubleday Anchor Books.

OFSTED/TTA (1997) *Framework for the Assessment of Quality and Standards in Initial Teacher Training 1997/98*, London: OFSTED/TTA.

THE PHYSICAL EDUCATION ASSOCIATION OF GREAT BRITAIN AND NORTHERN IRELAND (1974) *Man and His Movement*, Proceedings of the 75th Anniversary Conference, 17–20 April.

REPORT OF THE TEACHER'S CERTIFICATE WORKING PARTY, THE ACADEMIC COMMITTEE (1968) *Learning for Teaching*, University of Sussex.

RICH, E.E. (1970) *The Education Act 1870 — A Study of Public Opinion*, London: Longmans, Green & Co.

RIDLEY, A.E. (1895) *Francis Mary Buss and Her Work for Education*, Longmans.

SCHOOL SPORT FORUM (1988) *Sport and Young People — Partnerships and Action*, Sports Council.

SILVER, H. and TEAGUE, S.J. (eds) (1977) *Chelsea College — A History*, London: Chelsea College, University of London.

SPORTS COUNCIL (GL & SE Region) (1986) *Physical Education*, Joint Report of the London and South East Councils for Sport and Recreation.

WATSON, D. and TAYLOR, R. (1998) *Lifelong Learning and the University A Post–Dearing Agenda*, Falmer Press.

Official Publications

ASSOCIATION OF PRINCIPALS OF WOMEN'S COLLEGES OF PHYSICAL EDUCATION (1972) *Education and Physical Education — Complementary Studies?*, Conference Report.

ASSOCIATION OF PRINCIPALS OF WOMEN'S COLLEGES OF PHYSICAL EDUCATION (1975) *Human Movement Behaviour*, Conference Report.

BOARD OF EDUCATION (1937) *Physical Training and Recreation Act, 1937*, London: HMSO.

CANADIAN ASSOCIATION FOR HEALTH, PHYSICAL EDUCATION AND RECREATION (1948) *The Association's First Honor Awards*, Bulletin, 15, 6, June, p. 4.

COUNCIL FOR NATIONAL ACADEMIC AWARDS CALOUSTE GULBENKIAN FOUNDATION (1980) *Human Movement Studies*, Conference Report, University of Nottingham, 28–29 September 1979, London: CNAA.

DEARING, R. (1993) *The National Curriculum and its Assessment — final report*, London: Department for Education.

DEPARTMENT OF THE ENVIRONMENT (1975) *Sport and Recreation* (White Paper Cmnd 6200), London: HMSO.

ENGLISH SPORTS COUNCIL (1997) *England, the Sporting Nation — A Strategy*, London: English Sports Council.

GILCHRIST, J.R. (1978) *The Report of a Conference for Lecturers in Higher Education concerned with the Development, Submission and Validation of Courses in Human Movement Studies*, Dunfermline College of Physical Education, 11–15 September 1978.

NATIONAL COMMITTEE OF INQUIRY INTO HIGHER EDUCATION (1997) *Higher Education in the Learning Society* (The Dearing Report), London: NCIHE.

Journals

Chelsea Physical Training College/Chelsea College of Physical Education

Annual Leaflet — Old Students' Association 1909–1910, 1911, 1912, 1913, 1914, 1916, 1921.

Chelsea College of Physical Education Magazine, No I–XL 1920–1958.

Chelsea College of Physical Education Old Students' Association Magazine No 1–17, 1959–1976.

Ling Association — Physical Education Association

Journal of Scientific Physical Training, Vol I–XV No 45 1908–1922.

Journal of School Hygiene and Physical Education, Vol XVI No 46–XXIX No 88 1923–1932.

Journal of Physical Education and School Hygiene, Vol XXX No 89–XXXVII No 112 1933–1944.

Journal of Physical Education, Vol XXXVIII No 113–XLVII No 142 1944–1954.

Physical Education Vol XLVIII No 143–58 No 175 1955–1966.

British Journal of Physical Education 1967–1998.

Ling Association —

The Supplement Feb 1900–Dec 1903.
The Monthly Leaflet Vol 1 No 1 Jan 1904, Vol 67 No 10 Dec 1966.
Annual Reports 1899–1965.

Physical Education Association

Year Book 1974–75.

Unpublished Theses

WEBB, I.M. (1967) 'Women's physical education in Great Britain 1800–1966 with special reference to teacher training', Leicester MEd.
WEBB, I.M. (1977) 'The history of Chelsea College of Physical Education with special reference to curriculum development 1898–1973', Leicester PhD.

In Preparation

BAYLEY, S. and VAMPLEW, W. *The History of the Physical Education Association, 1899 to 1999.*

Index

Murdoch, E., 11, 139–66, 169
Murphy, S., 135
Musaryk, J., 60
Muska Mosston Spectrum of Teaching
  Styles, 154
Mynors, H.B., 108

National Association of Organisers of
  Physical Education, 53
National Champion Coaching Scheme,
  158
National Coaching Foundation, 157–8
National Coaching Foundation Consortium
  Council, 158
National College of Physical Training and
  Recreation, 54
National Committee of Inquiry in Higher
  Education, 165
National Curriculum, 9, 138, 152
National Curriculum Council, Physical
  Education Working Group, 152
National Curriculum Physical Education
  Working Group, 152
National Organisation of Girls' Clubs,
  26
The Nature of Physical Education, 140
Neuss, R., 158, 160
Newman, G., 36
Nonington College of Physical Education,
  6, 7, 8, 10, 55
Nuremburg Turnfest, 35

Oakden, E., 62
Odgers, P.R., 105
Office for Standards in Education
  (OFSTED), 157
Ogston, F., 2
Old Students' Association, 38–42, 103,
  163
  Annual General Meeting, 82, 100
  Annual Report to, 83
  bursary, 63
  Diamond Jubilee, 76
  founding members, 15
  Golden Jubilee, 68
  letter to, 127
  report to, 91, 106–7, 112–13
Old Students' Magazine, 26, 64, 86, 121
Oldland, P., 29

Olympic Games, 103, 159
O'Neill, J., 145
Osborne, W.A., 21
Österberg, E. Per W., 2
O'Sullivan, M., 108
overseas students, 99, 122, 133
Ovett, S., 123

Palmer, E., 71
Paris Hygiene Congress, 35–6
Parker, E., 23
Parker, M., 146
Parker, S., 142, 143
Partnership in Education Committee,
  157
Partnership Resource Scheme, 156
partnership school-based model, 156
Pearson, S., 101
Perry, E.M., 20, 21, 62
Physical Education, 151
Physical Education Association, 114
Physical Education in School and Teacher
  Education Group, 144
1937 Physical Training and Recreation Act,
  7
Pierce, G., 153
Pim, O., 7
Pollard, E.G., 79, 111
post graduate course, 91
Postgraduate Diploma, 134
Powell, C., 59
Prentice, R., 111
Prideaux, R., 144, 160
Professional Studies Association, 159

Ranelagh Club, 62
rations, 60–1
Recreation Service, 134–5
Recreative Physical Training, 53
Reed, E., 15
Rendel, L., 20
Representation of the People Act, 89
Research Assessment Exercise, 144, 145
Richardson, K.M., 49, 53
Rifkind, M., 10
Robbins Report, 90
Rogers, A., 11, 72, 75–6
Rollason, H., 103
Rowell, S., 143, 159